CRAFT
COFFEE

A MANUAL

CRAFT COFFEE

A MANUAL

brewing a better cup at home

Jessica Easto

with Andreas Willhoff

SURREY
BOOKS

AN AGATE IMPRINT

CHICAGO

Printed in China

Craft Coffee: A Manual
ISBN13: 978-1-57284-233-5 (trade cloth)
ISBN10: 1-57284-233-4 (trade cloth)
eISBN13: 978-1-57284-804-7
eISBN10: 1-57284-804-9
First Edition: November 2017

Surrey Books is an imprint of Agate Publishing.
Agate books are available at bulk and discount prices.
Visit agatepublishing.com for more information.

Contents

Introduction

CRAFT COFFEE CAN BE A POLARIZING SUBJECT. In the United States, coffee has had a long history of being made poorly and conveniently—and bought and sold cheaply. For many colonial settlers, coffee was liquid fuel, something that got their gears going in the morning and made them forget, if only for a moment, that they were slowly and murderously humping (European) humanity westward. It wasn't supposed to taste good, and for a while in the 19th century, it *couldn't* taste good; there were no adequate tools. People would burn coffee beans in a frying pan and then boil them with water (enter sugar and cream). In the later part of the 1800s, manufacturers started making fake coffee from various grains, which people continued to buy, despite being aware of the con, until they realized the additives usually included actual poisons, like arsenic and lead. Later came convenient preground coffee and later still, because ground coffee goes stale quickly, vacuum seals, both of which were, more or less, marketing gimmicks. The expectation that coffee is gross, convenient, and cheap is deeply engrained in the American psyche, and some people get prickly when others start talking about good-tasting, mildly inconvenient, relatively expensive coffee.

Let them prickle. Read this book. Make great coffee.

My coffee journey did not start out as a deliberate quest for the perfect cup. Instead, I found my way to craft coffee via a circuitous road largely paved with ignorance and pragmatism. My parents never drank coffee, and I had little exposure to it growing up. In high school, I ordered my first cup of coffee black—at a local diner—because I didn't understand that many people expect coffee to be vile and rely on cream and sugar to help them suffer through it. I accepted the thin, bitter brew without question. I had become a black-coffee drinker. Without the sweet embrace of cream and sugar, it didn't take me long to realize that different coffees have different tastes. I knew that diner coffee was markedly different from Starbucks coffee, and Starbucks coffee was distinct from my local independent café's coffee—but I never thought to ask why.

I also never lived near a café that offered manually brewed coffee—I didn't even know such cafés existed or that manual brewing methods had qualitative differences from machines. When I purchased my first pour-over device in graduate school, it was only because a machine seemed extravagant and unnecessary for the single cup I brewed each morning. I figured out how to work it well enough, but only occasionally did I brew significantly better coffee than that diner back in high school did. Then one day my friend Andreas (who is now my husband) came over and saw I had a manual coffeemaker. He happened to be a barista and seeing that I had never invested any time in learning how to use the device properly, he showed me a couple of easy ways to improve my brew. As it turns out, coffee—when brewed manually—can be controlled and even manipulated for best results every time. For me, this was a revelation.

By the time Andreas and I moved to Chicago after graduate school, independent roasters and cafés had been thriving for years, and it was easy to sample coffee made with high-quality beans from around the globe and brewed on any of several different devices. This coffee was flavorful, smooth, and full—a far cry from my first black cup.

Most people recognize that diner coffee often leaves much to be desired and turn to chains like Starbucks and Peet's for better alternatives. For many people, their first exposure to smooth, flavorful, high-quality coffee takes place at a small independent café. They then try to make the same coffee at home, but somehow, it never tastes as good as it does at the café. From there, it's hard to know where to turn. The internet, with its depths of overwhelming, conflicting information, can make it difficult for home coffee brewers to learn how to improve. Then there are baristas, who can cause a different kind of hesitation. The coffee world uses a lot of jargon, and as in any new community whose members talk to each other in code, it can be intimidating to approach a professional with questions—especially in the coffee industry with its unfortunate (although often undeserved) reputation for snobbery.

Today, many baristas are working to change this perception. Still, certain assumptions are often made in the professional coffee realm: this is the way coffee should taste, this is the way to make it, and this is the way to think about it. In reality, there is no one right way for any of it, and insisting that there is doesn't do curious home brewers like us much good. We all appreciate good coffee, but we don't have to appreciate it in the same way.

That being said, some professional brewing tactics may not be a good fit or even necessary for the home kitchen. Because we collectively know relatively little about why coffee does what it does on a scientific level, a lot of misinformation is out there—often in the form of techniques and practices that have little or no rationale behind them—and baristas aren't necessarily immune to it.

This book is not written from the perspective of a coffee professional. It's written from my perspective, as a coffee lover and home coffee brewer who has heard it all from the coffee professional who lives with me. I don't make assumptions about your coffee knowledge, budget, or level of fervor. Instead, I realize that coffee enthusiasts exist on a spectrum, and that you will need to (1) figure out where you fall on the spectrum and (2) make coffee decisions that reflect that. This book explores the full body of coffee knowledge and offers guidance, perspective, practical advice, and a healthy dose of my own (informed) opinion to help you make those decisions and develop your own preferences. My goal is to provide you with at least the baseline of knowledge you will need to forge a path toward your own perfect, delicious cup. Take what you want and leave the rest.

HOW TO USE THIS BOOK

This book is organized a bit differently than other coffee books. Chapter 1 contains what I consider to be the most important information when it comes to improving your brew at home: a solid grasp of the science of extraction and the factors that affect it. Understanding why coffee behaves the way it does means that when it comes time to brew, you will know how to troubleshoot less-than-stellar cups and replicate desired results day after day. You can manipulate the fundamentals of brewing coffee depending on what equipment, brewing device, and beans you decide to use, which is why I think you need to read about those fundamentals before you ever pour water over grounds. This is a book about *making* coffee, after all, and there's no reason to get distracted by how beans grow until you understand the basics of brewing.

Chapter 2 is all about guiding you toward the coffee equipment that is right for you. Like any hobby, coffee making requires a certain amount of gear. The coffee industry loves gear—new devices and contraptions hit the market all the time. Are they all necessary? No. The reality is you will likely brew on only one device (even if, like me, you own a dozen), which is why it's crucial that you purchase the device that best suits your lifestyle, taste preferences, and budget.

Not all brewing devices work the same way or produce the same coffee, however; each one brings pros and cons to the table, including how they affect the qualities of the cup. This chapter outlines the two major methods of brewing (pour over and full immersion) as well as 10 different manual brewing devices, paying particular attention to the factors you will likely care about the most when selecting your device: how easy it is to use, how easy it is to find, and how much money it costs. Brewing devices, however, don't exist in a vacuum. To properly brew café-quality coffee at home, you also must consider the other equipment involved—such as filters, grinders, scales, and kettles—that may or may not be required to optimally brew on a certain device and/or achieve your coffee preferences. Chapter 2 assesses those gadgets as well.

Only after you have selected your device and other coffee hardware should you start thinking about beans. Chapter 3 explores the complex world of high-quality coffee beans, which can taste quite different from each other depending on what kind of coffee they are, where they were grown, how they were processed, and how they were roasted. In my experience, the knowledge gap between coffee professionals and enthusiasts is often widest with regard to the beans, so this chapter tells you what you need to know and builds your bean vocabulary. Once you have an idea of what kinds of beans you might like, chapter 4 takes things a step further by explaining how to actually find and purchase high-quality beans, which can be a challenge if you don't know where to look or what to look for. When you finally get your hands on a bag, deciphering the label ushers in a new set of challenges, so this chapter ends with a section that teaches you how to decode coffee-bag jargon as well as how to store your carefully selected coffee once you get it home.

Next, I talk about coffee's flavors and how to develop your palate in chapter 5. I view the information in this chapter as bonus knowledge. You will know whether or not you like a cup of coffee simply by tasting it—it doesn't matter whether or not you understand why. But, developing a knowledge of coffee flavor and how it works can help you better identify the coffee you are most likely to enjoy and communicate your preferences to others, which can be fun. It also gives you a sense of what you should be looking for flavorwise before you starting brewing and evaluating cups at home.

Once you have your device, your coffee, and a grasp of what you like, you are ready to brew! The last chapter provides kitchen-tested instructions and specifications for the 10 brewing devices outlined in chapter 2. Some devices have multiple methods, and each method is labeled with icons that show what type of additional equipment I recommend for best results with that method. With your newfound coffee knowledge, you'll be on your way to making consistent, replicable results every morning.

Throughout the book, I have also provided tips and tests designed to help you troubleshoot your cup, but to make things even easier, I have included an appendix at the end that outlines common coffee-making mistakes and how to correct them for your next brew.

Where's the Espresso?

Most coffee books have sections on espresso and milk. I have deliberately excluded that discussion from these pages. Why? Well, the point of this book is to show that ordinary people can make extraordinary coffee at home, no matter their budget, skill set, or level of enthusiasm. I just don't think you can make extraordinary espresso at home without expensive equipment. Even the $500 espresso machine models you can get online don't really cut it, and professional-grade machines are well out of reach of most people's pocketbooks. Espresso machines are also more vulnerable to scale, so if you don't have some kind of pricey filtration system, you are either going to ruin your machine, make bad espresso, or both. Lastly, great espresso is all about fine-tuning. Tiny differences can make or break a shot. Professional shops fine-tune their shots throughout the day, and it doesn't seem practical for someone at home to pull a bunch of shots each morning until they get it right. Besides, this book has a lot of words in it already.

THE MANY WAVES OF COFFEE

According to a 2014 report by the National Coffee Association, a whopping 61 percent of Americans drink coffee on a daily basis. Though we may not always think of it this way, coffee is woven throughout much of the United States's history. It likely played at least a small part in colonial life since the earliest days of British settlement, as England had been introduced to coffee in the 16th century. But the beverage didn't become *popular* until the Boston Tea Party in 1773, when politics encouraged our citizens to turn their backs on Earl Grey and fall into the arms of coffee. Eighty-eight years later, the *New York Times* reported on a similar proposed tax, this time on coffee imports, designed to fund war efforts, saying, "All patriotic citizens feel that it is a sacred duty to support the Government in this trying hour, and to submit to any sacrifices that may be necessary to maintain the integrity of the Union." By that point, the United States was already consuming more coffee than any other nation—a quarter of the world's production, according to that same article.

Industry professionals often describe the history of US coffee consumption in three waves. The first wave of coffee started in the 1800s, when global coffee consumption exploded and big coffee outfits like Maxwell House, Hills Bros., and Folgers started growing to prominence—at least here in the United States. In general, market share—driven by speed, convenience, and caffeine—was more important than quality during this period. For the most part, these companies sold commodity coffee, that is, coffee that is bought and sold on commodity markets, as wheat, sugar, and other standardized "soft commodities" are. One way this is done is through futures on exchanges, such as the New York Mercantile Exchange and the Intercontinental Exchange. Commodity coffee, both then and now, involved a complicated web of exporters, importers, investors, buyers, and sellers, as well as prices that were subject to huge variations for a number of reasons, including those related to politics, weather, and speculation. The commodity coffee sold to the masses was not (and is not) always of the highest quality, but for much of coffee's history in the United States, quality considerations were, frankly, beside the point.

Eventually, enough people decided that the mass coffee product available to consumers did not pass muster. Growing antipathy toward low-quality coffee inspired the second wave of coffee, led by companies, such as Peet's Coffee & Tea and Starbucks, that valued something new: quality and community. To give you a sense of the timeline, Peet's opened its first store in 1966 in Berkeley, California; Starbucks opened its first store in 1971 in Seattle, Washington; and in 1978, the legendary Erna Knutsen—a secretary turned coffee broker who specialized in selling high-quality beans from specific origins to independent roast-ers—coined the term *specialty coffee* to better communicate the goal of her trade: to recognize the special qualities of individual beans. Achiev-ing this goal required placing new emphasis on proper processing, roast-ing, and preparation—that's specialty coffee in a nutshell.

From there, the philosophy and language of specialty coffee grew in-creasingly popular. In 1982, the Specialty Coffee Association of America (now known simply as the Specialty Coffee Association) was founded to help set standards for this burgeoning industry and to help its members communicate, innovate, and grow and market high-quality coffee to consumers. Along the way, specialty coffee establishments sold the idea and the experience of specialty coffee to a demographic—a large one, as it turns out—that was willing to pay a premium for it. Between 1987 and 2007, Starbucks opened an average of two new locations a day.

Significantly, specialty coffee has changed the way some coffee is bought and sold. A sizable portion of specialty coffee isn't sold or traded on commodity markets. Instead, large specialty coffee companies often contract directly with producers, and smaller roasters sometimes use importers that specialize in sourcing the highest-quality beans available. Specialty coffee shops are extremely popular (recent research estimates that there are more than 31,000 specialty cafés in the United States today compared with 1,650 in 1991), and from a consumer perspective, the beloved coffee-shop experience has arguably played a significant role in this growth. But somewhere along the way, the importance of the experience of specialty coffee had started, to some, to supersede the im-portance of quality.

So perhaps it comes as no surprise that many in the industry say we are currently living in the third wave of coffee. The term, first coined in 2002 by Trish Rothgeb of Wrecking Ball Coffee Roasters, generally refers to the growing number of importers, roasters, and baristas who, above all, treat the coffee bean as an artisanal food product, much as people do with cheese, wine, and (more recently) beer. In order to fulfill that mission, third-wave coffee professionals often adopt certain philosophies. They champion the unique qualities of individual beans, which, among other things, have led to new roasting techniques that leave beans distinctly lighter than more traditional roasting methods do— probably the most readily recognizable difference between second- and third-wave coffee for consumers. Additionally, there has been a growing emphasis on education and quality improvement. This has generated new research, programs, and certifications for people at all stages of the coffee trade—from producers to roasters to baristas—with the goal of sharing knowledge and techniques that benefit each step of the coffee-making process. Most third-wave professionals are also interested in ethics and transparency and strive to work fairly with producers, who have routinely gotten the short end of the stick. The third wave aims to show coffee producers proper respect for their work, both through fair compensation and in the way their coffee is presented to consumers.

SPECIALTY COFFEE VERSUS CRAFT COFFEE

Industry professionals and trade organizations use the term *specialty coffee* to distinguish coffee that meets their high standards from the majority of coffee found in the commodity trade. Likewise, they use the term *third wave* to distinguish specifically the latest generation of coffee, with its new emphasis on craft and ethics, from the overarching umbrella of specialty coffee. In other words, second-wave and third-wave coffee are both specialty coffee; their ideologies are just a bit different.

That being said, I am deliberately choosing not to use the term *third wave* in this book, even though the movement and I appear to have the same goals in mind. For one thing, it isn't very descriptive; *third wave* doesn't capture the defining characteristics of the movement and is, in some ways, inaccurate. For another thing, the media have all but turned the term into a pejorative, using it to remind us that a bunch of millennial hipsters are drinking fancy, fussy, overpriced coffee and trying to make something simple into something complicated for unfathomable, pretentious reasons. But making coffee a tiny bit more complicated can be a good thing. Let me explain.

In terms of ingredients, of course, coffee could hardly be simpler. But the coffee bean itself is incredibly complex, made up of thousands of compounds, most of which we don't fully understand—at least not on a scientific level. Archeological evidence suggests that humans have been making wine for about 8,000 years and brewing beer for about 7,000 years. Coffee, on the other hand, likely wasn't extracted and consumed until the 15th century, which means that compared with wine and beer, coffee lacks at least 6,000 to 7,000 years' worth of human knowledge and refinement. Making coffee, let alone making good coffee, is still a relatively new concept. Best practices for farming and processing coffee, for example, are still being developed all the time. The art of roasting—how roasters strategically manipulate coffee's compounds to unlock flavor—is in its infancy, as is our progress toward perfecting our brewing methods, the ways in which we extract flavor from coffee beans.

Despite being works in progress, all of these efforts to improve (and thus further complicate) coffee have already proven effective: coffee has never in the history of humankind tasted better than it does right now—and people are noticing. Today, the number of people interested in good coffee has reached a critical mass, one that has spawned hundreds of think pieces and spurred the second-wave Big Boys to make significant investments in the so-called third wave, whether they are buying up influential companies like Chicago's Intelligentsia or creating an ethos like Starbucks seems to be doing with its cold brew, its cascara syrup, and its Reserve shops. Many people still say there's no reason for coffee to taste good, but an increasing number of people (including you, probably, and me) say there's no reason for coffee to taste bad.

Having said that, it takes skill to make coffee taste good—skill on the part of the farmer, skill on the part of the processor, skill on the part of the roaster, and skill on the part of the coffee maker. Farming, processing, roasting, brewing: these are all, to some degree, manual skills that involve study or apprenticeship—a craft. This book focuses on the last part, brewing, which is among the most manual of skills—you are learning to brew coffee literally by hand as opposed to with a machine.

This is all a long-winded way of saying: I believe coffee is a craft and coffee professionals and enthusiasts are craftspeople. That's why I have taken to calling what is essentially third-wave coffee *craft coffee* instead. It is more descriptive; it makes more sense. The word *craft* implies a degree of skill and study—manual skill and manual study, at that. It also implies something small. Craft coffee's slice of the pie may be relatively significant—significant enough for coffee behemoths to suspect that they are missing out on a piece of the market—but it is still operating on a tiny scale. All craft coffee is specialty coffee, but not all specialty coffee is craft coffee. Craft coffee beans account for only a fraction of the total number of coffee beans produced each year. They are roasted, for the most part, carefully and in small batches. And if you add up all of the cafés that the top four craft coffee companies own, you get—as of this writing—just 52! Starbucks alone has 25,085 locations.

Another reason I like the word *craft* is that it doesn't imply, as *third wave* does, that contemporary coffee lovers discovered great coffee. It's important to remember that the desire for quality coffee is not strictly a 21st-century phenomenon. For as long as there has been coffee, there have been people humbly trying to improve their home brew and unlock the mysteries of the bean. In the past, those people probably felt as though they were merely shouting into the void (imagine trying to explain the science of extraction to cowboys or gold prospectors who boiled their coffee in the same piece of cheesecloth until it fell apart), but today, we owe these problem solvers a great debt.

In 1922, one such problem solver, coffee enthusiast William H. Ukers, finally published his 700-page opus, *All About Coffee*, after having taken 17 years to write it. In it, he noted that while coffee preparation in the United States had certainly improved in general, he hoped that soon "it may be said truly that coffee making in America is a national honor and no longer the national disgrace that it was in the past." It's been 95 years, and here we are, hanging our hopes on the same hook. Let this book help you join Ukers's league of problem solvers in whatever capacity you choose to participate.

CHAPTER 1
Brewing Basics

B EFORE YOU CAN IMPROVE YOUR BREW, you must have an idea of what's going on when water meets coffee. In this chapter, you may want to keep reminding yourself that coffee is simple—well, making it is simple, but the bean itself really isn't. The more time you spend trying to understand the bean, the more complexity it reveals. It's almost as if coffee beans do everything in their power to give you a hard time. They are, by nature, inconsistent, and if you want to optimize your cup, you must account for that irregularity. This chapter introduces you to coffee's inconsistencies and, based on the best knowledge the industry and science have to offer, outlines how water and coffee interact to make our beloved beverage. It also describes how (and why) you can manipulate factors such as brew ratio, dose, and grind size to optimize your brew. With a solid understanding of these concepts, you can create the cup of coffee you want day after day. Along with helping you to troubleshoot less-than-ideal cups, understanding coffee at its most basic level will help you make more informed decisions about the devices and coffee that are best suited for your lifestyle and preferences.

EXTRACTION

Extraction is the process of pulling flavor and texture compounds—insoluble oils, soluble gases, insoluble solids, and soluble solids—from the coffee grounds into the brewed coffee. In other words, it's what turns water into coffee. Obviously, you don't need to know the science behind how and why extraction happens in order to make coffee—you can just let the water do its thing. However, a solid foundation of extraction knowledge comes in handy when you are deciding what you like in a cup of coffee and how to replicate it day after day. The decisions you make—the device, the filter, the method, etc.—will all affect how your coffee extracts, and it will be difficult to manipulate brewing factors later on if you don't have a solid understanding of the basics. Let's start by looking at a few broad categories of coffee compounds that, in a sense, come alive when introduced to water:

- **Insoluble oils.** These oils are present within coffee beans but do not dissolve in water. Insoluble oils tend to be more visible in cups of coffee made with devices that use metal filters; they are partially or almost entirely trapped by cloth and paper filters. Insoluble oils can influence how coffee feels in your mouth. For example, particularly oily cups are often described as "creamy" or "buttery." If you look into almost any cup of coffee, especially if it's been sitting for a bit, you can usually see a faintly iridescent oil spill floating on the coffee's surface. That's from the insoluble oils.

- **Soluble gases.** These are gases that dissolve in the brewing water during extraction. They are the main contributors to coffee's aroma. For example, a cup of coffee might smell a bit like blueberries, or earthy, like hay. Different soluble gases are released at different temperatures, which is why you may notice that your coffee's aroma changes as it cools. As you likely know, aroma and taste are closely linked. The changing aroma is one of the main reasons why coffee's taste changes as it cools down.

- **Insoluble solids.** These are substances that do not dissolve in water, such as large protein molecules and tiny fragments of ground coffee beans (often called *fines*). Like insoluble oils, insoluble solids influence how coffee feels in your mouth and on your tongue. For example, a cup with lots of insoluble solids may feel kind of gritty. Many of the most popular brewing devices use filters to keep the majority of insoluble solids out of your cup.

- **Soluble solids.** These are substances that dissolve in the brewing water during extraction. They are particularly important because they determine how sweet, salty, bitter, sour, or savory the coffee will taste. In short, they largely determine a coffee's flavor.

Water extracts these compounds from the coffee grounds, and heat speeds up the process (cold water can do it, too; it just takes much longer). It happens in three stages: First, the hot water rinses the grounds of any surface material and displaces carbon dioxide (a by-product of the roasting process), which is why your coffee bed appears to breathe (aka *bloom*) when you brew fresh coffee. The carbon dioxide creates a barrier between the grounds and the water, so it's a good idea to wait until some of the gas dissipates before continuing your brew. Next, the soluble gases and soluble solids start dissolving in the hot water, creating that trademark coffee aroma and flavor. Finally, once these solubles are dissolved, osmosis pulls them away from the grounds.

These compounds don't all dissolve at once, however: coffee contains many different soluble solids that dissolve at different rates and impart various flavors to your cup. Here are a few of the more important ones:

- **Fruity acids.** These are among the smallest flavor molecules and tend to dissolve first. They give fruity and floral aromas to the cup. As their name suggests, they provide perceived acidity to a cup of coffee, but in high concentrations, they can make the cup taste gross and sour.

- **Maillard compounds.** These guys are produced during the Maillard reaction part of the roasting process (see page 146). Hundreds of compounds are produced from the Maillard reaction, and science is still sorting out exactly how they influence flavor and aroma. Some scientists say Maillard compounds can provide everything from grainy, nutty, or malty flavors to smoky, meaty, or caramel flavors in your cup.

- **Browning sugars/caramels.** These molecules are also created during the roasting process as natural sugars in the beans are caramelized. Some experts say they help contribute to perceived sweetness in coffee. They take a bit longer to dissolve than fruity acids. As you'll read later, the longer coffee is roasted, the more caramelized these sugars become. If roasting continues, the sugars can leave caramel country and enter carbonized territory—which means they are burning. Less-caramelized sugars (which taste sweeter) dissolve first, and highly caramelized sugars (which taste bittersweet) take longer to dissolve. This is part of the reason why darker roasts tend to be bitterer—there is less sweetness available to begin with. Sweetness in coffee often turns up as notes of chocolate, caramel, vanilla, or honey.

- **Dry distillates.** These are the molecules from the Maillard reaction and caramelization parts of the roasting process that lean more into burnt territory. They are more common in darker roasts, obviously, and impart tobacco, smoky, and carbon flavors. These molecules also tend to be bitter. These are the slowest molecules to dissolve, but they pack a punch. Even at low levels, they can mask the other flavors so that the entire cup just tastes bitter.

The goal of extraction is to achieve a balanced cup—that is, a cup in which the right amount of these dissolved compounds is present and contributing a pleasant mix of acidic, sweet, and bitter flavors. It's odd, but none of these soluble solids tastes particularly great on its own (see the experiment on page 18). Striking the right balance is a strange and subtle alchemy, one that is directly linked to time. If your coffee grounds are not in contact with the water long enough, then many of the soluble solids, save for the fruity acids, will not get a chance to dissolve. Without other flavors to dilute the acidic qualities of the fruity acids and add complexity, your cup will likely taste sour, unpleasant, and/or dull. In other words, your coffee is not extracted enough; it's *underextracted*. On the other hand, if your coffee grounds spend too much time with the water, you risk getting a higher concentration of dry distillates in your cup, which tend to overpower the other flavors with their bitterness. This is a cup that has extracted too much; it's *overextracted*. Keep in mind that all of this can happen in a relatively short amount of time—30 extra seconds could be enough to damage your cup.

What is the most important criterion for determining how well your coffee extracted? Taste. I'm not trying to be flip—it's just that the only thing that really matters in the end is how your coffee tastes, and it's important to remember that, despite everything I'm about to tell you.

Fun Extraction Experiment

Want to better understand how different flavor molecules extract at different rates? You can! Try an experiment in which you brew 400 grams (about 1⅔ cups) of coffee in four phases with your favorite pour-over device. You will need a gram scale (or really sharp eyes), the correct dose of coffee for your device, and four different mugs set out and ready to go. Set up everything as you would for a regular brew (see page 51), but only brew 100 grams (about ¼ of the water) into the first mug (phase 1). Quickly remove everything from the scale, set the next mug on top, transfer the dripper, and tare, or zero, the scale. Brew the next 100 grams (phase 2). Repeat the process for phases 3 and 4 until each mug contains about 100 grams of coffee. Now it's time to taste. Make sure to taste each sample in the order in which it was brewed and record your findings. How do the samples compare to one another? How does the phase 1 sample compare to the phase 4 sample? How does what you learned about extraction explain the differences in how the four samples taste? At the end, combine all four samples together into one mug. How does that taste? This experiment isn't perfect, but it should illustrate the different stages of extraction well enough.

STRENGTH AND YIELD

When coffee professionals evaluate the quality of a cup, they look at two things: strength and yield. The measure of these two factors is a good indicator of whether a customer is going to find the cup pleasant or not. Like I said, your taste buds will tell you whether or not you like a particular coffee, even if you don't realize they are responding to its strength and yield. But isn't life easier when we can use our words?

Strength is an easy concept to understand: it's the measure of the total dissolved coffee solids (TDCS)—another term for the soluble solids from the previous section—in a cup, usually presented as a percentage. If a cup is 1 percent TDCS, that means the other 99 percent is water. *Strong* cups contain more TDCS than *weak* cups.

"Strong coffee" is a familiar phrase that a lot of us use incorrectly. People often say "strong coffee" when they are referring to the flavor or the perceived caffeine content of a cup. Technically speaking, strength only refers to the *body* of the cup: how it feels in your mouth. A strong cup, one with a higher concentration of TDCS, might feel thick on your tongue. A weak cup, one with a lower concentration of TDCS, might feel closer to water, or *thin*. Whether you realize it or not, one of the ways your tongue decides whether you like a cup of coffee is by how it feels. If the coffee feels too thick or too insubstantial, you might be turned off. For more information on these distinctions, check out the Body section on page 191.

One weird thing about strength is that the difference between strong coffee and weak coffee is quite small in terms of the percentage of TDCS. For example, most people here in the United States would consider a cup that contains 1 percent TDCS and 99 percent water too weak and a cup that contains 2 percent TDCS and 98 percent water too strong. Most "good" cups of coffee fall somewhere between 1 and 2 percent TDCS, although it's always up to personal preference.

The second part of evaluating extraction is *yield* (sometimes called *extraction yield* or *solubles yield*), and it's a bit hairier to explain. Yield is a way to measure extraction, and it refers to the amount of material that the water has removed from the actual coffee grounds. Think of it like this: if you have a pile of coffee grounds, you are starting with 100 percent coffee material. The maximum amount of coffee material that is physically possible for hot water to remove (extract) is somewhere around 30 percent, and that would likely bear an utterly disgusting cup. Coffee professionals usually aim to extract somewhere between 18 and 22 percent of coffee material from the grounds.

Coffee that has a low yield (less than 18 percent of the coffee material has made its way into the cup) usually tastes underextracted, and coffee that has a high yield (more than 22 percent of the coffee material ends up in the cup) usually tastes overextracted. This all comes back to time: the longer that water and coffee mingle, the more opportunity there is for extraction.

The Takeaway

Your tongue can tell if your cup is over- or underextracted. In general, underextracted coffees lack complexity (meaning you are unable to taste multiple distinct flavors in the cup) and are often sour. Their aromas are normally faint and/or simple, and their bodies are thin. Overextracted coffees are often overly bitter and astringent (drying), which hides the yummy flavors in the cup. Their bodies are usually thick and syrupy. The best cups tend to be somewhere between under- and overextracted and are more likely to offer a range of pleasing flavors.

The Coffee Brewing Control Chart

For you visual learners, the Coffee Brewing Control Chart can help you wrap your head around strength and yield, which can help you understand how to correct over- and underextracted coffee until it's just right. How do coffee makers know what "just right" means? An MIT chemist named E. E. Lockhart developed the Coffee Brewing Control Chart in the 1950s to try to answer that question. He surveyed a bunch of US coffee drinkers

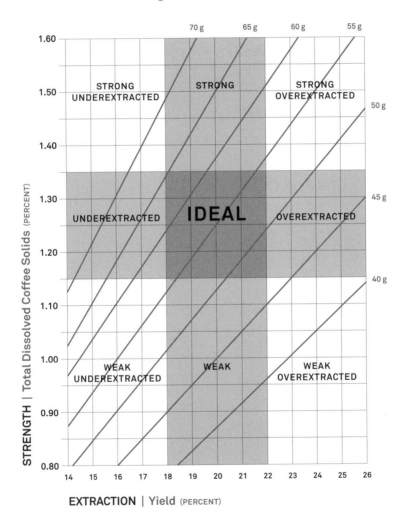

COFFEE BREWING CONTROL CHART
Brewing Ratio: Grams per Liter

about their preferences and found that most people prefer coffee that falls in the "ideal" square shown on the chart: an extraction yield between 18 and 22 percent and a strength measurement between about 1.15 and 1.35 percent. Lockhart's original findings are still supported by the Specialty Coffee Association (SCA) today—although these general preferences can vary around the world. While it may seem counterintuitive, you'll see that it is possible to brew a cup of strong, underextracted coffee and a cup of weak, overextracted coffee (actually, the latter describes typical diner coffee).

There are ways to calculate strength and yield with special tools and math (as indicated by the numbers on the chart), and it's tempting, even for professionals, to try this—but I'm not going to tell you how to do that here. It's nice to be aware of the ranges described in the chart, but I can't emphasize enough that you shouldn't let numbers distract you from taste. There is a sentiment among some coffee professionals that measurements like these encourage folks to stamp a cup of coffee as "good" based on calculations rather than taste. However, numbers don't tell the whole story—a bunch of different factors affect how coffee extracts, including the type of coffee, the processing method, and the roast. This means that even if two coffees have the same yield—20 percent, for example—they could still taste very different from each other.

The upshot of understanding how strength and yield work is that you will be able to experiment with both measures in your home brew. In order to do that most effectively, you'll need to understand the different brew variables that affect strength and yield—brew ratio, grind size, contact time, water, and temperature. These are the building blocks of every coffee recipe.

BREW RATIO AND DOSE

If you're going to make coffee, you need to know how much coffee and water to use. When I first started making coffee at home, I literally just guessed how much to use based on vague memories of what I had seen others do. If optimizing your cup is your goal, I don't recommend this method. Instead, you should consider two things: (1) how much coffee you want to end up with and (2) your personal preferences for strong or weak coffee.

Your brew ratio—the amount of coffee to water you use—has a direct effect on the strength of your cup. Remember, strength refers to the concentration of coffee compounds present in the brew, which affects the *mouthfeel* of your coffee, or how it feels in your mouth. The more coffee to water you use, the stronger your coffee will be. The less coffee to water you use, the weaker your coffee will be. The more coffee you start with, the more compounds end up in your cup.

> ### Brew Ratio and Taste
>
> **High brew ratio (too much coffee):**
> thick mouthfeel, muddled flavors, very aromatic
>
> **Low brew ratio (too little coffee):**
> thin mouthfeel, weak flavors, faint aroma

Lots of people will tell you that the correct brew ratio is two tablespoons of ground coffee for every six ounces of water. For his part, Beethoven reportedly counted out 60 whole beans for each cup of coffee he made. You can start with either of these tactics if that's easiest for you, but I (and most professionals) use a slightly different method of measuring coffee because consistency—being able to replicate desired results—is key, and the methods described earlier are not consistent.

The two-tablespoons method requires ground coffee, and if you are using fresh whole beans, you won't be able to measure until you grind them, which can be wasteful and expensive (high-quality beans aren't cheap). Beethoven's method removes the waste factor, but beans can vary greatly in size. Sixty beans from one type of coffee plant may end up providing significantly fewer grounds than 60 beans of another type of coffee plant. The solution? Use a brew ratio based on weight in grams.

Most coffee professionals in the United States use a brew ratio between 1:15 (that's 1 gram of whole coffee beans to 15 grams of water) and 1:17 as a starting point. That will get you close to the "ideal" range on the Coffee Brewing Control Chart. Yes, this means measuring both beans and water by their weight, instead of by their volume, which is what you're likely familiar with. Still, measuring both items with a single unit of measure means you can simplify this stage of the process by using only one piece of measuring equipment—an inexpensive kitchen scale.

How Much Does Accuracy Matter?

I know a lot of you will choose the two-tablespoons method, and that's fine. But for next-level brewing, I highly recommend measuring by weight and using a brew ratio for three reasons:

- It's more accurate.
- It makes it easier to troubleshoot/adjust your cup.
- It accounts for the variability in devices.

What some people may not realize is that the actual mass of the amount of coffee that fits inside a measuring spoon can vary greatly. Despite what you may have heard to the contrary, that's not something coffee people have made up to be complicated; it's science. It's why experienced bakers tend to measure by weight. One cup of all-purpose flour might not be the exact equivalent of the next cup you measure; maybe you inadvertently packed the second cup more, meaning there was more mass in that cup than in the first. Even a bit too much flour in baking can lead to less-than-ideal results.

For coffee, there's even more room for inconsistency. I already mentioned the fact that different coffee beans can vary significantly in size (just look carefully at your next bag of blended beans). This means the mass of one tablespoon of this bean might differ from the mass of one tablespoon of that bean. It's like the difference in weight between one cup of all-purpose flour and one cup of whole-wheat flour. These masses can differ by a gram or more, which is significant when you are dealing with relatively small measurements. Additionally, if you are measuring coffee grounds, the grind size also comes into play. A tablespoon of finely ground coffee will certainly have a different mass from a tablespoon of coarsely ground coffee. When the difference between your perfect cup and a not-as-good cup can be half a gram or less, it's critical to get exact measurements. The same is true for water—a tablespoon of water is supposed to weigh about 14.8 grams, but try weighing tablespoons of water and see how often that ends up being the case.

Measuring by weight, however unfamiliar, is the only way to ensure precise, consistent brew ratios and consistent cups. Otherwise, you may luck out with a delicious cup, but it will not be a result that's easily replicated unless you record the ratio for future use. After all, coffee has only two ingredients—even small variations affect the taste. When you do something consistently, it makes it easier to know what to adjust, if need be. For example, if your coffee feels quite thick and overwhelming in your mouth (strong), you might be using too much coffee, and next time you can use less. If it feels too watery (weak), you might be using too little coffee, and next time you can use more.

Lastly, ideal brew ratios vary depending on the device you are using. As you'll see in the next chapter, devices are specifically designed to optimize extraction, but their designers have different ideas about how to go about doing that. How your device works to extract coffee can certainly affect the brew ratio (or ratios) that tend to work best with it.

How to Calculate Dose

The amount of coffee that's used in a brew ratio is called the *dose*. Calculating dose requires math. I hate math because in sixth grade I failed my advanced placement test, but my teachers decided to advance place me anyway, which prompted a six-year struggle through AP classes that I'm clearly not over yet. But even I can calculate dose. And the good news is that once you figure out your dose, you can use the same numbers over and over again without having to calculate anything! The other good news, which I mentioned before, is that my brew ratios let you measure both water and coffee by weight in grams, which makes things very easy. Huzzah metric system!

The first things you need to know are what size your brewing device is and how much coffee you want to end up with. (Don't under- or overfill your device—choose one that's the proper size for the amount of coffee you want to brew.) Let's use a small BeeHouse dripper as an example. The manufacturer says it is designed to hold grounds for one to two cups of coffee. Let's say you want one cup. One cup is eight fluid ounces. One fluid ounce of water is 29.57 grams. Let's start with a 1:16 brew ratio and see what that means for your coffee dose (to make things easier, I've rounded all of the measurements to the nearest whole number):

Cups of Coffee	Water (fl oz)	Water (g)	1:15 Dose (g)	1:16 Dose (g)	1:17 Dose (g)
1	8	237	16	15	14
2	16	473	32	30	28
3	24	710	47	44	42
4	32	946	63	60	56
5	40	1,183	79	74	70
6	48	1,419	95	89	83

Since you already have the calculation for the 16 part of the ratio (237 grams), all you have to do is divide it by 16 to get the coffee dose. That ends up being 15 grams (actually about 14.8, but I find it easier to adjust my dose if I start with whole numbers). This means you would start with 15 grams of coffee beans and 237 grams of water, grind, brew, and see how that tastes. Depending on what you think of the taste, you can adjust your dose accordingly, half a gram or so at a time. (As a heads up, 15 grams might be a lot more coffee than you're used to using. One of the most common mistakes of people making coffee at home is not using a big enough dose. If you try using a 1:16 brew ratio and think your dose looks like too much coffee, I urge you to follow through and see what happens before reducing the dose.)

You can also apply the chart to different quantities and different devices. If you were brewing for a crowd using a large Chemex, you could use the chart to see that you would start with 1,419 grams of water and between 83 and 95 grams of coffee beans to brew six cups. However, if you own multiple devices, note that you likely will not be able to use the same brew ratio across all of them. As you'll see in chapter 6, the ratios I use vary from 1:12 to 1:17, depending on the device.

Once I figure out the brew ratio I like for the device I'm using, I write it down and use it each time I make coffee. Most craft coffee shops do too, and that ratio becomes part of the device's *base specifications*, or *base specs*. The point isn't to reinvent the wheel each time you brew. Instead, you can use the base specs as a starting point. A coffee shop might adjust its specs daily (or at least every time they're working with a new batch of coffee), a process called *dialing it in*, in order to optimize quality. At home, I rarely tweak mine. The base specs usually work well enough.

Choosing the Right Dose
Bad: Guessing
Okay: Two tablespoons of ground coffee per six ounces of water
Better: 1:15 to 1:17 whole beans to water in grams

GRIND SIZE AND CONTACT TIME

Grinding coffee involves breaking whole coffee beans into smaller pieces. A whole bean, with its relatively small surface area, does not afford water much opportunity to penetrate it and extract the good stuff. Also, trying to extract coffee from whole beans would take forever, which isn't practical. That's why beans are ground up into big (*coarse*) or small (*fine*) pieces before being used—it makes it easier for water to extract coffee from them. Understanding how grind size affects extraction will help you adjust your cup to suit your preferences.

Grind size has a significant effect on your coffee's extraction and, by extension, its flavor. Finer grounds give your dose a greater overall surface area than coarser grounds, which translates to more room for water to flow in and extract flavor. This means that if you start using finer grounds without changing anything else about the way you currently make coffee, you will end up with a higher extraction yield than usual. When water has more opportunity to penetrate the grounds and dissolve the coffee's flavor compounds, more dissolved material ends up in your cup.

Of course, more isn't always better. Because extraction happens faster with finer particles, you can easily overdo it. Brewing methods that use finer grounds tend to require less contact time with the water to make a yummy cup. Likewise, brewing methods that use coarser grounds tend to require more contact time with the water.

While finer grounds may extract faster, they don't necessarily help the coffee brew faster. This is because grind size can drastically affect *flow rate*, or how quickly water passes through a pile of coffee (this applies to pour-over brewing methods more than full-immersion brewing methods; see page 46). Coarse grounds have more space between them, which means water can pass through them more quickly. Finer grounds are more compact, so water moves through them more slowly. Think of it like this: Would water travel faster through a column of gravel or a column of sand?

Unfortunately, there isn't one special grind size that will guarantee you a better cup; great (or terrible) coffee can be made with all manner of grind sizes. To make things more mysterious, there are no universal grind sizes and no standardized language to talk about grind size beyond the terms *fine*, *medium*, and *coarse*, which are highly subjective. Further, different grinders come with different nomenclature. One grinder set to 14 might not produce the same size grounds as a different grinder set to 14. Other grinders may not even use numbers. There are scientific ways

GRIND REFERENCE CHART

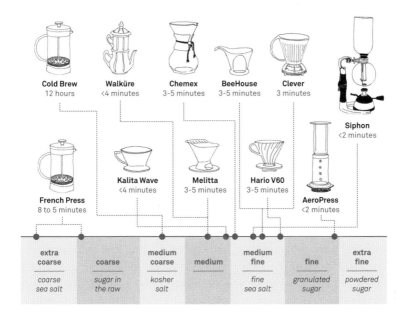

extra coarse	coarse	medium coarse	medium	medium fine	fine	extra fine
coarse sea salt	sugar in the raw	kosher salt		fine sea salt	granulated sugar	powdered sugar

Cold Brew 12 hours
Walküre <4 minutes
Chemex 3-5 minutes
BeeHouse 3-5 minutes
Clever 3 minutes
Siphon <2 minutes

French Press 8 to 5 minutes
Kalita Wave <4 minutes
Melitta 3-5 minutes
Hario V60 3-5 minutes
AeroPress <2 minutes

to measure particle size, but you need extra equipment, and it simply isn't practical for the home brewer (or anyone).

For these reasons, it's often simpler to compare the size and texture of the grind with more familiar kitchen items, like salt and sugar. In the Grind Reference chart above, I've illustrated the spectrum of grind sizes, along with a tactile comparison and the brewing devices covered in the next chapter that typically use each size.

Different devices generally work best within a certain range of grind sizes to better control the flow rate. If you use grounds that are too coarse for a device, the water will pass through them so quickly that you'll end up with underextracted coffee. On the other hand, if you use too fine a grind, the water will move through the grounds at a snail's pace (or even stop!), and you'll end up with overextracted coffee. This is why, if you're in a rush, you can't just tighten the grind to make your coffee brew faster.

One big indicator that your grind size is too fine for your device—at least if you're using a pour-over device—is the state of your coffee bed: if it looks muddy, the grind is likely too fine. Another indication is your water takes too long to draw down through the coffee bed. In chapter 6, I provide a target drawdown time for each of the pour-over methods. Overshoot that time and your grind might be too fine; finish ahead of schedule and your grind might be too coarse.

Devices also tend to be associated with certain windows of brewing times. A French press is among those with the longest brewing times and an AeroPress is among those with the shortest brewing times. That isn't to say there is a single correct combination of grind size and contact time for each device, even if the manufacturer says otherwise. You can find multiple ways to make a great cup of coffee on one device; it's just that success is probably more easily obtained in the windows described in the chart—at least for beginners. However, some devices are more versatile than others. For example, this book provides specs for both an eight-minute and five-minute French press method, and the coffee community seems to crank out endless wild recipes for the AeroPress.

It's important to note that grind size is never truly uniform because roasted coffee beans, by their nature, break up irregularly. All grinders produce a distribution of grind sizes, from relatively large chunks to tiny fines. This is one of the reasons why it's important to use a good grinder (and why I suggest that if you buy only one coffee implement, it should be a burr grinder), but I'll discuss this further on page 84.

Grind Size and Taste

Too fine = thick mouthfeel, bitter flavors
Too coarse = thin mouthfeel, flat or sour flavors

WATER

Coffee is 98 to 99 percent water. Water is both an ingredient and, because it is a solvent, a tool. That means water deserves our attention. To start: funky-tasting water will produce funky-tasting coffee. In the United States, most of us are blessed with ready access to water. However, not all water is created equal. When making coffee, fresh, good-tasting water is key. For beginners, if you already have fresh, good-tasting water that flows directly from the tap, then go ahead and use it. If you don't—that is, if the water has a perceptible smell or taste of any sort—consider using a simple carbon-filter pitcher or a similar device (assuming you're not already doing so). Our water here in Chicago happens to taste like chlorine, as if the city is diluting pool water and running it through the pipes. My carbon-filter pitcher does a great job of filtering out that taste—in fact, a standard carbon-filter pitcher will filter out any chlorine tastes or odors (probably the most common issues with tap water in the United States) as well as a few kinds of metals. A variety of other more expensive filtering options are out there, but for home coffee brewers, a carbon-filter pitcher is likely all you need to fix subpar water.

When using a filter, however, the goal is not to remove *everything* from your water. That's because water contains a bunch of minerals and other substances that help it to be a good solvent. For example, magnesium and calcium are particularly good at extracting coffee flavors. Soft or distilled water (water in which most or all minerals and impurities have been removed) is not a good coffee solvent. Distilled water may be necessary for your disgusting neti pot, but you should never use it to brew coffee—it cannot pull enough flavors from the coffee grounds, so your cup can end up tasting overly acidic (sour). However, mineral water is not the best option for brewing either, even though it might be chock-full of calcium and magnesium. Mineral water is often *too* hard, which results in dull, bitter coffee that lacks pleasant acidity.

A common complaint from those who have well water is that it's too hard and causes non–coffee-related problems, like scaling and the need for extra soap when cleaning. Because of this, many households with well water use softening systems. If you're in this situation and your coffee isn't tasting good, try comparing coffee made with hard water to coffee made with soft water. If you can tell a difference, start using the water with the better result. If you don't like either, you can try using natural bottled spring water (which is different from mineral water).

Many professional coffee shops have reverse-osmosis systems that filter their water and then add the right amount of calcium and magnesium back in. I have even seen shops sell their reverse-osmosis water to customers. This is completely unnecessary and almost criminal—there, I said it! A handful of companies also sell the right mix of minerals to turn distilled water into perfect coffee water. I haven't yet tried that myself, but I suppose it's good to know that it's an option.

The SCA provides standards on water quality, which I've included below. The middle column is what the SCA suggests is perfect, and the right column offers wiggle room in some areas.

Characteristic	Target	Acceptable Range
Odor	Clean/fresh, odor free	
Color	Clear color	
Total chlorine	0 mg/L	
Total dissolved solids (TDS)	150 mg/L	75–250 mg/L
Calcium hardness	4 grains or 68 mg/L	1–5 grains or 17–85 mg/L
Total alkalinity	40 mg/L	At or near 40 mg/L
pH	7.0 mg/L	6.5–7.5 mg/L
Sodium	10 mg/L	At or near 10 mg/L

For beginners, this chart should at least suggest that freshness, cleanness, and the absence of chlorine are the most important factors to consider when assessing brewing water. For home brewers who are interested in water, it's worth noting that the chart is sometimes vague and sometimes specific. Regardless of your level of interest in brewing water, you should know that it is unlikely that the water you have at home falls within all of the SCA's ranges, and the chart certainly has its flaws. For example, recent studies suggest that the importance of something like TDS (how many minerals and other elements are in your water—not to be confused with TDCS, the term I use to specifically refer to the amount of dissolved coffee particles in coffee) as a measurement in and of itself is exaggerated. It's also not practical for home brewers to test their water for all of these characteristics. I think of the SCA's water standards as more of a "control what you can" type of guidance. Maybe you can't control the number of TDS in your water, but water that tastes like chlorine? That you can control.

People who are super interested in water should read *Water for Coffee* by barista Maxwell Colonna-Dashwood and MIT coffee scientist Christopher H. Hendon. It explores how and why water changes coffee from a scientific perspective and suggests that many coffee professionals put too much emphasis on, for example, TDS. Determining the perfect water for brewing coffee is a developing science and is not completely applicable to the home kitchen, but the book offers a few points that are worth emphasizing to home brewers:

- **Water makes coffee different from other craft products.** The quality of coffee is determined by its flavor, just like with wine or beer. You can talk about the processing, mouthfeel, and flavor notes of all three beverages. But coffee beans also must be prepared (not just processed) with water, making it fundamentally different from wine and beer, which do not require any such preparation. On top of that, water is the primary ingredient in our beloved coffee, and it is not constant—it can vary from town to town. This means that about 99 percent of coffee's composition is ever changing—that's remarkable!

- **Different types of water have various effects on coffee's flavor.** Because water varies from place to place and it's not practical (or necessary, frankly) to make it uniform, you will get different results in your coffee cup depending on the kind of water you use. Even if there were a way to ensure that all of your other brewing variables stayed the same, using a different type of water than usual could have a drastic effect on your coffee's flavor. This means that if you move or go on vacation, the specs that worked so well for you at home might not work so well in your new place— or maybe it works better!

All of this is simply to say that home coffee brewers should respect water and do what they can to control their water quality: filter out chlorine and avoid using distilled water or mineral water. There also may come a time when your water just doesn't work with a specific type of coffee. Coffee is roasted to work with the roaster's water, which might not align with what you have going on at home. In reality, it's unlikely that this difference is going to affect your cup so much as to make it undrinkable. Any water issue is more likely to manifest like this: you have tried everything and your coffee never tastes right. Maybe it's your water.

TEMPERATURE

Conventional coffee wisdom says the ideal brewing temperature for water is usually between 195°F and 205°F (except for cold brew; see page 60). Note that this range is lower than water's boiling point of 212°F— that's the main takeaway here: water at a boiling temperature is too hot for making coffee.

Water temperature is important because it influences how the soluble compounds in coffee dissolve. The low end of the ideal temperature range is 195°F because it's harder for water colder than that to dissolve many of the compounds that contribute pleasant flavors to your cup, meaning it might take longer for the water to do so. Water that's too hot

Heat Retention

At my house, I use a standard electric kettle to heat my water because it's super fast, and I can't stand to wait for water to boil. If I'm using a pour-over method, I transfer the water from the electric kettle to a gooseneck kettle, and the whooshing of the water during the transfer cools it down enough (on average, to close to 205°F) to be ready to pour so I don't have to wait. (There are electric gooseneck kettles, but I like the setup I have now.)

You may have noticed that professional baristas often return the kettle to the heat source at times when they aren't pouring, like after wetting the filter (see page 54). I'd say typically this isn't necessary, especially if you are heating your water on a stove.

I'm a generally curious person, though, so I did some water temperature retention tests (warning: this goes kind of deep). In the past, I've defaulted to waiting only 30 seconds between taking the kettle off boil and pouring the water because a minute just *seemed* too long. However, when I tested this theory at home, I was surprised by how well my kettle retained heat. After 30 seconds, my water temperature was a rock-solid 210°F every time I tested it. After a full minute, it only dropped by another degree or two. At a minute and 30 seconds, it was around 207°F and after two minutes, it was around 203°F. After three entire minutes, the water only lost about 12°F on average, registering at 200°F during most tests—still well within the ideal brewing temperature range. How quickly the temperature of your water drops has a lot to do with your environment. On the day of testing, my room temperature was 78°F, and I used a kettle made of stainless steel, a material that retains heat well. If you're interested in water temperature, try this same test in your own home with your own kettle.

(like at the boiling point) dissolves too many compounds too quickly, which can result in bitter or astringent coffee.

Professional baristas use special equipment—usually water towers or kettles with induction plates that can gauge and hold certain temperatures—to ensure that the water they use is always on point. Although similar equipment is available to you, it's probably not strictly necessary for home brewing. You could simply use a digital-read thermometer to check your water temperature while you heat it, but another approach is to take the kettle off the boil for about 30 seconds to a full minute before pouring. For the home brewer's purposes, this should do just fine.

It should be noted that the act of pouring into a brewing device or brewing vessel *significantly* reduces water temperature. In one test, I noticed that when poured directly off boil into unheated ceramic mugs, my water immediately cooled to 200°F and, outside the warm embrace of stainless steel, continued to lose heat quickly until it reached around 160°F. That's why many baristas try to account for this loss by preheating their devices and coffee mugs with hot water. These are both attempts to reduce the amount of heat lost as the heat transfers from the brewing water to the device and from the coffee to the mug, respectively.

All things considered, I doubt the heat retention of a device or vessel perceptibly changes the flavor of the brew. Under normal kitchen circumstances, I generally don't bother to preheat my device unless it's a by-product of my rinsing a paper filter—although it certainly doesn't

Elevation and Water Temperature

For every 500-foot increase in elevation, the boiling point of water decreases by 1°F. That means in a place like Denver, which is 5,280 feet above sea level, the boiling point of water is around 202°F, as opposed to the standard 212°F. Pretty wild! What does this mean for coffee folks who are living a mile up in the air? The boiling point of coffee is smack dab in the ideal temperature range for making coffee. As discussed, boiling coffee at sea level is generally a no-no, but in a place like Denver, maybe you can tool around with it. (For example, Boxcar Coffee Roasters in Denver makes its coffee using a boiling method.) Have fun!

hurt anything if you do. Preheating ceramic, at least, does seem to slow down heat loss. In my tests with preheated mugs, the water temperature still immediately dropped to around 200°F, but the inevitable drop to even lower temperatures was markedly slower—meaning your coffee has a better chance of staying warmer for longer.

POUR

When using a pour-over method, the way you pour the water over the grounds can affect the way your coffee tastes. Specifically, the pace and control of your pour have the biggest impact. There are probably as many perfected pour techniques as there are professional baristas, yet there isn't much literature on the subject of pouring. It's sort of an abstract concept, and it can sound a little ridiculous when you get down to it, but since you're going to have to pour that water at some point, you might as well learn how pouring can affect your brew. Is pour technique beginner-level stuff? Probably not. Is a super-refined pouring technique strictly necessary for homemade coffee? No way. But beginners can apply a couple of easy pouring concepts and still taste a difference in their cup.

As I discussed previously, the amount of contact time the water has with the coffee directly corresponds to how many flavor molecules dissolve. As you'll see a bit later on, the extent to which you agitate the water can also affect extraction. In other words, pouring quickly and sloppily can significantly (and negatively) influence the final outcome. Speaking as someone who used to just dump the water over the grounds, I can assure you that a slow, controlled pour bears noticeable results.

Performing this slow, controlled pour is easiest with a gooseneck kettle (see page 97). No, you don't *need* one—and I've included methods in this book to make pouring easier if you don't have one—but it certainly helps you control and direct the flow of the water.

There is much debate in the professional coffee community about two different types of pouring methods: continuous pouring and pulsing.

I think either one is fine for the home brewer, but there are a few things to keep in mind no matter which technique you use:

- **Don't flood the coffee bed.** The point of pour-over methods isn't to drench the coffee grounds and have them soak in a pool of water. You want to keep the water level relatively stable so you can ensure that fresh water is continuously replenishing the bed as coffee drains from the bottom of the device. Why is this important? Fresh water is a better solvent than coffee water. (Of course, there are exceptions; see the V60 method on page 248.)

- **Pour toward the middle.** For most of your pouring time, you should be sticking relatively closely to the middle of the coffee bed. If you pour around the sides of the device, the water can make channels along the walls and bypass most of the coffee grounds. You can tell whether you're hitting the sides of the device by taking a look at the filter once the water draws all the way down. There should be a thin layer of coffee, mostly made up of fines, around the sides of the filter just above the bed. If there are clean patches of filter (called *balding* in the biz), then you know water was hitting the sides of the device and taking the path of least resistance downward. The other issue with this is what's called *fines migration*. Because fines tend to stick to the sides of the filter, water can wash them to the bottom of the filter, where they clog up everything, sending your contact time straight to hell.

- **Evenly distribute the water.** Although it's best to stick to the relative middle of the coffee bed, you never want to pour directly into one spot. This will create a channel that allows water to bypass most of the grounds. To avoid this, try to pour in a rhythmic pattern of small circles or figure eights or whatever your heart desires. Professional baristas do this in lots of ways (and many have strong opinions about which is right), but for the home brewer's purposes, the point is to keep the water moving so it is evenly distributed across the entire bed. When the water drains through the grounds, the bed should be as flat as possible. If you notice slopes or divots once all of the water has drained, you know that you've been favoring one area over another.

- **Keep the coffee in the coffee bed.** While it's common to see fines stuck to your filter, you don't want to see thick walls of grounds stuck all the way up the sides of the brewing device. (Unless there is an exception, which there always is; again, see the V60 method on page 248.) Large chunks of grounds stuck to the filter above the bed are called *boulders*. The thicker and higher the boulders are on the sides of the filter, the less coffee is actually coming into contact with the water for the correct amount of time. In some of my brew methods, I recommend taking a quick lap or two around the outer reaches of the bed to make sure you are pushing those grounds back down into the slurry.

- **Make your time.** Besides making sure the coffee is evenly and completely in contact with the water, the controlled pour is also supposed to control the time in which the coffee is in contact with the water, the brewing time. This book's specs outline the target brewing time for each method in chapter 6. For pour-over methods, this includes the time you pour and how long it takes the water to filter through the bed once your final beverage weight is met. If you pour too fast, the water won't get a chance to extract all of the goodness from the grounds. If you pour too slowly, you might end up with overextracted coffee. Remember, if you feel like you are pouring as slowly as you can and the water is still draining too quickly, your grind might be too coarse. If you are consistently hitting your brew-time mark but the water is drawing down achingly slowly, your grind might be too fine. (See page 27 for more on this.)

Getting the hang of pouring takes time, but it gets easier the more you do it. Eventually, you, like professional baristas, may develop a muscle memory that makes pouring second nature. Will that happen to you? Who knows! But good pouring technique is fairly simple to master either way.

Continuous Pouring

Plenty of baristas feel that if you're preparing pour-over coffee, you should be continuously replenishing the water in the device with a slow, steady stream from your kettle. This is called *continuous pouring*. The goal is to keep the slurry at a low, consistent height and to keep the flow rate constant throughout the length of the pour. Ideally, the stream of water should never break, not even to a dribble.

Advocates of this method often say it's gentle (little agitation), meaning you can use finer grounds that can potentially result in a tastier cup. Many also claim that devices like the V60 and the Chemex literally *require* such slow, controlled pouring because the devices themselves do very little to control flow rate.

This kind of pouring is essentially impossible without a gooseneck kettle, and it certainly requires a bit of effort to master. For best results, the kettle should be about three-quarters full (the flow rate out of the spout changes more drastically as the water level in the kettle decreases, which can be tricky for beginners), and it can feel a bit heavy at first. Over time, people supposedly develop a "barista muscle," and it becomes easier for them to hold and control a full kettle in one hand for the entire pour time. (I, for one, remain a weakling to this day.) It's also helpful to practice pouring into your device with a filter but without the grounds. Practice continuous pouring with a familiar amount of water—say, 250 to 400 grams. Time yourself and start over if you break your stream. See how slowly you can go. If you can pour 250 continuous grams of water in three minutes or longer, you can probably do anything.

Agitation happens when the coffee grounds move around in the water. Agitation exposes coffee particles to fresh water more quickly, which in effect speeds up extraction. A certain level of agitation happens with most devices because you must introduce the water at some point, and that's going to stir things up a bit. As the water level rises and falls, the coffee grounds move with it—that's more agitation. Most of the time, you probably want to keep extra agitation, beyond what's happening as you pour the coffee, to a minimum. However, some methods, particularly full-immersion methods, may benefit from a quick stir or two. How do you know how much to agitate? It's just something you'll have to pick up with practice. But in the beginning, it's a good skill to keep in mind and work toward developing.

Pulsing

Pulsing is a different kind of pouring technique. Instead of continuously pouring the water, you take breaks at certain intervals to allow the water to drain. How often you break and for how long is highly variable—everyone has their own opinions about what's best for what kind of device. Generally speaking, one break every 50 to 60 grams is fairly standard.

While pulsing involves taking a break in between pours, that doesn't mean it'll draw out the brewing time. Pulsing necessitates pouring faster (because of the breaks), and the target brewing time on a pour-over device generally remains the same whether you pulse or continuously pour.

In my experience, pulsing is more forgiving and easier to master than continuous pouring. Pulsing is way less stressful for one thing, and it lets you easily make adjustments to your speed as you go. Pulsing also allows you to brew smaller batches of coffee and still maintain the proper contact time.

Blooming

No matter which technique you use, *blooming* your coffee—that is, thoroughly prewetting the grounds with a small amount of hot water before you continue pouring—is another easy way to improve your cup. It sounds silly: How could just wetting the grounds and waiting have a significant effect on the end flavor of the cup? But it seems to. At base, the heat and moisture provided by the bloom prepare the coffee for extraction, and they do so in two ways:

- **Releasing carbon dioxide.** Fresh coffee contains a lot of carbon dioxide because it gets trapped in the beans during the roasting process. When you wet coffee grounds, they swell and bubble as the carbon dioxide is released. (One good indicator that your coffee has gone stale is that there is little to no bubbling during the bloom). Coffee naturally off-gasses carbon dioxide, but hot water speeds up the process. Carbon dioxide, as anyone who has drunk soda water can tell you, is bitter. Blooming makes sure all of that bitter carbon dioxide doesn't end up in your cup.

- **Beginning the extraction process.** Blooming ensures that the beans' carbon dioxide gets out of the way of the other solubles before real extraction starts. If the carbon dioxide isn't released, the gas repels the water, providing the other solubles with a protective shield. This makes it more difficult for the water to reach these solubles, which makes it harder for you to make a tasty cup.

How much water should you pour for a bloom? A good rule of thumb is to double the weight of your dose and use that amount of water. For example, if your dose is 14 grams (about 2 tablespoons) of coffee, your bloom weight would be 28 grams (about 4½ tablespoons) of water. You want enough water to soak the grounds but not so much that it streams through the device (some dripping is okay). Adding too much water at once can trap the carbon dioxide and defeat the purpose of the bloom.

How long should you wait before continuing with the brew? A good bloom time is about 30 to 45 seconds, depending on the coffee's freshness, roast, and dose. For example, fresh, light-roasted coffee usually needs a longer bloom time, as do bigger doses. Once the bubbles start to slow, that's a good sign that the bloom time should be ending.

At this point you might be thinking: Why only 30 to 45 seconds? Why not wait until *all* of the bubbles have completely subsided? For one, the bubbles usually don't stop. Two, if carbon dioxide is escaping, you can bet your butt that other volatile aromatic compounds are escaping as well. Volatile aromatics are incredibly delicate and prone to wafting off into the ether—that's why they are called volatile!—but it's important to keep them in the coffee because they greatly contribute to flavor (aroma is a big part of flavor; see page 193).

> **Zero That Scale!**
>
> Don't forget to zero your scale before you start pouring water for the bloom. The weight of neither the device nor the coffee should be included in the bloom weight.

DIALING IT IN

As mentioned earlier, when coffee professionals use the phrase "dialing it in," they are talking about using trial and error to determine the correct brew variables, or specs, for a cup of coffee (or a shot of espresso). In other words, they're talking about fine-tuning their brew. As you've seen, all of the brew variables discussed in this chapter can affect the outcome of the cup, so it's important to get them just right.

Professional baristas may need to tweak some of these variables as often as daily. This is because brew variables simply are not constant. As previously discussed, grind size is not uniform, and water temperature can vary throughout the brewing time. On top of that, the device, type and age of the bean, pouring consistency (in the case of pour-over methods), and even the weather outside can all affect how a cup turns out—yes, even temperature and humidity can influence the way your coffee brews! That's because coffee is hydroscopic, which means it sucks moisture from the air. This plumps up the beans (at least on a molecular level), which may make them denser once they are ground. One solution for this might be to coarsen the grind. This issue is more common with espresso, but it's a good example of how certain nonobvious variables can affect the cup and force some changes to the base specs.

Another common instance of specs needing to be tweaked is when super-fresh beans are used instead of not-so-fresh beans. A professional barista might use a slightly finer grind than usual with very fresh beans because they contain a lot of carbon dioxide and the gas can interfere with extraction. A finer grind can help counteract this interference early on, and as the week goes by, the barista may loosen the grind accordingly.

While you are learning and dialing it in at home, be sure to change only one brew variable at a time. That way, you can track your progress. If you change two or more variables at once, you'll never be able to draw a definitive line between the adjustment and the result. It's also easier to understand and remember each variable's effects when you test them individually. For example, if your coffee is too strong and you think either the brew ratio or the grind setting is off, only change one at a time to see which one is the problem.

As you brew more and more coffee, the process will become less like trial and error and more like concrete decision-making. You'll eventually be able to identify problems and ways to solve them quickly without using a lot of guesswork. You can also learn some tips and strategies for troubleshooting problems in the Appendix (see page 251).

CHAPTER 2

Choosing Hardware

Y OU MAY BE WONDERING why this chapter comes before the chapter on beans, which would seemingly be the first step to better coffee. Let me put it to you this way: you can put the best beans in the world into a horrible automatic machine and it will turn them into bad coffee as quick as you please (you'll learn why in this chapter). If you don't have a device with the *potential* to make great coffee, then even great beans can't make it happen.

The simple fact is that the device you choose to brew on—and how you choose to brew with it—has a measurable impact on your cup. You have a series of important device-related choices ahead of you, and this chapter will help you make them. There is a ridiculous number of options in the world of brewing devices, but the first favor I did for you is reduce that number. This chapter focuses on 10 devices, including my favorites. Any one of them could be a great choice, but the point of this chapter is to help you make the best choice for *you*. That's why I focus on the factors that tend to be most important to home brewers looking to buy a new brewing device: ease of use, availability, and affordability.

However, you can't make a good purchasing decision without considering the other types of equipment you want (or don't want) to invest in—most brewing devices require a bit of company. This chapter outlines some of the other additions you can make to your brew bar—filters, grinders, scales, kettles, and more—and how they can improve (or damage) your cup.

FULL-IMMERSION VERSUS POUR-OVER BREWING DEVICES

There are two primary ways to manually brew coffee: the full-immersion method and the pour-over method. When choosing a brewing device, this is the first decision you'll have to make: Which method do you want to use? As you'll see, the kind of method you choose will affect not only the characteristics of your brew but also how much money you spend, how much time and energy you use making coffee, and how much additional equipment you might need.

Full-immersion (often simply called *immersion*) brewing involves essentially the same process as what you would use to steep tea. The water is introduced all at once, and the grounds soak fully submerged. The water then penetrates the grounds to extract the flavor and texture compounds. At the very end of the brewing process, the grounds are filtered from the coffee.

Pour-over brewing, on the other hand, involves pouring water over the grounds and through a filter. The key there is to introduce the water slowly throughout the length of the brew cycle. As it washes through the grounds, the water takes the coffee's flavor and texture compounds with it.

One big advantage of immersion devices is that they tend to be a bit easier to master than pour-over devices because they do not require a high level of technique or any special equipment. Immersion brewing is a set-it-and-forget-it way of making coffee. In contrast, pour-over devices require a certain degree of technique to make sure enough water is reaching the grounds for the correct length of time. Such precision generally warrants an extremely slow and controlled pour, a feat most easily accomplished with a gooseneck kettle. This kind of attention to detail is less important when it comes to immersion brewing, so if you aren't interested in investing in extra equipment right off the bat, you may want to reconsider using a pour-over method.

Keep in mind, however, that all devices exist on a spectrum. As you'll see in the device profiles starting on page 69, some pour-over devices require less technique (and less additional equipment) than others.

A NOTE ON THE AUTOMATIC COFFEE MACHINE

Even though coffee is simple, I've just spent several thousand words talking about its various facets and making suggestions that will help you replicate coffee from a shop at home. It's not difficult to see why pushing a single button on an automatic coffee machine is much more tempting than dealing with any of this.

The problem is that most standard automatic coffee machines will never replicate coffee-shop quality at home—even if you opt for drip coffee instead of pour over when you go out. That's because most automatic machines simply aren't designed for optimal coffee brewing, for two main reasons:

- Most automatic machines cannot reach the proper brew temperature quickly enough or maintain it for the length of the brew cycle.
- Most automatic machines do not achieve the proper contact time.

In other words, automatic coffeemakers have temperature and time working against them.

On the other hand, a manual device allows you to easily beat a typical automatic machine on both fronts. Here's an anecdote to put this into perspective. At the office where I work, we mostly use a Melitta pour-over system, but we also have a standard automatic coffee machine. When we make pour-over coffee, we do not consistently or precisely measure the water or the beans, and we don't use a gooseneck kettle. We don't have scales or even volumetric measuring cups, and we don't use a good grinder (yet). In short, there is very little special technique involved with our pour-over method. We have work to do, after all! Still, coffee made with the pour-over system is *perceptibly* better tasting than that made with the automatic machine, even though the automatic machine is arguably making coffee more consistently than we humans are. But, at the very least, we humans are bringing the water up to the correct temperature, and the design of the Melitta device slows down the pour time—even if we pour into it as much water as we can as quickly as we can.

Does using the Melitta this way result in craft coffee-shop coffee? Not usually, but sometimes it does. Either way, it is good enough for the context of our situation—and, again, it is *perceptibly* better than the coffee made with the machine. I cannot stress this enough. It's crazy!

This isn't to say that no automatic machines can brew high-quality coffee. Most coffee shops use automatic drip machines that can produce delicious coffee, but those are for commercial use and baristas calibrate them regularly. The Specialty Coffee Association (SCA) tests consumer-grade coffee machines each quarter, and if a machine meets its standards (mainly the time and temperature considerations described previously), it becomes an SCA Certified Home Brewer, and you will likely be able to make a good cup with it. As of this writing, that list includes the following machines:

- Bonavita 8-Cup Digital Coffee Brewer model BV1900TD *(retail: $199.95)*
- Bonavita 8-cup Coffee Brewer model BV1900TS *(retail: $189.99)*
- Behmor Brazen Plus Customizable Temperature Control Brew System *(retail: $199)*
- KitchenAid Custom Pour Over Brewer model KCM0802 *(retail: $230)*
- KitchenAid Pour Over Coffee Brewer model model KCM0801OB *(retail: $199.99)*
- OXO On 12-Cup Coffee Brewing System *(retail: $299.99)*
- OXO On 9-Cup Coffee Maker *(retail: $199.99)*
- Technivorm Moccamaster *(retail: $309 to $360)*
- Wilfa Precision Automatic Coffee Brewer *(retail: $329.95)*

This isn't an exhaustive list of automatic coffeemakers that can make high-quality coffee, but it's a good place to start your research if you are in the market for one. As you can see, they are all rather pricey, which makes them inaccessible to a lot of people who want to make coffee at home.

It's also important to realize that simply owning a machine doesn't mean you'll be able to make foolproof coffee without thinking about anything. The machine may take care of water temperature and brewing time for you, but you still need to make decisions about the brew ratio, the grind size, and what kind of coffee to use, and you need to operate the machine according to the manufacturer's instructions.

BASIC SETUP AND TECHNIQUE: FULL IMMERSION

STEP 1: Put the water on to boil.

STEP 2: Weigh (or measure) and then grind the beans.

STEP 3: Add the ground beans to the device. If using a scale, place the device on the scale and zero it out.

STEP 4: Add the water until the proper weight (or volume) is reached. Wait the recommended amount of time.

STEP 5: Filter/plunge the brew.

STEP 6: Decant and serve immediately.

Use the Full Immersion basic setup and technique for:

The French Press page 212   The Abid Clever page 224
The AeroPress page 219

Use the Pour Over basic setup and technique for:

The Melitta page 232   The Kalita Wave page 240
The BeeHouse page 235   The Chemex page 243
The Walküre page 237   The Hario V60 page 246

Note: The Siphon requires a modified setup (see page 228).

BASIC SETUP AND TECHNIQUE: POUR OVER

STEP 1: Put the water on to boil.

STEP 2: Weigh (or measure) and then grind the beans.

STEP 3: Fold the filter, if necessary, and place it in the device.

STEP 4 (optional): Thoroughly rinse the filter with hot water and discard the rinse water.

STEP 5: Add the ground beans to the device. If using a scale, place the device on the scale and zero it out.

STEP 6: Start a timer and bloom the coffee according to the recommended time and weight (or volume).

STEP 7: Add the water until the proper weight (or volume) and time are reached.

STEP 8: Allow the coffee to draw down.

STEP 9: Serve immediately.

HOW DO FILTERS FACTOR IN?

Almost all coffee devices need some kind of filter to keep grounds out of the final brew. If you are currently using an automatic coffeemaker, then you are likely familiar with the wavy, flat-bottomed filters that work with many of those machines. Manual brew methods use an array of different filters—generally a far cry from the wavy kind—that are designed to work with specific devices (I talk about these more specifically in the device profiles starting on page 58). These filters come in different shapes, are made from a variety of materials, and are not always readily available to you—all factors to consider before you settle on a device. For example, if you don't want to mess with purchasing filters at all, you may want to choose a device with the filter already built in.

The filter you use, I would argue, has a greater effect on the quality of your brew than the device itself. The oldest and most primitive forms of filters, such as those found on the French press (metal) and Walküre (ceramic), trap insoluble solids (the grounds) and allow liquid to pass through, making the brew more drinkable. Although these filters are fine enough to trap most of the grounds, they still allow insoluble oils and solids—also referred to as *sediment*, the very fine wisps of suspended particles you may see floating near the bottom of your cup—through. These filters tend to yield coffee that feels heavy on the tongue (because of the suspended sediment) and features robust notes (because of the flavor-packing oils).

Meanwhile, paper filters, which date back to the early 20th century, are designed to trap finer sediments and insoluble oils, leading to what professionals call a *cleaner cup*. Some people prefer this to the fuller-bodied feel of coffee made with metal or ceramic filters, but others don't—it's completely based on personal preference.

Paper Filters

The first paper filter was patented in 1908 by Melitta Bentz, a German housewife who would later become the namesake of one of the most

> ### Bleached (White), Unbleached (Natural Brown), and Bamboo Filters
>
> All paper is brown in its natural state. Natural brown filters are the same as white ones—they just haven't gone through the whitening process. Manufacturers claim that there is no difference, taste-wise, between a natural and a whitened filter, but I disagree. Natural filters tend to give coffee a papery taste.
>
> If you see a white coffee filter, it's been processed. That doesn't mean, however, that it was bleached with chlorine, as was common in the past. Today, most quality white paper filters are whitened with oxygen, so you can use these filters without worrying about chemicals leaching into either your coffee or the environment.
>
> For many people, the environment is still a big concern when it comes to using paper filters. Most paper filters are 100 percent biodegradable and can be composted along with the coffee grounds, but you should always verify that information with the manufacturer of the specific filter you're using. Some manufacturers are also starting to use bamboo, which is considered a renewable resource, in their paper products.

successful manufacturers of coffee devices and accessories in history. Before paper filters, most people brewed coffee with linen filters or used filterless devices, such as percolators, which were messy and apt to produce bitter, burnt coffee. A daily cup of coffee created a lot of sludge for wives to scrape from the bottoms of their kettles, so one day Bentz took a brass pot, punched holes in it, lined it with a piece of her son's blotter paper, placed it over a coffee cup, and the first paper filter and dripper device was born. It kept the grounds out of the cup and was easy to clean up and throw away. Bentz and her family immediately set up shop to sell the revolutionary paper filters to coffee-loving Germans and, eventually, the world.

Her company, Melitta, became a pioneer of filter innovation. By the

1910s, Bentz's filter had morphed into a circular shape, and by the 1930s, it had become the now-recognizable cone shape, complete with a matching cone-shaped dripper. All modern cone-shaped filters and devices are based on this simple but elegant design. Melitta also was the first company to offer unbleached (natural brown) paper filters and, later, filters whitened with a nonchlorine bleaching process—both of which are industry standard today.

While Melitta is still a leader in coffee and coffee accessories, paper filters now come in a variety of shapes and sizes to fit different devices. For example, AeroPress filters are small and round, while Kalita filters are reminiscent of those used in automatic machines.

THE IMPORTANCE (OR NOT) OF WETTING YOUR FILTER

No matter what device you choose, if you use a paper filter, most coffee professionals recommend thoroughly rinsing it with hot water before you pour in the grounds and letting the water drain into your brewing vessel before you start brewing. There are several theories for why this is important. For one, wetting the filter improves the function of most cone drippers, and some drippers even depend on it.

Wetting a cone filter creates a seal between the filter and the angled walls of the device. It's not a complete seal, though—each device has (or should have) its own unique way of allowing for air movement. For example, the Melitta, BeeHouse, and V60 all have various types of signature ribbing along the interior walls of the dripper, which creates pockets through which air can pass. The Chemex filter, when properly wetted, creates a seal along the smooth sides of the funnel while reinforcing two air channels on opposite sides of the device. These features are all designed to regulate airflow. If there is no airflow, the wet filter will essentially create a vacuum, which slows or stops the flow rate. With too little airflow, the water will mingle with the grounds too long and extract the nastier qualities of our beloved, bitter beans. If there is too much airflow, the water will pass through the grounds too quickly, resulting in weak and unsatisfying coffee. Wetting your filter ensures that your device is firing on all cylinders from beginning to end.

The most popular manual coffee devices aim to strike a perfect balance between seal and airflow to guarantee a consistent rate of extraction. Designers, as you may have gathered by now, perpetually try to reinvent the humble cone dripper. Some are interested in achieving science-based coffee perfection, while others, it seems, are more interested in aesthetics. If you are tempted to purchase one of these newfangled, aesthetically pleasing drippers, investigate the method by which it allows for airflow. If there is none (you'd be surprised), she's not the device you're looking for.

Additionally, wetting your filter rinses away much of the filter's papery taste so it doesn't end up in your cup. For me, this is the most compelling reason to wet the filter because my taste buds can tell if I don't. I find that natural brown filters, in particular, need a good rinse before use.

Not convinced? Try wetting your filter and tasting the resulting water. You will likely be able to detect the papery taste right away. In a blind taste test, Andreas, I, and all of our subjects were able to identify the water that had gone through a brown filter—even after the filter was rinsed—and most of us could identify the water that had gone through a dry white paper filter. If you cannot immediately taste any paper in the brown-filter water, compare it with a sample of fresh, clean, boiled water. In this experiment, it was very difficult to distinguish between the clean, boiled water and the water that had passed through a rinsed white paper filter—which is why I almost exclusively use white filters at home.

There's no doubt that paper-flavored water will affect the taste of your brew—coffee is 99 percent water, after all. A word of warning: If you're anything like me, once you identify a paper taste in your coffee, it will haunt you for the rest of your life. This is especially true if you ever drink coffee out of a paper to-go cup—you will taste all paper, no coffee. Proceed with caution.

Lastly, wetting your filter and letting the hot water drain into your brewing vessel warms up the vessel. This last reason is perhaps the least important, but it stems from the idea that great coffee requires a consistent temperature.

How much does all of this *really* matter? The evidence is in your cup. I rinse because I taste paper in my coffee if I don't.

Permanent Filters

An alternative to paper filters is to use a permanent filter, which can be made of metal, ceramic, or cloth. In some cases, a particular device comes with a permanent filter, as with the mesh plunger on the French press or the crosshatch ceramic screen on the Walküre. However, with a bit of research, you can find individually sold permanent filters that are essentially just more durable versions of many of the paper filters described in this book.

As previously mentioned, using a permanent filter will absolutely affect the flavor of your brew. No matter how fine the mesh is or how tightly woven the cloth is, a permanent filter of any kind allows more fines and oils through than a paper filter does. This isn't necessarily a bad thing—it all depends on your preferences.

If you're using the right grind size and fresh, well-roasted coffee, the extra sediment and oil shouldn't be an issue when the coffee is brewed properly. However, stale coffee (or off-the-shelf preground coffee, which you can consider stale) delivers a particularly bad result when used with permanent filters. Stale coffee means compounds in the bean (particularly oils) have started to oxidize. Oxidation—the process by which oxygen helps turn one thing into another—is usually bad news for any food product, but it's particularly bad for coffee because oxygen turns yummy coffee flavors into bad-tasting coffee flavors in a hurry. Since many permanent filters do not trap as much oil as paper filters, all of those off flavors can make it into the cup.

Relatedly, permanent filters are at greater risk for residue buildup—

coffee oils that have oxidized so much as to become rancid. This buildup can certainly affect the way your brew tastes—and not for the better. Always be sure to thoroughly clean your permanent filters after each use to rid them of leftover coffee oils.

Cholesterol and Unfiltered Coffee

Studies have shown that drinking large quantities of coffee that has not been filtered through paper may slightly increase your cholesterol levels. The cholesterol-raising compound (called *cafestol*) is found in coffee oils, which are trapped by paper filters. It should be noted that coffee has been both condemned as a poison and proclaimed a curative since it was popularized hundreds of years ago. I have read the cholesterol–coffee literature, but that obviously does not make me a doctor. If you're concerned about this facet of unfiltered coffee, do your research and consult a physician.

CLOTH FILTERS

Many people turn to permanent, reusable filters for environmental reasons. If you like the taste of paper-filtered coffee but want a reusable option, cloth is a good choice. Some devices, like the siphon, are designed to work with special cloth filters, but you can find relatively inexpensive cloth alternatives to fit most devices, including the V60 and the Chemex. Cloth filters trap insoluble solids and oils almost as well as paper filters (I can't tell the difference, personally), but they are a bit fussier. For one thing, you need to boil them before the first use in order to sanitize them and then boil them every couple of months for cleanliness. It's also recommended that you store cloth filters in water in the refrigerator between uses. Without proper care, these filters will become foul and, when used, impart disgusting flavors to your cup.

FULL-IMMERSION DEVICES

The French Press (Press Pot, Coffee Press, or Cafetière)

Known by many names around the world, the French press likely is one of the oldest brewing systems that uses a filter. I say "likely" because no one is quite sure when the method came to be—or where for that matter. Some sources say that the press was being used in France as early as the 1850s. Before filters, people boiled their coffee grounds together with the water in one pot. Folklore has it that, one day, a Frenchman realized that his water was boiling, but he had forgotten to add the coffee. When he poured the coffee in, all the grounds were floating on top of the water, rendering it undrinkable. The crafty Frenchman found a metal screen, placed it on top of the pot, and pushed it down with a stick to trap the coffee—*et voilà,* he had made a French press! The coffee tasted delicious (probably because it wasn't boiled and burnt to hell) and the Frenchman never looked back.

Rich, full-bodied taste

COST   ● ● ● ● ●

AVAILABILITY   ● ● ● ● ●

TECHNIQUE   ● ● ● ● ●

Method on page 212

A 2014 *New York Times* article lends credence to this story—at least in terms of the time period. According to the report, two Parisians—a metalsmith and a merchant—received a joint patent in March 1852 for a device that used the basic principles of the French press. The patent described the filter as a piece of pierced tin covered in flannel on both sides. This filter was attached to a rod, which the user was meant to press into a cylindrical vessel. Sounds familiar, huh?

Despite this, the press did not become well-known in Europe until the 20th century, and some sources insist that the first "official" French press wasn't patented until 1929, when Italian designer Attilio Calimani filed his invention for an "apparatus for preparing infusions, particularly for preparing coffee." In the 1950s, Faliero Bondanini—also Italian—improved the design and filed a patent for his own "coffee filter pot." He started manufacturing the device and—with distribution by large kitchenware companies such as Bodum—its popularity greatly increased across Europe. However, it took even longer for the press to gain popularity in the United States.

Today, French presses are available almost anywhere kitchen goods are sold, in a variety of sizes and materials, including glass and plastic. Although the French press has been tweaked here and there over the years, modern devices employ the same admirably simple design: pour, wait, press, and enjoy. Because of this, the method is great for beginners or those who are interested in more straightforward handmade coffee. The French press requires no special skills or kettles. Generally speaking, you can go about the rest of your morning while the coffee brews.

The French press is also one of the most versatile coffee devices. You can make cold brew (see page 217) and tea in it—you can even froth milk in it for café au lait or hot cocoa. If you prefer a device that can be used multiple ways in the kitchen, strongly consider the French press. The one downside is that it's relatively difficult to clean. However, that's no excuse—to ensure that you don't get a buildup of grounds and oils, I recommend a thorough washing (yes, by disassembling the plunger) after each use.

HOW IT WORKS

When you use a French press, the coffee grounds are in contact with the water for a relatively long time, so it is important that you use very coarsely ground coffee. This will slow down the extraction rate and ensure that you don't end up with bitter, overextracted coffee.

Because the (usually metal, usually mesh) filter does not trap all of the grounds, it's important to drink or serve the coffee relatively quickly—the fines that end up in your cup will continue to extract. The longer the coffee sits, the more you risk an overextracted cup. (This is also a good reason to use a burr grinder; see page 87.) However, fines aren't all bad. They contribute to the mouthfeel of the cup, making it heavier and more velvety, which—while it stands in stark contrast to paper-filter methods—contributes to that distinct French press quality that many people enjoy.

The French press method produces a unique-tasting cup, period. French press coffee is usually bolder and richer than other coffees, bringing out the beans' darker qualities, such as chocolaty, earthy, or floral notes. Much of this is due to the fact that a French press filter allows the

COLD BREW

Cold brew has been around for a long time—possibly since the discovery of coffee itself—and craft coffee shops have been using this method of preparation for many, many years. It has gained popularity in recent years as bigger coffee chains have adopted the practice. Its rich, bold flavors, smoothness, and low perceived acidity make this drink incredibly palatable. Because the coffee is brewed with cold water and stored cold, there is less dilution when ice cubes are added (iced coffee is hot coffee poured over ice, which results in instant dilution), if you add ice cubes at all. It's no wonder this method has become a coffee fixture in the warmer months.

What you might not know is that cold brew is easy to make at home, and a variety of devices are available to help you do it. In this book, I've included the most basic method using a French press, along with one for the Clever because its design lends itself to the task. Cold brew is the ultimate set-it-and-forget-it method. It's quite economical to make it at home, too. Cold brew is very forgiving, so even less-expensive blends can turn into wow-factor beverages. Additionally, a typical batch that is properly stored in an airtight container in the refrigerator can keep for one to two weeks.

Even cold water can extract flavor from coffee. Extraction with cold water just takes a lot longer than with hot water—sometimes as long as 12 to 15 hours. Your patience will be rewarded, though. The long brewing times coffee's essential oils to stay in the brew—there is no paper filter to trap them. Because the French press tends to highlight more robust flavors, I recommend using roasts that highlight the qualities of the bean, rather than the qualities of the roast.

Some coffee professionals tend to dismiss the French press, perhaps because it makes it harder to produce more delicate flavors in the coffee. Others believe the French press is one of the purest ways to make coffee as it's the closest to the *cupping* method, a highly regimented process that coffee professionals use to taste new coffee.

tend to bring out sweet, rich flavors in the coffee—and there is very little perceived acidity. The oxidation and degradation of the coffee molecules—the same processes that turn hot coffee into gross coffee if left to sit too long—are slowed down when coffee is brewed with cold water. Recall also that coffee solubles dissolve at different rates, and those that are linked to overly bitter flavors dissolve last. That's why overextracted coffee—the kind that has spent too much time with hot water—tends to taste bitter. With cold brew, because the water takes so long to dissolve the solubles, many of those bitter compounds are not dissolved, even after 12 to 15 hours of brewing.

Because not all coffee molecules dissolve in cold water, more coffee is needed to make up for it. Both of the cold brew concentrates I use have a brew ratio of about 1:6, which is a much higher concentration of coffee than any hot brew method uses. However, the concentrate can be diluted to your liking. Adding water allows you to adjust the strength of your brew.

Cold brewing coffee often brings out a completely different flavor profile than hot brewing does. I once had a cold brew that tasted like a delicious, ripe tomato—something I've never tasted in hot-brewed coffee before. For a fun experiment, make a batch of cold brew and taste it side-by-side with the same coffee that's been brewed with hot water.

The AeroPress

I think it's safe to say that the Aero-Press is the only coffee device manufactured by a company that is better known for making flying discs. It is the result of years of research by engineer Alan Adler, the founder of Aerobie and the designer of its famous flying disc (along with all of the company's other products). His goal was to create a device that made the perfect single serving of coffee.

Although it's a relative newcomer on the coffee scene (it was released in 2005), the AeroPress is well loved for its simplicity and speed. There likely isn't a faster brewing time with such tasty results. The AeroPress is also

Fast-as-hell brewing time

COST   ● ● ● ● ●

AVAILABILITY   ● ● ● ● ●

TECHNIQUE   ● ● ● ● ●

Method on page 219

lightweight and durable (made of BPA-free plastic), making it particularly easy to travel with. It is also incredibly versatile. There are dozens and dozens of AeroPress recipes. Unlike some other devices, it seems to work well with any number of grind sizes, brewing times, and water temperatures. The coffee community even developed a new way of using the device, called the *inverted method.* In this book, I've included a method very close to the one Adler intended as well as an inverted one.

Additionally, people like to experiment with the kinds of drinks the AeroPress can make. The manufacturer suggests that the AeroPress can make a beverage that tastes akin to espresso, and then users can add the appropriate amount of milk to make espresso drinks, such as lattes and cappuccinos. It can also make tea. I'm not sold on the authenticity of AeroPress espresso drinks, but that doesn't mean they won't taste good or that you won't prefer them to regular coffee. Give it a try! If you like experimenting and using multitasking kitchen implements, this is certainly a device to consider.

Due to the device's growing popularity, it is widely available on the internet and in brick-and-mortar stores. Many craft coffee shops sell the AeroPress, but you can also get it (as of the time of this writing) at large retailers such as Target, Bed Bath & Beyond, Crate and Barrel, and Williams Sonoma.

Also, you don't need a slow-pour kettle to make great coffee with the AeroPress. It's designed to drain directly into a coffee cup, so you don't need extra carafes or servers. It only comes in one size, but the same device can make one to four servings faster than anything else out there (including typical electric coffeemakers). Coffee made with the Aero-Press tends to have less perceived acidity, as it uses a finer grind and a lower brew ratio, both of which up the body and lessen the acidity. If you are sensitive to acidity, you may want to try this device.

AEROPRESS FILTERS

These small, circular discs are manufactured to fit exclusively in the narrow brewing chamber of an AeroPress. They are made of a paper similar to that of the Melitta filter, although AeroPress filters do not sport the perforation that Melitta filters often do. AeroPress filters are sold in packs of 350 for about $8 (your first 350 are included with the purchase of the device) and are often sold at craft coffee shops.

Unlike other paper filters, AeroPress filters stand up relatively well to reuse because their shape makes them easy to rinse and dry. If you do plan to reuse an AeroPress filter, make sure you thoroughly clean it and let it dry completely. Leftover oils and the funk that often follows dampness do not make for good coffee. Lastly, licensed AeroPress filters only come in white; the manufacturer recommends that those of you who want natural brown filters make your own. Using the white filter as a template, you can cut your own out of a brown paper filter of your choice. Metal disc AeroPress filters are also available from third-party vendors.

HOW IT WORKS

The AeroPress is a type of hand press—you might think of it as a giant syringe. The coffee is poured into a brewing chamber along with the water, and then you insert a plunger and press down, forcing the coffee through the paper filter and the plastic, perforated cap at the bottom of the brewing chamber and into your cup. It's kind of like a French press, but it differs in a few important ways.

First, the AeroPress is designed to use circular paper filters, while the French press has a metal filter. The paper filter allows you to use a much finer grind—and therefore get a much quicker extraction time—than with the French press. This tends to give AeroPress cups a full-bodied, nuanced taste without the silt left behind by a metal filter. Additionally, with the Classic AeroPress Method, the water in the brewing chamber is pushed through the grounds by a pillow of air, not by the plunger itself, which allows for more even pressure.

To clean up, simply twist off the cap, hold the AeroPress over the trash or compost bin, and plunge until the compressed puck of coffee pops out, filter and all. Thoroughly rinse and dry the device, and you are good to go for next time. Every so often, you may need to wash the plunger with hot, soapy water, but this device is low maintenance.

The Abid Clever

Designed and manufactured by the Taiwanese company Absolutely Best Idea Development (or Abid for short), the Clever dripper hit the coffee scene in the late 2000s. Unlike other brewers, the Clever only comes in (BPA-free) plastic and in one size. The Clever *looks* like a standard pour-over device— it is conical in shape and even uses a paper filter (#4 Melitta cone filters work well), but it actually brews more like a French press. Its design is meant to make handmade coffee as easy as possible, and it's one of the least fussy methods in this book.

No muss, no fuss

COST   ● ● ● ● ●
AVAILABILITY   ● ● ● ● ●
TECHNIQUE   ● ● ● ● ●

Method on page 224

The Clever certainly has a user-friendly design. A regular tea kettle, for example, won't stand in the way between you and a great cup of coffee, as it might with other devices. It's also designed to drain directly into a coffee mug, so no extra carafes are needed. Cleanup is much easier than with other immersion methods, like the French press, because all you have to do is remove and discard the filter. The Clever is ideal for someone who likes the easy, hands-off approach of immersion methods but prefers the cleaner taste of paper-filtered coffee. It can also be used to make cold brew (see page 227).

One downside is that the Clever is not as widely available as other brewing devices. Most major retailers do not carry it, and although you may find one for sale at a craft coffee shop, they are not all that common. It's purchased easily enough on the internet, however.

HOW IT WORKS

Although the Clever borrows its shape from cone drippers, it's still a full-immersion method, with the grounds and water steeping together for the length of the brew cycle. The base of the device is watertight, and the slurry will not drain until you engage the release mechanism by setting it on top of a carafe or coffee cup. Just pour the water into the Clever, wait out your brewing time, and set the device on your cup to drain.

Some professionals feel that the Clever loses too much heat during the brew process. Others feel that the design clogs the filter too often with fines, which extends the contact time and can lead to overextracted coffee. Andreas and I don't really think the heat-loss argument is well founded. When professionals "cup" coffee, it often sits there, uncovered, for 12 to 15 minutes before it's tasted, and heat loss is rarely discussed in that context. However, we have found that using finer grounds in the Clever sometimes leaves us with a clogged filter.

The Siphon (Vacuum Pot)

For more than a century, people have been using the siphon (aka *vacuum pot* or *vac pot*) to make delicious coffee. It all started in 1830, when S. Loeff from Berlin filed a patent for the device, although it didn't gain commercial success until the 1840s, when a French woman named Marie Fanny Amelne Massot improved the design and patented it under the moniker Mme. Vassieux. Her design paid close attention to aesthetics—the device featured a metal frame that held two vertically hung glass globes; the top one was capped with a crown.

Over the years, the siphon's design has been tweaked, but its principles have remained the same. Even today, the brewing method itself seems designed

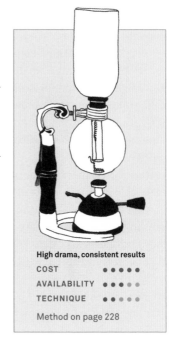

High drama, consistent results

COST   ● ● ● ● ●

AVAILABILITY   ● ● ● ● ○

TECHNIQUE   ● ● ○ ○ ○

Method on page 228

for theatrics (or at least a science experiment). You get the impression that the siphon was always meant to be on display, perhaps entertaining guests in a Victorian parlor somewhere. Even though some of the glamour was reduced by the time the siphon was first manufactured and sold in the United States (under the name Silex) in 1910, it has remained an object of wonder and amusement. This is perhaps why it has seen something of a resurgence in the coffee community in recent years.

Today, many siphons are sold by Hario and Yama, two Japanese companies that sell a variety of coffee equipment, as well as a well-established coffee brand called Bodum. They come in a range of sizes, including three-cup, five-cup, and eight-cup models. If you don't purchase a stovetop model, note that siphons also require a heat source, which is sometimes sold separately. The butane-burner models are more affordable, but companies also make flameless heat sources for the siphon, which run a couple hundred bucks or more. If you opt for a stovetop model, it's recommended that you also buy a heat dispersion plate to set between the device and the burner. The Bodum brand is available at higher-end retailers, such as Crate and Barrel, but you'll likely need to rely on the internet to find the Japanese brands.

Indeed, a major drawback of the siphon is that it's quite expensive. But it's so fun to use! The whole device is a bit delicate and should be handled with care, so if you're a bit clumsy, this likely isn't the device for you. Although the siphon is not the most practical of devices, I would argue it's one of the most consistent methods of making coffee, as much of it is automated—there is very little human intervention beyond choosing a dose and reading a thermometer. KitchenAid makes an automatic siphon, which, while not a manual brewing method, is still interesting.

SIPHON FILTER

Both Hario and Yama siphons require small, circular cloth filters. The Bodum model has a plastic filter built into the machine. Although the cloth filter is reusable, you need to treat the filter with special care if you want it to work properly and last for a while. The first time you use a cloth filter, boil it for a few minutes before you brew with it. After using it, thoroughly rinse it, and store it in clean water in the refrigerator. Then, before each use, soak the filter in clean, warm water for about five minutes. It's also recommended that you boil your cloth filter every once in a while to keep it fresh. Spoiler alert: if you don't take proper care of it, your coffee will taste like a dirty sock.

HOW IT WORKS

The siphon uses an immersion method, but it's quite distinct from other immersion methods. The water is heated in the lower globe by a heat source. The difference in pressure eventually forces the water up through a glass stem into the top chamber, called the *hopper*. Once the temperature is stabilized (around 202°F) in the hopper, it's time to add the grounds. It looks like the water is boiling, but it's not—it's just agitation from the air that's also getting sucked through the stem and into the hopper. This is the water that extracts the coffee, and when the brewing process is complete, the heat source is removed, and the pressure changes again, pushing the brewed coffee back into the bottom vessel. The hopper is fitted with the filter, which prevents the grounds from escaping into the bottom chamber. What results is a smooth, rich brew with very little sediment.

Percolator, Alligator

Maybe you are wondering why I have not included the percolator in this book. While it has loyally served the needs of coffee-drinking folk for more than 200 years, it has not served them well. Percolators fundamentally make it difficult to brew decent coffee as they force boiling water through the coffee grounds only to recirculate it multiple times. This often leads to a burnt, overextracted brew. While I do not doubt that some coffee enthusiasts have reined in the percolator beast and made it do their bidding, I don't think this device is a good one for home-brew beginners.

POUR-OVER DEVICES

The Melitta

Despite the fact that the Melitta was the first cone-shaped pour-over system created—Melitta Bentz invented the coffee filter in 1908 (see page 52), and the device soon followed—I've rarely seen it hanging out on brew bars. You will, however, see other manufacturers' tweaks on Bentz's original design, several of which I discuss in this chapter. I cut my home-brewing teeth on this device, and it was the first one that

The original pour-over device

COST   ● ● ● ● ●

AVAILABILITY   ● ● ● ● ●

TECHNIQUE   ● ● ● ● ●

Method on page 232

allowed me to taste the different flavors in coffee. The Melitta may not be as flashy or trendy as other devices, but it gets the job done, and its design makes it forgiving.

Melitta products are accessible and affordable, which is a big plus when you're new to the pour-over game. The six-cup plastic model retails around $10.99 and can usually be found at big-box retailers (as well as the internet, of course). For those of you who are looking for an upgrade from plastic kitchenware, Melitta drippers also come in ceramic. If you're new to pour over and aren't looking to break the bank, the Melitta system may be a good place to start.

MELITTA FILTERS

Melitta cone filters (also known as *wedge* filters) are great for beginners because they fit a variety of devices and can usually be found at any grocery store (and often even drug stores). Before I got into coffee, I remember seeing the distinctive green-and-red packaging everywhere and thinking, "What the hell are these for?" There's also a good chance you are already using this brand's flat-bottomed filters in your automatic machine. You'll find the cone filters in the same grocery aisle as the flat-bottomed ones. If you don't want to mess with special-ordering filters, Melitta cone filters are a good place to start. A pack of 100 filters runs between $6 and $8.

Circular and wider at the top, the Melitta cone filter tapers to a flat edge at the bottom. Both the bottom and one side of the filter are crimped. To use, take a flat, unopened filter and simply fold the bottom crimp up, then fold the side crimp over. I like to make sure the crimps are folded to lie against opposite sides of the filter. It helps the filter sit in the device and provides extra insurance against breakage (although I've never actually had one bust). Open the filter, place it in the device, and you're ready to go.

Melitta cone filters come in several sizes to match the sizes of the devices—the #2 and #4 are the most popular. Be sure to choose the size that fits your device. Although I have been known to jury-rig filters in a pinch, it's not advisable. You can't expect a device to work properly if you aren't using the appropriate component parts!

Devices That Work Well with Melitta Cone Filters		
• Melitta dripper	• BeeHouse dripper	• Abid Clever dripper

HOW IT WORKS

The Melitta is the original wedge-shaped dripper. Drippers must rest on some kind of vessel (a mug or a carafe) and require the use of a filter, which must be purchased separately and inserted into the dripper. When you pour water into the dripper, it makes its way through the coffee bed, through a filter, through a drain hole, and into the waiting vessel. The Melitta's cone shape is flat across the bottom, and it requires similarly shaped filters. Ribbing along the dripper's interior walls helps regulate airflow, and there's one medium-sized hole at the bottom (compared with the single large hole in some other pour-over devices and the two holes in the bottom of the BeeHouse). This design slows down the rate at which water can make it through the coffee bed, a quality that generally makes devices more forgiving. When the device controls a good part of the flow rate for you, your pouring technique doesn't have to be very nuanced.

The Melitta's design does seem to make it more prone to fines migration than other devices. Because there is only one relatively small hole for the water to drain through, it doesn't take much for fines to clog up the works and reduce the flow rate even more. I advise you to aim your pour away from the sides of the device as much as possible.

The BeeHouse

Based on the classic Melitta design, the BeeHouse is an updated wedge-shaped cone dripper that comes in two sizes. It very closely resembles the Melitta dripper, but where the Melitta has one drain hole at the bottom, the BeeHouse has two. The ribbing along the interior wall of the dripper is also a bit different, and the BeeHouse only comes in ceramic. If you like to pour directly into your coffee mug, the BeeHouse is an attractive op-

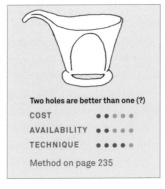

Two holes are better than one (?)

COST   ● ● ● ● ●
AVAILABILITY   ● ● ● ● ●
TECHNIQUE   ● ● ● ● ●

Method on page 235

tion. It fits most coffee cups, and the base of the dripper features windows so you can see how close you are to maximum capacity. As a pour-over device, the BeeHouse inherently requires more technique than immersion devices, but it's one of the easier pour-over devices to use. For example, I feel it's much easier to master than, say, the V60 (see page 79)—it's probably my second-favorite device, for what that's worth.

Additionally, the BeeHouse is an attractive option for those who do not want to worry about special filters. The BeeHouse is compatible with

Melitta filters (the large can use #2 or #4, and the small uses only #2), which can be found in almost any grocery store. Because of this and its relatively inexpensive price tag, the BeeHouse is a great way to introduce yourself to pour over.

One downside is it's not available at bigger chain retailers, although it is a bit more common to see them for sale at craft coffee shops than the Clever dripper. There is always the internet.

HOW IT WORKS

The BeeHouse works like a standard pour-over filtration system. However, its design (namely, the two drain holes) restricts water flow more than other devices, such as the V60 and the Chemex (see page 77), which means it tends to be more forgiving of imperfect technique than those other devices. Because the design takes pressure off your pour time, you might find the BeeHouse less stressful to use than other pour-over devices. Grind size is the primary factor in determining the flow rate with a BeeHouse, so feel free to experiment with different sizes and see how they affect your brewing time.

Like with most cone-dripper coffee, a BeeHouse cup is clean, but the longer brewing time provides a chance for sweeter flavors to come through. Some professional baristas feel that some complexity is lost with the BeeHouse and that it is perhaps fundamentally incapable of achieving the greatness of the Chemex or V60. I find, however, that it provides consistent results for the home brewer, no matter what kind of coffee you use.

The Walküre

Made of four sections of high-quality porcelain, the Walküre (pronounced VAL-kur-ee; *es ist deutsch!*) has been around for more than 100 years. It's still made, along with other porcelain goods, in the same factory in Bayreuth, Germany, that Siegmund Paul Meyer opened in 1899. High demand for his products prompted Meyer to launch the Walküre line of home goods in 1906. With its beautiful design and simple brew method, the Walküre is the perfect option for someone who wants a pour-over device that's both easy on

Purist's dream

COST	● ● ● ● ●
AVAILABILITY	● ● ● ● ●
TECHNIQUE	● ● ● ● ●

Method on page 237

the eyes and easy to use—and full disclosure: this is my favorite device.

In my experience, the Walküre is relatively forgiving. It doesn't require a paper filter, but it produces a cleaner cup than other paperless brewers, such as the French press. The Walküre's ceramic filter allows oils and other insolubles through, but the slow pour makes it easier to produce a more delicate, complex cup. You should still be wary of over-extraction from the fines sitting in the decanter, but that is easily avoided by serving the brew right away.

I'll admit that the Walküre is one of the more esoteric devices in this book. You certainly won't find it at home goods stores, and it's also less likely that your local coffee shop sells it than other less popular devices, such as Clever drippers. It is, of course, available on the internet, particularly on coffee-supply websites. The other downside of the Walküre is it's on the pricier side. The smallest Karlsbad (0.28L), which is more traditionally styled, runs about $89, and the small Bayreuth, which has a sleek, modern look, runs closer to $110. The prices only go up from there—a medium size (0.38L), which is the one I use, and a large size

(0.85L) are also available. Another thing to consider is that the smallest Walküre can't make multiple servings of coffee at once. I can make two modest cups with the medium size, but it's probably best to think of it as a single-cup brewer.

HOW IT WORKS

We need to talk about the Walküre's components, starting from the counter up. First, there is a decanter with a handle and a spout for pouring. Next, there is a cylindrical brewing chamber, which has a double screen of cross-hatched porcelain at the bottom. This is the device's built-in filter. The grounds sit directly on top. Next, there is a dispersion plate that hangs inside the brewing chamber. To use it, you pour the water onto the plate, and it slowly drains through holes along the rim to the grounds below. Last is the lid, which fits atop both the dispersion plate, to keep heat in during the brew, and the decanter, for when you are ready to serve.

I am reminded of the designer's ingenuity each time I brew with the Walküre. There are so many advantages, starting with the dispersion plate. This unique feature controls even the sloppiest of pours—the water can drain only so quickly through the holes, and when it does, it showers evenly over the bed at a consistent rate. It also keeps agitation to a minimum. Because of this, you don't necessarily need a slow-pour kettle or a steady hand. The other advantage is you don't need filters. The built-in filter looks improbable, but it effectively traps a surprising number of fines. In fact, because of the way the device is designed, the coffee bed itself acts as a filter, trapping fines before they can make it into the cup (this is sometimes called *cake filtration*). Some fines obviously do get through, but because of how the spout is positioned on the decanter (at least with the Karlsbad), I find that very few fines end up in the cup, although you may notice some in the decanter when you clean it.

The Kalita Wave

Kalita is a Japanese company that got its start making paper filters in Tokyo in 1958. It has since expanded its manufacturing to coffee brewing implements, like kettles and the Wave. The first Kalita dripper was manufactured in 1959, and its original design is said to have been strongly influenced by that of the Melitta, although it featured three holes to Melitta's one. (I'm not sure if

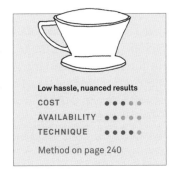

Low hassle, nuanced results

COST	● ● ● ● ●
AVAILABILITY	● ● ● ● ●
TECHNIQUE	● ● ● ● ●

Method on page 240

it's a coincidence or not, but even the names and the logos are similar.) Since then, Kalita's original dripper has evolved into the Wave, a unique pour-over device with a distinctive flat-bottomed design.

The Kalita Wave is available in two sizes, #185 (big) and #155 (small), each of which requires its own-sized filter. The device can be purchased in ceramic, glass, or stainless steel. As of this writing, familiar kitchenware retailers do not carry the Kalita Wave, although you might find it at your local craft coffee shop, particularly if the shop uses the Wave for its pour-over coffee. Like the BeeHouse, you may need to turn to the internet to purchase this device.

Many professionals feel that the Kalita Wave is a versatile, forgiving device. The dripper's design does a good job of regulating water flow, which helps make up for user error, but it can make it difficult to use a continuous pour method with the Kalita Wave, especially if you are working toward the top end of its capacity. Therefore, I recommend using a pulse method for this device, which makes it a good choice for those who are just starting out with pour over.

KALITA WAVE FILTERS

Kalita Wave filters look a lot like your standard flat-bottomed wavy filters, but they are not! They are specifically designed to work with the

Kalita Wave dripper. When you drop a Kalita Wave filter into the Wave, you'll notice it doesn't touch the bottom of the device, which is intentional. Like the Chemex, Kalita Wave filters play an integral role in the function of the device. Their accordion-wall design is meant to suspend the filter inside the dripper. This is designed for temperature control; the pockets of air that form between the filter and the sides of the device, as well as between the filter and the bottom of the device, are said to insulate the slurry. With other cone drippers, the filter lies right up against the wall of the device, and some people believe the material of the dripper, particularly when it's metal or plastic, can draw heat away from the brew and affect extraction. You may be able to find Wave filters at a local coffee shop. If not, they are sold online for around $10 to $13 for a pack of 100. Make sure you are purchasing the correct filter size for your device.

HOW IT WORKS

The Kalita Wave is in the cone-dripper family—meaning it works on the same principles as other pour-over drippers—but its three triangulated holes and flat bottom set it apart and, some believe, give it some advantages. The design of the device makes a shallow, flat coffee bed, which discourages agitation more than other cone drippers. This kind of coffee bed also makes it difficult for water to create channels, leading to more even extraction. It tends to use a coarser grind than other pour-over devices, and its design minimizes turbulence. With the help of its filter, the design of the Kalita also encourages the water to go downward toward the coffee bed, instead of bypassing it, as can happen with other cone brewers. Additionally, a raised Y-shaped ridge on the bottom of the device prevents the filter from creating a seal and restricting airflow too much.

Because of these characteristics, the Kalita's brewing time is relatively long, and it can tease out character and complexity from a variety of different coffees. You can choose to brew into a carafe or directly into your cup. Kalita also sells branded glass servers and decanters for those who want to keep it in the family.

The Chemex

Invented in 1941 by German designer Peter Schlumbohm, the Chemex Coffeemaker is one of the few products to achieve icon status in both popular culture and the art world. If you missed the Chemex sitting in the background of Megan Draper's California kitchen on *Mad Men*, then take a trip to the Museum of Modern Art in New York, where it is the only coffeemaker in the museum's permanent collection.

Ralph Caplan, a design critic and professor at the School of Visual Arts in New York, has described Schlumbohm's invention as "a synthesis of

Mid-century modern cool, clean taste

COST	● ● ● ● ●
AVAILABILITY	● ● ● ● ●
TECHNIQUE	● ● ● ● ●

Method on page 243

logic and madness." Many of Schlumbohm's designs were influenced by his background in chemistry and his interest in marketing—his products were often practical and capable of appealing to a wide audience. The Chemex is patented as a "filtering device" and was intended for uses inside and outside of the kitchen, such as laboratory filtration.

Today, the Chemex is available in several sizes—3 cup, 6 cup, 8 cup, and 10 cup—and each size comes in two different styles: the classic wooden-collar look (pictured) or the sleek glass-handle look. Both styles are made of glass and require the use of special Chemex filters. The Chemex is one of the most popular pour-over devices right now (as of this writing, the Chemex factory in Massachusetts is struggling to keep up with demand). You can find it for sale in almost any coffee shop and at many chain retailers, such as Bed Bath & Beyond and Williams Sonoma.

The Chemex requires more technique than other devices, and it may require more practice to get it right. Unlike some other pour-over models, the larger Chemex sizes are capable of making fairly big batches of coffee. Many people say Chemex coffee has a very distinct taste—it's incredibly clean, that is, free of silt and coffee oils. It's kind of the opposite of a French press if that appeals to you.

CHEMEX FILTERS

Because the Chemex is so popular right now, you may be able to purchase Chemex filters from your local coffee shop or large home goods retailer. Otherwise, you'll need to order them online. These filters are quite a bit more expensive than Melitta and V60 filters—a pack of 100 costs between $8.90 and $17.50, depending on where you purchase them.

Unlike Melitta and other wedge-shaped filters, Chemex filters come to a point at the bottom. Chemex filters can be white or natural, circular or square, and they are significantly thicker (20 to 30 percent, according to the manufacturer) than other types of filters, which allows them to trap more oils and sediments. Because of this, the Chemex produces a distinctly clean-tasting brew. Many people will tell you that the filter is what makes Chemex coffee different from any other.

Obviously, these filters are specifically designed to be used with a Chemex. In addition to being thicker, they are much larger than most other filters. Unlike Melitta filters, Chemex filters don't have a seam. Instead they are folded (you can fold them yourself or buy them prefolded). The shape of the filter is crucial to the function of the device. When the Chemex filter is properly wetted, it creates a seal against the glass, except for two air vents—the grooved spout and the gap opposite the spout—which allow for proper airflow to help regulate the rate of extraction. When correctly folded, a Chemex filter has a layer of paper on one side and three layers of paper on the other side. The three layers are placed on the spout side of the device, creating extra reinforcement for the spout air channel. If the filter is placed the opposite way, it may collapse into the spout mid-brew, which will break airflow and drastically increase your extraction time, resulting in overextracted coffee. Chemex filters come in a variety of sizes, so be sure to choose the filter that fits your device!

HOW IT WORKS

It's not hard to see the scientific influence in the Chemex's deceptively simple design. Essentially, it is a glass flask that nips inward in the middle, giving it the shape of an hourglass. The funnel on top holds the paper filter, while the bottom half serves as a carafe. The genius, though, is hidden in two subtle design elements: the pouring groove and the shape of the funnel, both of which work in concert with the Chemex filter to ensure a proper rate of extraction.

However beautiful and ingenious its design, the Chemex is not very forgiving. If you use grounds that are too fine, it will be obvious, as your water may come to a standstill. The thick Chemex filter also has a pointed tip that makes it highly susceptible to the effects of fines migration, which makes it particularly frustrating to try to use a blade grinder with a Chemex (you'll see why on page 85).

That being said, in the right hands, the Chemex can produce more nuanced cups than some other devices, as it gives the brewer complete control over certain variables, such as flow rate. When you use a Chemex, your brewing technique controls the flow rate more than the design of the device. Since the Chemex puts technique front and center, it is a favorite in craft coffee shops around the country.

The Hario V60

Although the V60 is a relatively new take on the old cone design (it was first released in 2005), it's probably among the most prized devices in craft coffee shops today. The V60 is made by Hario, a Japanese company that started in 1921 as a heat-resistant glass manufacturer and evolved to be one of the most recognized names in coffee implements. It comes in two sizes: #01 (small) and

Control freak heaven

COST   ● ● ● ● ●
AVAILABILITY   ● ● ● ● ●
TECHNIQUE   ● ● ● ● ●

Method on page 246

#02 (large), both of which require the use of special #01 and #02 V60 filters, respectively. The device is available in plastic, ceramic, glass, or steel, each of which comes with a different price tag (surprise: the plastic option is the most affordable).

The device does very little to regulate flow rate, which means it's up to the brewer. In my opinion, the V60 and the Chemex are among the most difficult devices to master. The V60 is not impossible to brew on, but it does require a certain level of technique (especially if you are new to pour-over brewing)—and a slow-pour kettle. If you aren't interested in learning technique or purchasing extra equipment, don't bother with this one.

I've seen V60s for sale at almost every craft coffee shop I've been to, and as of this writing, retailers such as Williams Sonoma, Crate and Barrel, and Bed Bath & Beyond also have it in stock.

HARIO V60 FILTERS

Made in Japan—an epicenter of craft coffee culture—V60 filters use a lightweight, high-quality paper. These filters are very similar in shape to Melitta filters, but they taper to a sharp point (like the Chemex filters). To use, fold the filter at the seam and place it in your device.

Due to the V60's popularity in craft coffee shops, many shops usually sell both the device and the filters, making for an easy purchase if you happen to live close to any. The cost of V60 filters is comparable to that of Melitta filters (between $5 and $7 for 100), but, as mentioned previously, they are not quite as ubiquitous.

HOW IT WORKS

The V60 is a variation of the classic dripper filtration system. Its name reveals its distinguishing design: the sides of the device, which look like a V, funnel down at a 60-degree angle to an open base with one relatively large hole at the bottom. This shape, combined with the device's signature spiraled ribbing, is said to allow coffee to drain from both the bottom and sides of the device, allowing for a more even brew.

The V60 is generally more sensitive to brewing variables than other devices—in fact, I might say it's the most difficult method to master. Because of the large hole at the bottom, you really need a slow, continuous pour to ensure that the water doesn't just go whooshing out the bottom, making a gooseneck kettle essentially a requirement. On the other hand, there is a good reason why it's used in so many coffee shops: it can produce a very nuanced cup. Some feel it can produce the *best* cup, more so than any other device.

ADDITIONAL EQUIPMENT GUIDE

Most brewing devices require additional equipment, and if you don't own that equipment already, you have to factor it into your decision about which device to use. The rest of this chapter goes deep into the three types of additional equipment—grinders, scales, and kettles—that I recommend for optimal brewing and why I think each deserves a place on the brew bar. Ideally, you would own all three, but I realize that is not always possible or preferable.

Bearing that in mind, I have designed this guide to help you select a device based on how gadget-tolerant you are. It recommends certain devices depending on whether you're willing to buy one, two, or three pieces of additional equipment. No matter which category you fall into, I've made device and equipment recommendations that will set you up to make an optimized cup. Additionally, I chose the brewing methods for this book with these recommendations in mind—every method in chapter 6 corresponds to the amount of additional equipment you're willing to purchase.

If, at this point, you still have no idea what device to choose, this guide might be a good place to start. If you already own some equipment, the guide can help you choose a device with the least amount of additional investment—or if you already have a device, it can help you make decisions about the next steps to take as you read through the rest of the chapter.

Lastly, the guide will help the cost-conscious among you stay within your budget. Whether we like it or not, whether it's a self-imposed factor or not, price is still a barrier of entry when it comes to making coffee at home. As you've seen, the cost of a device alone can run the gamut from about $10 to over $100. But in addition to the cost of the device, you should also consider the cost of the extra equipment that will help you optimize your cup.

You can, of course, make coffee without any special equipment, but the point of this book is to help you optimize your brew—and equipment plays a leading role in doing that.

ONE PIECE OF ADDITIONAL EQUIPMENT	TWO PIECES OF ADDITIONAL EQUIPMENT	THREE PIECES OF ADDITIONAL EQUIPMENT

Burr Grinder	Burr Grinder + Scale	Burr Grinder + Scale + Gooseneck Kettle
If you're willing to buy only one tool, make it a burr grinder. I'll talk about this more on page 87, but for now, just know that it will noticeably improve your cup, even if you change nothing else.	If you're willing to get two implements, make the second one a gram scale. There's only so much you can do without accuracy and consistency. See page 90 for more.	If you're willing to go all in, your third tool should be a gooseneck kettle. While much delicious coffee can be made without it, many cone-dripper methods are less frustrating when you're able to use a slow, consistent pour (see page 97).
BEST RESULTS WITH: AeroPress Cold Brew	BEST RESULTS WITH: Clever French press Siphon Walküre *Plus column 1*	BEST RESULTS WITH: BeeHouse Chemex Hario V60 Kalita Wave Melitta *Plus columns 1 + 2*

GRINDERS

In the early days of global coffee consumption, everyone bought their beans whole and ground them fresh before use. It wasn't until the 1900s that the Big American Coffee Oligarchy and its stalwart crew of marketing men started making headway with their vacuum seals and preground beans. "Convenience!" they said. "It's what you need!" Coffee marketing in the United States has almost uniformly put cost and convenience ahead of quality, and that message, despite recent trends, still holds strong today.

The fact of the matter is that coffee is delicate—it's made up of hundreds of flavor and aromatic compounds that start to deteriorate if mishandled. Grinding your coffee fresh is one of the easiest ways to prevent such mishandling and thus improve your cup—that's why I suggest that if you are only willing to invest in one piece of coffee equipment, you should make it a decent grinder. It is paramount for two things: the flavor of the coffee and the efficiency of the brew.

Most coffee aficionados will tell you that coffee quickly starts to lose flavor and aromatics as soon as it's ground. Many of the delicate compounds that make coffee taste great are locked in the bean's structure, but breaking that protection apart via grinding exposes them to air, moisture, and light—the ever-present banes of a coffee bean's existence. All of those compounds will start to noticeably diminish—at least to the trained palate—about 30 minutes after grinding. And like the proverbial man who went out for cigarettes, once flavor is gone, it's not coming back. But to be honest, a person with an average palate likely wouldn't be able to detect any diminished flavor until about an hour or more after grinding. (Most of the anxiety surrounding lost flavor is related to espresso, which uses a very fine grind, giving the coffee more surface area and thus more opportunity for flavor to escape.)

But there is another practical reason—one that I think is even more important than freshness—to skip preground beans: doing so will up your extraction game. Recall from chapter 1 that for best extraction, the size of your grind needs to align with the device you're using. Brewing devices that take longer to brew generally need larger grounds; brewing devices that are quick tend to require smaller grounds. Here's why this matters to you: the odds that your preground beans are the correct grind size for your device of choice are slim. A can of preground coffee and a French press, when used together, are unlikely to bear tasty results because that preground coffee is not ground specifically for a French press (and it's probably stale). By grinding the beans yourself, you can tailor the grind size to your particular device. Similarly, being able to adjust the grind size allows you to troubleshoot your brewing process; buying preground beans eliminates that option.

In sum, for best results, buy whole beans and grind them just before use. Still sounds like a pain in the rear, you say? Let me put it into perspective: according to *Uncommon Grounds* by Mark Pendergrast, during the Civil War, Union soldiers carried around whole coffee beans and ground them fresh with grinders built into their guns' buttstocks. If they could manage to grind their own beans in the face of bloody, hand-to-hand combat, you can manage to do so at home. But unless you have a Civil War–era Sharps carbine lying around, you'll need a grinder.

Blade Grinders

Most devices that you see marketed as coffee grinders are blade grinders, which use a rotating metal blade to chop the beans. The cheapest grinders hold the beans in the same chamber that houses the blade and require the user to push and hold down a button to activate the blade.

The longer you hold down the button, the finer your grind will be. Most blade grinders make it easy to check on the state of the grounds—simply pop off the lid and take a peek. If the grounds are looking too coarse, take them for another spin. In theory, this sounds like a simple way to get freshly ground coffee. But if you are interested in making a consistently better cup at home, I think a blade grinder will end up being a frustrating device to work with.

When you use a blade grinder, some coffee beans get pulverized while others remain coarse. You generally end up with an inordinate number of fines and a wide range of other grind sizes, no matter what you do. It's the nature of the blade grinder's design: the chamber doesn't allow for much movement, so the beans at the bottom (nearest to the blade) get chopped more finely than the beans at the top. I actually use blade grinders quite regularly (we have one at my place of employment), and I've tried almost everything to make the grind more consistent: grinding a small number of beans at a time, gently shaking the device in an attempt to redistribute the beans, pausing every few seconds to stir the grounds with a spoon. These tricks help a little, but they always seem like wasted efforts when I pour the fresh grounds into the filter and find an entirely whole bean at the top and fines packed into clumps around the blade.

Simply put, blade grinders are really bad at grinding coffee evenly.

Let me tell you why this is a problem. Too many fines will clog up your paper filters like silt in a stagnant pond, which slows—or stops!—water flow. Your cup will take an excruciating amount of time to make, and it likely will end up being overextracted (read: gross and bitter). Even worse, some metal filters, such as those on French presses, cannot trap fines, which means fines end up in your cup and continue to extract. Yes, French presses are designed to keep some fines in the cup, but too many will turn your delicious full-bodied brew into a dirty, muddy mess.

Generally speaking, you want your grind to be as consistent as possible so that each particle extracts at a similar rate. The smaller the particle, the faster the water can penetrate it and extract its flavor. The more consistent the grind, the more consistent the extraction. Imagine that you are chopping up potatoes to fry. You'd want each piece to be about the same size so that they all cook evenly and get done at the same time. If they were all chopped to different sizes, some might burn while others might remain raw. The same concept holds for coffee grounds. When all of your grounds are consistently sized, they all will be done around the same time. A consistent grind will also make it easier for you to figure out what went wrong if you end up making a less-than-desirable cup— and you'll be better able to troubleshoot that cup as needed.

Burr Grinders (Burr Mills)

If you are interested in easily improving your daily cup of joe, I wholeheartedly recommend investing in a burr grinder. Burr grinders are designed to grind beans to a uniform size. They work by pushing the beans between two grinding surfaces called *burrs*. The spaces between these surfaces can be manually adjusted. The smaller these spaces are, the finer the grind will be, and the larger these spaces are, the coarser the grind will be. To use a burr grinder, just pour the beans into the chamber, set your grind size, and flip the switch. On most models, the grounds fall into a detachable container for easy pouring.

Burr grinder

The downside to burr grinders is that the electric (i.e., convenient) models are generally more expensive than blade grinders. The best burr grinders offer a wide range of settings, and decent ones can range from $130 to $800. If you can't (or don't want to) spend that much cash, a hand-crank model will run you about $25 or more. As an added bonus, these manual grinders tend to be lightweight and compact, making them especially useful for camping and traveling. Yes, you'll need to use a bit of elbow grease, but if your morning coffee ritual already takes five attentive minutes, what's one minute more for perfectly ground coffee?

Hand grinder

It's worth noting that even burr grinders do not grind beans to a completely uniform size. One of coffee's unique properties is that it breaks apart in unpredictable ways. This makes it impossible to grind each bean to a universal size and shape, which means there will always be some tiny broken fragments (fines) with a burr grinder. The difference is that with a blade grinder, you'll have a wide spread of different grind sizes, from the tiniest particle to, in some particularly dismaying cases, a whole bean, while a burr grinder generally reduces that distribution, which allows for more even extraction.

I think any burr grinder—even the cheapest one—is better than no burr grinder. Andreas and I happily used a Baratza Encore for several years before upgrading to the Virtuoso. When traveling, we used a Porlex JP-30 (until we gave it away), and now we use a Hario for our manual-grinding needs while on the road.

Fines: Pure Evil?

Fines are widely accepted to be bad because they have so much surface area that they are presumed to extract almost instantly, which could lead to overextracted coffee if there are too many of them. Recent and convincing research by coffee scientist Christopher H. Hendon suggests that the number of fines is not what causes uneven extraction—it's the distribution of the particles. Generally speaking, fines are okay as long as you take measures to limit the number of them in your coffee (i.e., by using a burr grinder). There is also some evidence to suggest that freezing your beans allows them to be ground more uniformly.

POPULAR GRINDERS

Model	Burr or Blade	Electric or Manual	Price
JavaPresse	Burr	Manual	$20
KitchenAid BCG110B	Blade	Electric	$26
Hario Skerton	Burr	Manual	$40
Porlex JP-30	Burr	Manual	$57
Baratza Encore	Burr	Electric	$129
Baratza Virtuoso	Burr	Electric	$229
KitchenAid KCG0702ER	Burr	Electric	$250
Baratza Sette	Burr	Electric	$379

Your Local Coffee Shop's Grinder

All reputable craft coffee shops use high-quality burr grinders. If you are fortunate enough to live near one of these shops, you may be able to purchase whole beans *and* ask for the beans to be ground in-house. Now, you may notice that this flies in the face of what I said at the beginning of this section: don't buy preground beans. Some coffee people might even say that having a coffee shop grind your beans for you is sacrilege and mourn the loss of all those delicate flavors and aromatics—but hear me out.

My major concern with preground beans is the grind-size issue. At a coffee shop, you will likely be able to ask for your beans to be ground to correspond with the brewing device you plan to use at home. If you say something like, "Can I get these beans ground coarse enough to use with my French press?" the barista is probably going to know what to do. No, you won't be able to tinker with that particular spec at home, but the barista will be able to get you the grind size you need, and I'm willing to bet that those preground beans will be easier to work with than any grounds that have been mangled by a blade grinder.

As for the issue of lost flavor and aromatics, there are always things you can do to get more flavor out of older, diminished coffee (namely, add a bit more coffee to the dose to compensate for any lost compounds), but there's not much you can do about uneven grounds and uneven extraction rates. In fact, Andreas gives new employees old beans during their training to test their skills, and on more than one occasion, I've been able to produce surprisingly good results from months-old beans.

To be clear, I'm not encouraging you to use year-old beans—especially if they are preground. But if you normally finish a 12-ounce bag of coffee in two weeks or less (that's about 14 [12-ounce] cups), I think you'll still be able to make a tasty cup at home with preground beans from your local shop. Just be sure to properly seal the bag and store it as recommended (see page 181).

Tips

If you do choose to get your coffee ground at a shop, I suspect you will get better results by using those grounds in an immersion device. If you are using a device like an AeroPress or a French press, you can easily adjust the brewing time to match the grind size if needed.

I recommend avoiding the grinder at the grocery store, even though it's likely a burr grinder, because (1) it's probably never cleaned, (2) the burrs likely don't get replaced as frequently as they should, and (3) many people will have used it to grind dark-roast beans, which means your coffee will be contaminated with stale fines and oxidizing (i.e., rancid) oils from other beans.

SCALES

In the United States, many people hear the term *kitchen scale* and their blood boils. Americans hate kitchen scales. They love measuring spoons, and they love measuring cups. A scale—a machine—makes things seem more complicated, and no one wants to complicate a simple task like measuring. So it should come as no surprise that many are skeptical about the necessity of using a scale to make coffee. It can seem like one step too far, I suppose. But let's get real: this

Digital kitchen scale

is a multipurpose item that's going to make your coffee life (and kitchen life, if you have one) easier. There is nothing simple about measuring cups or spoons, as anyone who has had to mince herbs before measuring them, scrape out syrup from a tablespoon, or wash multiple spoons, cups, and bowls after cooking can tell you. Here are the reasons why I think a kitchen scale is a great addition to your home brew bar if you're willing to purchase *two* additional pieces of coffee equipment:

- **Accuracy.** As discussed previously, certain ratios of coffee to water (based on weight in grams) are most likely to get you in the ideal range of extraction and strength. This range is captured on the Coffee Brewing Control Chart (see page 21)—a chart that has science on its side. I believe a good starting brew ratio, one that will get you a great cup most of the time, is between 1:15 and 1:17. An inexpensive kitchen scale will allow you to measure both water and coffee in grams, which will make your coffee routine a whole lot easier. The most accurate way to measure anything is by weight—how could you compare the mass of coffee to the mass of water otherwise? That's right: you can't. You are going to have to use a scale. You are going to have to let go of your tablespoons and US customary units in general. Say good-bye to them. You don't need them. You think you do, but you don't. Bye-bye, US customary units!

- **Consistency.** Coffee beans can vary so much in size and density that measuring by volume can be surprisingly inconsistent. If you use a tablespoon (or guess) to measure your dose, you will end up using a different amount of coffee each day. That means you will never be able to consistently replicate yesterday's cup. And that's not even taking the water into consideration. I gather that weighing water is what really turns people off from the idea of using a scale. It sounds like madness—madness! But think of it like this: if you measure the water before boiling it, there is no way for you to account for any that is lost with evaporation and steam. Steam is your carefully measured water saying, "See you never!" If you measure your water as you pour it, you don't need to worry about steam and its utter disregard for you. If you'd rather not leave the quality of your cup up to chance, a kitchen scale will allow you to steer the ship every time.

- **Easy troubleshooting.** When your brew ratio becomes a constant, you are better able to tweak your specs to get a perfect cup. Let's say you decide to try a new type of coffee one morning. You go through your regular routine, but the resulting cup is too strong. A set of potential actions unfurls before you, the first of which is: reduce your dose. You can do that easily now that you have a scale. You know exactly how much coffee you started with, so you can easily reduce that amount next time.

- **Less waste.** Specialty coffee isn't cheap. If you're not measuring accurately, there is a good chance you are using too many beans, which means you are wasting precious coffee! Also, if you are using a tablespoon to measure *ground* beans, which some sources suggest, as opposed to whole beans, you are certainly wasting beans. If you grind the beans before you measure them, it's unlikely that you are guessing the correct number of beans every time. How many cups of coffee do you currently get out of your 12-ounce bag? With accurate measuring, you should be able to get about 14 (12-ounce) V60 cups, 21 (8-ounce) AeroPress cups, or 10 (16-ounce) Chemex cups.

It may not seem like it at first, but I promise that a kitchen scale allows you to think *less* about your coffee and to make fewer movements during your routine. Using a scale makes measuring a seamless part of the coffee-making process. I encourage you to brew directly on the scale so that you don't need to use multiple measuring devices or stress about getting exact measurements before you start brewing. This is especially true for measuring the amount of water to heat in your kettle. In fact, you should always heat a bit more water than you need. Once it's hot, place your brewing vessel and brewing device (with coffee added) on the scale, zero the scale, and pour the water over the grounds until the scale reads the weight you want it to read. Easy! There's no guesswork, no worry of evaporation, and no disruptive hunkering down to check the level of your brew. The extra hot water in the kettle can be used for lots of things. Before you start brewing, for example, I recommend wetting the coffee filter first (see page 54); or, while the coffee brews, some people like to pour a little hot water into their waiting coffee cups to preheat them. But the most practical use for extra hot water is rinsing the brewing device immediately after using it. It makes cleanup a snap.

What kind of kitchen scale should you choose? First of all, it doesn't need to be expensive. A perfectly functional kitchen scale costs about $15 to $20. Of course, there are always more expensive options. Many professional shops use fancy scales, such as the coveted Acaia models, which can sync with your phone, monitor flow rate, and track bloom time. They can cost upward of $100. Is that necessary for you? Of course not. But keep the following in mind before you purchase a scale:

- **Readability to the tenths place.** It's best if your scale can read to a tenth of a gram, which is important for dosing. Cheaper scales might read only to a whole gram or a half gram, which leaves significant room for error, and scales that read to the hundredths place are often unable to hold as much weight as is necessary to brew.

- **Weight capacity of at least two kilograms.** That's 2,000 grams. You need enough capacity to hold not only your water but also the device itself. The six-cup Chemex and the Walküre, for example, each weigh well over 500 grams on their own.

- **Large enough surface for your device and/or vessel.** The bottom of your device or the vessel you are brewing into should fit completely on the surface of the scale to ensure accuracy.

- **Tare function.** Most scales do, but always make sure your scale can tare, or zero, after an object has been placed upon it and measured. This is essential because you'll need to tare the scale after adding your device, grounds, and vessel to it before you can measure your pour.

You don't need to break the bank with a scale (unless you want to), but I do recommend buying at least a cheap one for simplicity and accuracy. If you are dead set on never using a kitchen scale, you will, of course, still be able to make coffee; you'll just be doing so while enduring a self-imposed hardship—mark my words!

POPULAR KITCHEN SCALES

Model	Readability	Capacity (g)	Features	Price
Smart Weigh TOP2K	0.1 g	2,000	N/A	$14
Jennings CJ4000	0.5 g	4,000	N/A	$26
Hario VST-2000B	0.1 g	2,000	Built-in timer	$57
Acaia Pearl	0.1 g	2,000	Built-in timer, mobile app for tracking specs	$139

KETTLES AND THERMOMETERS

For most brewing methods, you'll need some kind of kettle to heat the water. A standard tea kettle is a common kitchen device, so there's a good chance you already have one. If this is the case and/or you are not interested in investing in a *third* piece of coffee equipment, a tea kettle will work well for many of the methods in this book, particularly the immersion methods. To be clear, I don't think you will gain that much by using a special kettle for methods like the French press, the AeroPress, or even the Walküre or Clever.

You may want to choose your device based on the kind of kettle you already have. However, for methods where speed and control are more critical (such as the Chemex and V60), you may consider purchasing a gooseneck (sometimes called a *slow-pour* or a *swan-neck*) kettle. Let's take a look at the options for both standard and gooseneck kettles.

Standard Tea Kettles

A standard stovetop tea kettle can cost anywhere from $20 to more than $100. They are usually made of some kind of metal:

- **Aluminum.** This is usually the least expensive kind of kettle, but it can get dinged up and tarnished easily.

- **Copper.** Besides being easy on the eyes, copper is a great conductor of heat. But it also is pretty expensive and on the softer side, making it prone to blemishes. Copper also tarnishes, although it can be polished back to shine.

- **Cast iron.** Cast-iron kettles are usually coated in enamel. This metal heats evenly and retains heat very well. A bit of maintenance is required to prevent it from rusting, but a cast-iron kettle should last a lifetime, if not several. Cast iron tends to be heavy, though, which matters if you are a weakling like me.

- **Stainless steel.** This is a great option for kettles because it's durable (less prone to dings and dents) and easy to clean. My home kettle is made of stainless steel, and it resists wear very well.

Kettles can also be made of glass. Tea kettles come in all kinds of colors and styles—something you might want to consider since you'll likely be looking at it every day. However, you don't want appearance to be your sole consideration. I, for one, have been burned (literally and figuratively) by a pretty-looking kettle. Don't underestimate the importance of:

- **How easy it is to add the water.** On a lot of kettles, the handle arches over the opening where you add water. Depending on the design, this can make it annoying to pour water into the kettle from pitchers and other vessels.

- **How heatproof the handle is.** You would think manufacturers wouldn't even make kettles with handles that get piping hot, but you'd be wrong. Make sure the handle is well insulated.

- **How much water it can hold.** Water capacity is usually more of an issue with gooseneck kettles, but you want to make sure any kettle you have can hold enough water for the device you plan to use (plus a little extra).

- **How easily it pours.** Easy pouring is most important when looking for a gooseneck kettle, but you should be able to pour water easily and smoothly from any kettle. Many regular tea kettles tend to dribble water down the side if you pour too slowly.

Tea kettles can also vary in the speed with which they boil water and how well they retain heat. You don't want to be waiting around all day for your water to boil. If you are really impatient (like I am), you might also consider an electric kettle (see page 99).

Gooseneck Kettles

Because pour-over methods require such a controlled, slow pour, a specially designed kettle known as a *gooseneck kettle* has evolved from the standard tea kettle design. This kettle has a long, skinny, curved (like a goose's neck!) spout that is usually attached near the base of the kettle. This spout allows for slow, smooth,

Gooseneck kettle

continuous pouring. It also allows you to direct the water stream exactly where you want it to go.

If you are interested in pour-over methods, I recommend investing in a gooseneck kettle for your third home-brew purchase. It can be difficult to control the results of your cup without one, and it's difficult, if not impossible, to get a slow, smooth pour out of a tea kettle: the water usually comes out too fast and causes much agitation, or it comes out too slowly and dribbles down the side of the kettle. Is it impossible to make pour-over coffee without a gooseneck? Of course not. In fact, I personally brew that way multiple times a week at my office, where we have a Melitta dripper but no gooseneck. The coffee I make that way still tastes better than it would out of the automatic coffeemaker, so there's that. But a gooseneck kettle is similar in price to a regular tea kettle (anywhere from $25 to more than $100—although a midgrade gooseneck probably is slightly more expensive than a midgrade tea kettle), so it's worth considering.

When choosing a gooseneck, you want to consider the same things as you would with a regular kettle. However, there are a few extra important details to keep in mind:

- **Size.** Some gooseneck kettles do not hold as much water as regular tea kettles. I would say about 1 to 1.2 liters (1,000 to 1,200 grams) of water is the average capacity. Additionally, some designs don't work as well when the kettle is completely full, though this usually isn't an issue for typical small-batch brewing. Because the spout is attached near the bottom of the vessel, boiling can cause some of the water to boil out of the spout. This is a common criticism of the Kalita Wave 1-liter kettle, the kettle I use at home. However, I've never personally experienced this issue, likely because I remove the kettle from the heat at the first sign of boiling. But the subject brings me to my next point.

- **Lack of whistling.** Most tea kettles whistle when the water boils, alerting you that it's time to come off the heat and preventing you from boiling the kettle dry. Most goosenecks *do not* whistle. You can tell when it's time to take a gooseneck off the heat by the sound of the roiling water inside it or by watching how the steam leaves its spout (it vents in rhythmic fits and bursts). The point is you must watch gooseneck kettles more carefully than regular kettles. Boiling the kettle dry is very hard on it, and you never want to lose much water to evaporation anyway.

- **Water control.** Not all goosenecks are made equally, and some certainly control flow rate better than others. I never really thought about this until Andreas and I upgraded our Bonavita stovetop kettle to the Kalita gooseneck we use now. Although Bonavitas are used in professional shops, I struggled with ours, routinely pouring too quickly for my BeeHouse. When I switched to the Kalita, I actually started pouring too slowly. The difference between the two was mind-blowing. However, some kettles, including the Bonavita, can be fit with flow-rate restrictors to help you out. These restrictors are a less expensive alternative to purchasing a high-end kettle.

Because gooseneck kettles can be unfamiliar, I've provided a short list of popular options at a range of different price points. Note that the full capacity might not be the same as the practical capacity and that the price is suggested retail—you will likely be able to find all of these at certain retailers for less. Also, there are many, many other options; use this table as a starting point.

POPULAR GOOSENECK KETTLES

Model	Material	Full Capacity (g)	Induction Compatible	Price
Bonavita BV3825ST	Stainless steel with BPA-free plastic accents	1,000	N/A	$40
Hario Buono 120	Stainless steel	1,200	Yes	$67
Fellow Stagg	Stainless steel	1,000	Yes	$69
Kalita Wave	Stainless steel with wood accents	1,000	Yes	$105

Electric Kettles

Electric kettles have been around since the late 19th century. They include their own heating element, so there is no need to use a stovetop. Modern versions can bring water to temperature quickly, turn off to prevent boilover, and/or hold specific temperatures. They are extremely convenient, and I personally love them.

Electric kettles come in standard and gooseneck versions. In fact, you can purchase electric versions of both the Bonavita and the Hario

Duck, Duck, Gooseneck

Gooseneck kettles are the target of a lot of antipathy. Poor (pour?) goosenecks! It's really undeserved—especially because the price range is similar for gooseneck and standard kettles. I have had extensive experience using both, and for pour-over methods, the gooseneck, hands down, makes what I'm doing (directing water—let's not lose sight of that) easier and more consistent. I've read elsewhere that some consider goosenecks for the home brewer to be overly complicated, expensive, and prone to losing heat if not used properly. I don't get it. It's just a kettle with a different spout, and you should use it the same way as you would a regular kettle. No, it's not necessary to have a gooseneck, but if it makes pouring easier and doesn't cost that much more, then why not get one? It doesn't make you complicated—it makes you a person who bought a kettle. On the other hand, abstaining from the gooseneck life does not make you a coffee philistine. If you don't want to buy one, plenty of brewing methods get great results without a gooseneck kettle.

kettles mentioned in the table on the previous page. In addition to making coffee, electric kettles are also great for making items like tea, hot cocoa, and rice noodles because they boil water so quickly. If you drink tea, an electric kettle that can be programmed to hold a certain temperature can be extremely useful because most tea is better when steeped at lower temperatures. (Although, for similar reasons, this function is great for coffee as well.) The feature eliminates the need to wait for the water to cool off or use a thermometer.

At our house, Andreas and I use the economical Melitta 40994, which is a 1.7-liter electric kettle, in conjunction with the Kalita stovetop kettle. The electric kettle brings the water to boil super fast, and I find that transferring it to the Kalita cools it off just enough to be the perfect temperature for most brewing methods. However, if the Kalita

Wave kettle came in an electric version, I'd probably cut out the middleman and just use that.

When choosing an electric kettle, keep the following in mind:

- **Minimum and maximum capacities.** Most electric kettles can hold more water than standard kettles, which is great for people who want to make larger batches of coffee (especially if the model has a temperature-hold feature). However, most electric kettles have water minimums, too. Our Melitta's is 0.5 liters (500 grams), which is usually a bit too much for my normal serving. I just use the extra water to wet my filter and rinse my device after use.

- **Limescale buildup.** Electric kettles are prone to limescale buildup: chalky deposits of minerals that can affect the appliance's performance. Proper care and maintenance can prevent this.

As with standard stovetop kettles, the spout on an electric kettle isn't as much of a concern if you are planning to use immersion methods.

Thermometers

The other part of the kettle equation is the thermometer. We've discussed how water temperature affects the extraction of coffee. All in all, I would say perfect temperature is not as critical as some other details, like grind size, and it's easy enough to keep your kettle off heat for a few moments so the temperature can reduce (when it's not boiling, you know it's cooler than 212°F).

However, a digital instant-read kitchen thermometer is nice to have for various uses (cooking meat, baking, etc.), and a decent one only costs around $8. (An analog thermometer will work too if that's what you have; you will just have to wait longer to read it.) You can even find thermometers that clip to the side of your kettle, which might be worthwhile because steam burns! Just make sure whichever model you choose can read beyond the boiling point of water.

Alternatively, some electric kettles come with temperature-read and -hold functions, and you may be able to find a stovetop model, like the Fellow Stagg pour-over kettle, that has a temperature gauge built into the device itself.

BREWING VESSELS, SERVERS, AND THERMOSES

Many of the brewing devices in this book are sold separately from any kind of brewing vessel or carafe. Most devices, including the AeroPress, Clever, Melitta, BeeHouse, and V60, fit directly on top of a standard coffee mug (about three inches in diameter). When brewing directly into your cup, note that most pour-over devices (except for the BeeHouse and Melitta, which have windows) are kind of hard to see through. If you aren't measuring carefully, you'll want to monitor how full your cup is. A clear glass mug easily solves this issue.

However, if you are making more than one cup of coffee, you are going to need a brewing vessel. Most coffee equipment companies, including Melitta, Hario, and Kalita, make brewing vessels that perfectly fit their drippers. However, a cheaper alternative (and my personal preference) is to purchase borosilicate glass Griffin beakers like those you used in science class. You can get a 600-milliliter beaker for about $9 from certain online retailers, while brand-name servers can cost $20 or more. The 600-milliliter beaker has enough capacity for most large pour-over

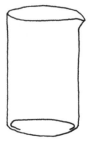

Griffin beaker

batches and a diameter of about 3.5 inches, which fits most pour-over devices (except for the BeeHouse). These beakers are also extremely durable because they are made for science experiments and can withstand extreme temperature fluctuations—which cannot be said for all glass. One benefit of purchasing a brand-name pour-over server is that you know you'll be able to brew directly into it. It also generally comes with a lid, while a beaker does not, but I usually don't leave coffee sitting around at home.

If you like to make extra coffee and/or keep some coffee warm for later, you'll need an insulated vessel. Whether you are looking for a thermal carafe or a thermos, note that those with a double wall and a vacuum chamber retain heat the best. Most thermal carafes and thermoses are made of stainless steel, although some are made of glass. With any insulated vessel, I find that a thorough scrub is a must after each use, as lingering coffee oils quickly go rancid and can give freshly brewed coffee an off flavor.

No Vessel? No Problem

If you don't want to bother with a coffee server, choose a device with one built in, such as the Chemex, siphon, or Walküre. Technically, you can serve from a French press, too, but it's recommended that you transfer the brew into cups immediately to prevent overextraction.

The Limits of Keeping Coffee Hot

Scientists think there may be some evolutionary basis for the fact that most people love hot coffee or cold coffee but generally detest everything in between (most people like drinking coffee at 150°F to 180°F). Unfortunately for us, coffee cannot stay hot indefinitely. It's a common scenario: you brew a delicious cup, life gets in the way, and your coffee is tepid by the time you get the chance to finish it.

The best way to keep your coffee warm, as it turns out, is to never let it cool down in the first place. To ensure that your coffee stays the right temperature for the longest period of time outside of a thermos, preheat your brewing vessel or carafe. This is accomplished easily if you are wetting your filter before brewing (see page 54). Just use hot water to rinse the filter into your brewing vessel, and you've killed two birds with one stone.

Coffee can stay surprisingly fresh for several hours in a high-quality preheated thermos or insulated carafe. Once coffee's temperature falls below about 175°F, however, its chemistry starts to change, resulting in increasingly sour or bitter flavors as the temperature continues to drop. But even if a thermos could keep coffee at a constant temperature forever, the coffee would still oxidize (because there is oxygen in water). Oxidation happens when oxygen molecules from either the air or the water in the coffee mingle with other molecules to create entirely different compounds that, unfortunately, taste different from the original ones. This gives the coffee its stale taste. Oxidation happens to coffee left at room temperature, too, although obviously much faster. It can be fun to taste how coffee's flavor changes as it cools, but at a certain point, it all goes south. Because of this, most professional shops keep their drip coffee in insulated urns for a limited amount of time, anywhere from 15 minutes to an hour.

You may be thinking: well, I can just reheat my coffee if it gets cold. But before you turn to the microwave, hear me out. Reheating coffee usually results in an undesirable outcome. As discussed, coffee is fragile and its molecules are untethered. Lukewarm coffee has already had its flavor changed by the cooling process, and reheating will break down what good-tasting molecules remain into more bad-tasting molecules. What results is a sour, bitter, astringent, woody-tasting cup. Next time you get the urge to microwave your coffee or set your (heatproof) vessel over the stove, try pouring your tepid brew over ice instead.

CHAPTER 3
The Coffee

Now that you know what kind of device and equipment to use, it's time to turn your attention to the bean. This chapter examines many of the factors that make coffee taste the way it does, from the different types of beans and where they're grown to how they're processed and roasted. For something that's so small and unassuming, the coffee bean is utterly complex, and after many centuries of consumption, it is still revealing its mysteries to us. For most of coffee's history, the art of roasting, growing, and processing—some of the biggest factors when it comes to how coffee tastes—were learned through trial and error or apprenticeship. The idea of scientific coffee research is a relatively new one, and there is still much to learn about how factors such as roast, varietal, and origin affect the coffee you drink.

BEANS

In the previous chapter, I stressed the importance of choosing a device that lets you manually adjust the brew variables that an automatic machine does not—even high-quality beans will yield low-quality coffee when brewed in a poor-quality automatic coffeemaker. But it's important not to underestimate the power of great beans. Manual devices and manual techniques can only do so much, and no matter how much you perfect your technique, you won't be able to shift the quality meter that much if you're starting with horrible beans. In fact, coffee scientist Christopher H. Hendon suggests that the outcome of any given cup is dependent on four key variables: the quality of the green (unroasted) coffee beans, the roast, the water chemistry, and the brewing technique. However, he doesn't give each of these equal weight.

Hendon says the quality of the green coffee beans has the largest influence on the outcome of the cup. Its impact is huge compared with those of roast, water chemistry, and brewing technique (to emphasize, this chart is assuming that the brewer is trying and *has* technique; an ill-equipped automatic machine in place of the Brewing slice would destroy the rest of the pie). Another way to look at this is to realize that there are limits to what a great roaster and a great brewer can do to improve coffee's quality. Neither can bring low-quality or defective beans back from the dead. Because the quality of green coffee beans is so important, let's start by tackling the difference between arabica and robusta beans.

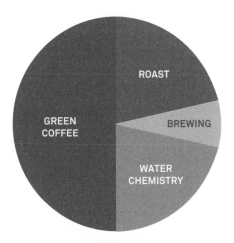

What influences cup quality?

A Tale of Two Species

Coffea, the coffee plant, is a flowering tree that produces small red or purple fruit called *cherries*. Coffee cherries are drupes (stone fruit), but unlike more familiar drupes such as peaches and apricots, they are grown for their seeds (coffee beans) rather than for their flesh. Each cherry usually contains two coffee beans. According to the National Coffee Association, a single coffee tree produces about 10 pounds of coffee cherries a year, which equals about 2 pounds of green coffee beans. Coffee beans weigh less after roasting, so it's safe to say that an entire coffee tree produces less than two pounds of roasted coffee per year!

A few species of coffee plants grow in the wild, but only two matter to us: *Coffea arabica* and *Coffea canephora*. They are better known as arabica and robusta, respectively. Most of the commercial coffee grown in the world (70 to 80 percent) is arabica. Originating in the forests of Ethiopia and Sudan, arabica is of distinctly higher quality than robusta. Robusta, which was discovered in 1898 in western and central sub-Saharan Africa, tends to be bitter and unbalanced due to its comparatively low acidity, lipid content, and sugar concentration. I've seen it described as tasting like "burnt tires" and "a wet paper bag," so that gives you an idea of what to expect. However, robusta plants produce about twice as many pounds of beans per plant and impart to those beans almost double the amount of caffeine as arabica plants. They are also generally resistant to the diseases known to destroy arabica fields (e.g., coffee berry disease and coffee leaf rust).

Yes, robusta is robust—in every sense of the word—and its heartiness, productiveness, and aggressive flavor make it less expensive to cultivate and buy. From an economic standpoint, robusta beans cost about half as much as arabica beans, and historically it has not been uncommon for big US commodity brands (aka the common household brands you find at every grocery store) to use robusta in their blends. Today, you'll find robusta mostly used as filler in lower-quality, mass-market coffee products. Additionally, almost all instant coffee is robusta. However, higher-quality robusta is often still used in espresso blends, particularly Italian-style espresso blends, as it's thought to provide the desired bold flavor, add extra caffeine, and enhance the *crema* (the thin layer of caramel-colored foam on top of an espresso shot). But generally speaking, most craft coffee roasters likely would never consider using robusta outside of espresso blends. This makes it irrelevant to our discussion, which is why I'll focus on arabica from here on out.

To be clear, not all arabica beans are created equal. Green coffee beans are graded and scored before they are exported to the United States (coffee is usually transported in its green state to maintain its

> ## Green Coffee Prices
>
> The pricing sweet spot for a typical specialty roaster might be between $2.50 and $6 per pound for green coffee, but the most expensive beans, often sold at auction, can cost $20, $50, or even $100 per pound. (However, prices that high tend to be linked to rarity or novelty as opposed to top-notch quality.) In contrast, commodity coffee at the time of this writing is about $1.45 to $1.55 per pound. High-quality beans require a tremendous amount of human attention and care, which is reflected in the price. This is why craft coffee costs more than commodity coffee.

freshness; roasted coffee turns stale rather quickly). First, the beans are sorted according to size, shape, weight, color, and defects—all of which are associated with quality—at the processing mill. The specific terminology of this complicated system can vary from country to country, but the idea is to separate the beans into categories from highest quality to lowest quality.

Because no one can determine how coffee will taste just by looking at it, people called Q graders brew and taste (i.e., *cup*) samples of roasted beans right at origin to determine their quality and assign a score to each lot. They score the beans from 0 to 100 based on standardized SCA criteria. To be considered specialty-grade coffee—the grade that specialty and craft roasters use—beans must receive a score of at least 80. While a coffee review website might mention such scores, you're unlikely to see them on a bag of beans or hear a barista talking to customers about them. Scoring is pretty inside baseball.

What makes a bean bad? Defects, subpar growing conditions, and faulty processing methods—all of which are distilled in the taste of the cup—will reduce a bean's score. However, lower-scoring beans are cheaper, so they are still used in plenty of mass-market coffee products. Conversely, craft roasters and shops strive to select the highest-quality green coffee available to them within their budget. They try to partner with farmers and importers that treat coffee production like a craft. Together, coffee producers, importers, roasters, and craft coffee shops have all been raising the bar; as a result, a greater variety of high-quality beans are available than ever before.

VARIETALS AND CULTIVARS

I've already discussed the differences between the species arabica and the species robusta, but there are also several different types of arabica, known as varietals. According to the SCA, a varietal "retains most of the characteristics of the species, but differs in some way." In other words, it is genetically and characteristically distinct from its parent plant. Often, a varietal is born when a plant spontaneously produces a mutation or crosses with another varietal, creating traits in the resulting plant that coffee producers find desirable.

A *cultivar* is a varietal that humans deliberately cultivate, such as when scientists cross two coffee plants to create a new plant with more favorable traits. It's rare to see or hear the word *cultivar* used outside of the scientific community, however; the coffee industry uses the word *varietal* as an umbrella term for both varietals and cultivars. A bag of coffee may name varietals even if what's inside of it is technically a cultivar. For the sake of consistency with the industry, I will stick with the term *varietal* here.

Within the world of *Coffea arabica*, there are two primary varietals: typica and bourbon. To understand where these came from, we have to go back to Ethiopia, coffee's birthplace. According to the SCA, coffee was first exported from Ethiopia, its homeland, to Yemen, which is just across the Red Sea from Ethiopia. Yemen, in turn, transported coffee plants all over the world. Those that were taken to Java (an island of Indonesia) are said to be the ancestors of what we know today as typica. Those that ended up on Île Bourbon (a French island known today as Île de la Réunion) are the ancestors of bourbon. (You may have guessed that the French are responsible for this terminology, but note that the coffee varietal is not pronounced like the whiskey; it's pronounced burr-BONE). From there, many new varietals developed from the original typica and bourbon plants.

As mentioned earlier, arabica plants are more susceptible to disease and generally yield less coffee than their robusta counterparts. But because arabica beans are of much higher quality than robusta beans, farmers are constantly trying to find the best arabica varietal, one that produces good yields and does not fall to disease. Over the years, this has led to numerous types of arabica plants—too many to describe here. Let's take a closer look at a few you are most likely to hear about or see listed on a bag of coffee. Note that although each coffee varietal has certain characteristics, it can be difficult to predict exactly how any given varietal will taste, as flavor is so heavily influenced by the coffee's specific growing conditions.

Typica and Related Coffees

One of the grandmothers of arabica varietals, typica is still grown all over the world today, especially in Central America, Jamaica, and Indonesia. It often contains what industry folks call a *malic acidity*, kind of like what you might taste in an apple. High-quality typicas usually produce a *clean cup*, which means the coffee is free of off-flavors and negative attributes related to defects. Additionally, typicas are often noted for their sweetness and body. Compared with bourbon plants, typica plants have longer seeds and yield about 20 to 30 percent less coffee. They can also fall prey to all major coffee pests and diseases. In sum, typica plants are capable of producing beans with high cup quality, but they are relatively delicate and low producers. Many of the varietals described in the following sections were created in the hopes of remedying these problems.

MARAGOGYPE/MARAGOGIPE

Pronounced mara-go-HEAP-ay, this varietal is a natural mutation of typica that was discovered in Brazil around 1870. Although it's relatively low yielding, everything about the maragogype plant is huge: its general size, its leaves, and its beans. Because of these large beans, it takes a bit more skill on the roaster's part to get the final product right. Maragogype is not grown often (its low yield is not worth it to many farmers), but its relative rarity seems to pique people's interests and give it some allure. At its best, maragogype's cup quality is considered among the highest of all coffee beans.

KENT (K7)

This was the first coffee plant cultivated for leaf-rust resistance (although it's now susceptible to new strains of the disease). Most people believe this varietal was derived from typica grown on the Kent estate in India, but it has since been planted all over the country. A version of Kent called K7 is popular in Kenya.

KONA

Kona coffee is one of the most expensive and prized coffees in the world. It's not a true varietal (although growers sometimes call it "Kona typica"), as its distinct taste doesn't come from its genetic makeup. Instead, it comes from the unique (and highly regulated) growing conditions and methods of the Kona region in Hawai'i. Kona farmers were among the first to treat coffee cultivation as a craft—and at a time when few were doing so. (Today, producers everywhere are doing the same thing, and when that aligns with ideal growing conditions, you get superior coffee, even outside of Kona.) You can think of Kona as a brand name of typica. The Kona region isn't very big, which makes this coffee relatively rare, and because of this, you are most likely to see "Kona blends" (which can contain as little as 10 percent Kona) rather than pure Kona coffee. Is this coffee worth the hype? I've personally never tasted it, but

I've noticed a growing sentiment among coffee people that suggests it may be a little overrated. That being said, I would *definitely* try it if given the chance!

BLUE MOUNTAIN

Like Kona, this is another branded typica (some Blue Mountain growers may use other trees, but most use typica), this time from the Blue Mountains of Jamaica. The Coffee Industry Board of Jamaica oversees this coffee's growth and processing, and all Blue Mountain coffee sold under that name has been certified by the board. Blue Mountain is said to produce a cup that is well balanced, with bright acidity and almost no bitterness. Like Kona, it's expensive, and I've heard people question whether the price and hype are warranted.

Bourbon and Related Coffees

This is the other grandmother of arabica coffee. Because of its high yield, bourbon rose in popularity quickly after its development on Île Bourbon, and it's now grown all over the world. Bourbons tend to be sweet, complex, and delicate with crisp acidity, although, like most coffee beans, bourbon beans can taste different depending on where they are grown. While most coffee cherries are red, some bourbon plants can produce cherries that are pink, yellow, or orange. (Occasionally, you may see coffee labeled as "pink bourbon" or "red bourbon"—now you know that those names refer to the color of the coffee plant's fruit.) A number of popular varietals have stemmed from the bourbon plant, and despite the coveted characteristics of bourbon, some of these varietals have replaced bourbon plants in many parts of the world because they produce higher yields or are more resistant to disease.

CATURRA

A natural dwarf mutation (meaning the plant is short) of bourbon first found in Brazil in 1937, caturra is more productive and more disease resistant than its mom, bourbon. It's now popular in Colombia, Costa Rica, and Nicaragua, although Brazil still grows a decent amount of it. Caturra tends to produce cups that have bright, citric acidity and low-to-medium bodies. While the cup quality is good, it's usually considered to be of lower quality than bourbon. When the two varietals are compared, caturra tends to be less sweet and less clean in the cup. Some roasters compare it to pinot noir, as it can have an astringent quality similar to what tannins give red wine.

SL28 AND SL34
Commissioned by the Kenyan government in the 1930s to identify a high-quality, high-yielding, and disease- and drought-resistant coffee plant, Scott Laboratories selected SL28 and SL34 (both generally considered to be of bourbon descent). Though SL28 is not high yielding or disease resistant, its beans are considered to be of a deliciously high quality. In fact, some say its characteristics (juicy body, black-currant acidity, intense sweetness, tropical flavor notes) are unlike those of any other coffee in the world. SL34 is a bit more productive than SL28, and although it's still considered a high-quality bean, it's not considered as exciting or flavorful as SL28.

TEKISIC
This relative of bourbon was developed in El Salvador by the Salvadoran Institute for Coffee Research (ISIC) and was first released for commercial production in 1977. The tekisic plant, which has a slightly higher yield than bourbon (but is still considered relatively low yielding), produces small cherries and beans. However, coffee professionals tend to consider it of excellent quality when grown at high elevations. It's said to be sweet, with notes of caramel or brown sugar, complex acidity, and a heavy mouthfeel. According to World Coffee Research, the name comes from the Nahuatl word *tekiti*, which means *work*—very apropos considering the ISIC spent almost 30 years developing it.

VILLA SARCHI

This is a natural dwarf mutation of bourbon that was first cultivated in the town of Sarchi, Costa Rica, in the mid-1900s. Today, Villa Sarchi is still relatively rare outside of Costa Rica. It's more productive than its parent, bourbon, and it's known to do particularly well on organic farms and in extremely high-elevation environments, as it is resilient in the face of strong winds. The quality of the cup can vary greatly based on how the beans were processed, but its flavors are generally fruity, sweet, and acidic.

PACAS

Pacas is another natural dwarf mutation of bourbon, this time from El Salvador. It was discovered in 1949 and named after the family who owned the farm where it was found. In the cup, it's said to be similar to bourbon, but it tends to be less sweet. The pacas plant is slightly more productive than bourbon due to its small size, which allows the producer to plant more of it in the same area. Today, it's most commonly grown in its home country and Honduras.

Crosses of Typicas, Bourbons, and Their Relatives

PACAMARA

This is a cross between pacas and maragogype. Like its maragogype parent, pacamara's cherries and seeds are relatively big. The cup profile is said to be quite unique, with floral notes and lots of acidity. Professional cuppers often consider this bean to be among those of the highest quality when grown in the right conditions. On the downside, these plants are extremely susceptible to coffee leaf rust.

MUNDO NOVO

In the 1940s, the Instituto Agronômico de Campinas (IAC) in Brazil decided to cultivate this natural cross between typica and bourbon (a variety called red bourbon, to be exact). Some sources say as much as 40 percent of coffee plants in Brazil are mundo novo. The plant is relatively productive (about 30 percent more than bourbon) and disease resistant, which producers tend to like. A typical cup may have notes of dark berries, chocolate, citrus, or spice.

CATUAÍ

This varietal is a cross between yellow caturra and mundo novo that was also created by Brazil's IAC. Like its caturra parent, the catuaí plant is relatively short and more productive than bourbon. Now grown all over Latin America, it produces red and yellow cherries, although some roasters believe the red is superior to the yellow. A typical cup is high in acidity, and the best cups are considered of good but not exceptional quality. According to World Coffee Research, the word *catuaí* is derived from the term *multo mom*, which means *very good* in Guarani, an indigenous language in South America.

Arabica/Robusta Hybrids

You know by now that due to robusta's inherently poor quality in the cup, craft roasters rarely use it outside of espresso blends. But robusta does yield a lot of fruit and is significantly more resilient than arabica. Forced to choose between the pros and cons of each species, growers have not stopped hoping there is a way to get the best of both worlds. Enter hibrido de Timor, aka the Timor hybrid, a naturally occurring cross (many say the *only* naturally occurring cross) between an arabica plant and a robusta plant that was discovered on its island namesake of Southeast Asia. In the late 1970s, Timor plants were taken to the Indonesian islands of Sumatra and Flores, where they continued to evolve, especially in breeding programs designed to perfect the plant so that it produced high-quality beans. The plant is supremely resistant to coffee leaf rust, unlike most arabica coffee plants, but because of its low cup quality, it is not very popular among craft roasters. There continues to be interest in some of its progeny, however.

CATIMOR

A cross between Timor and caturra, catimor might be one of the most popular hybrids among craft coffee professionals. It was developed in Portugal in the late 1950s and is now a popular plant in Central America. It's very productive and is resistant to coffee leaf rust and coffee berry disease. Catimor has plenty of arabica influence, but its robusta genes still tend to rear their dull, overly bitter heads if given the chance. However, in the right hands, catimor can make a decent cup, and you may see it listed on bags of craft coffee. There are several varieties of catimor, including Costa Rica 95, lempira, and catisic.

CASTILLO

I need to tell you a story for this one. In the 1960s, the Colombian government's National Coffee Research Center (Cenicafé) started experimenting with different catimor varieties to produce a high-quality, high-yield, disease-resistant plant. In the early 1980s, after several rounds of breeding, Cenicafé released a line called Colombia, promoting its high cup quality and disease resistance. When coffee leaf rust was discovered in Colombian coffee fields (which grew primarily caturra), this new variety was primed to take over. However, Cenicafé never stopped developing coffee plants, and in 2005, it released a better-tasting improvement on Colombia: castillo. Today, most of Colombia's coffee fields have been replaced with castillo. There has been a bit of drama about castillo in the coffee world, with both producers and graders being suspicious of its quality, especially compared with caturra. However, castillo's cupping scores have been comparable to caturra, and baristas have been known to use castillo beans in industry competitions.

RUIRU 11

This varietal has a story similar to that of castillo, except it was the Kenyan government that funded the catimor research (Ruiru 11 is named after the research station where it was developed). In this case, the researchers experimented with several arabica plants, including SL28, to develop a high-quality cup that retained the disease-resistance of the catimor plant. Despite their efforts, experts tend to feel that Ruiru 11 will never match the high quality of SL28. The Kenyan government never gave up, though, and recently, an improved form of Ruiru 11 called Batian matured and hit the market. Because Batian is genetically closer to SL28 and SL34 than Ruiru 11 is, it seems to have a better cup quality. You may see Ruiru 11 and/or Batian, along with SL28 and SL34, on bags of single-origin Kenyan coffee.

Heirloom Varietals

Some arabica coffees don't fit neatly on the family tree under typica or bourbon. These are the plants that continued to evolve on their own in Ethiopia and Sudan, separately from the plants brought to Yemen that turned into typica and bourbon.

ETHIOPIAN HEIRLOOMS

There are literally thousands of different Ethiopian heirlooms, each a natural descendant of wild coffee plants. Many villages have their own varietal, which they have cultivated to work with the growing conditions of their location. These varietals are often called *heirlooms*.

GESHA/GEISHA

Gesha (often spelled "geisha") is the breakout star of the aforementioned heirlooms. It was transported from the small town of Gesha, Ethiopia, to Costa Rica. Gesha grows well only in particular microclimates with high elevations (one of which is the area around Boquete, Panama), making it a rather rare bean. It is highly prized in the industry for its superior quality and intense flavors, which can have notes of bergamot, berry, citrus blossom, and honey. Because exceptional geshas can command high prices, producers in Central and South America have started cultivating it more often in recent years.

ORIGIN

High-quality coffee grows well only in a certain part of the world: at high elevations in countries that generally fall between the Tropic of Cancer and the Tropic of Capricorn—an area otherwise known as the Bean Belt. More than 50 countries (commonly referred to as *origins*) grow coffee, although not all of them export specialty coffee to the United States. A couple of countries, like Vietnam, grow mostly

Why Does Most Good Coffee Come from Volcanic Soil?

You'll notice that many of the highest-quality coffee beans are grown near volcanoes. It's not just a coffee thing—high-quality grapes, wheat, tea, and other agricultural products are also known to thrive in volcanic soil. Why? For one thing, volcanic soil contains what is perhaps the widest range of minerals of any soil. Scientists believe volcanic soil contains both major and minor minerals as well as trace minerals and rare earth elements, like nitrogen, calcium, zinc, phosphorus, potassium, and boron. All of these enhance soil biology, which plants need to grow. The soil near an active volcano is also replenished naturally during eruptions. As with all farming, growing coffee plants removes minerals from the soil. If proper techniques (or fertilizer) aren't used to maintain healthy levels of nutrients, the soil becomes dead and unproductive. Volcanic eruptions keep the soil nearby fresh and fertile. If not near an active volcano, most coffee is grown in mountainous regions. Mountains were created by tectonic activity, which also tends to bring vital coffee nutrients to the Earth's crust.

robusta, which isn't relevant for our purposes. A few others focus on low-quality arabica beans destined to become instant coffee and other forms of commercial coffee. And some countries, like Thailand and China, are just starting their specialty coffee programs and don't yet produce enough high-quality product for us to see it commonly in the United States.

However, the highest-quality coffee in the world requires more than the right coordinates on a map. Everything about the coffee's environmental growing conditions (called *terroir* in the industry) can affect its flavor. Coffee thrives best in mineral-rich soil. It also prefers warm, tropical climates with plenty of rain. The right amount of shade and a high elevation encourage slow bean growth, which gives the bean more time to develop nutrients that result in desirable flavors. Although there are exceptions, some of the highest-quality coffee is grown in the shade and/or at high elevations.

In addition to terroir, high-quality coffee also needs the care and attention of skilled coffee producers. Some countries, like Colombia and Kenya, have governments and infrastructure that greatly support their coffee producers. Meanwhile, producers in some other countries struggle to gather the resources necessary for high-quality coffee production for various reasons: economic instability, political unrest, a lack of best-practices education, or a lack of necessary infrastructure. As you'll see, a few countries are newcomers to the specialty market, and the movement toward growing high-quality coffee is being bolstered by individual producer entrepreneurs, coffee importers, and/or specialty roasters.

Craft coffee roasters are particularly interested in how origin influences taste, which is why they commonly sell "single origin" coffee instead of or in addition to blends, which contain beans from multiple origins. Because flavor is influenced by so many factors, it can be difficult to make generalizations about what *all* coffee from a particular origin tastes like. But to give you a basic idea of where coffee grows and how that influences coffee characteristics, this section covers 23 origins that produce the specialty beans most commonly used by US roasters.

Most countries have multiple growing regions, which I outline in the following pages. However, it's important to note that very few countries have explicitly designated the names of their growing regions, and the names that importers and roasters use to describe them on packaging are largely unstandardized. In fact, they sometimes don't align with geographical or geopolitical regions. The names of cities, for example, are commonly used to describe "growing regions," even if the beans are grown in areas surrounding the city. I have tried to use the terms that seem to be the most common.

In addition to a brief description of each country's growing regions and coffee characteristics, I also added a snapshot of each origin that I thought would be useful to home brewers who want to know more about where their coffee comes from. I included a rough estimate of each country's elevation (how many meters above sea level, or masl, it is) and the type of processing (see page 142) that is common to the origin, as both are linked closely to flavor. I also included the number of 60-kilogram bags the country exported in the 2014–15 growing season to give you a sense of its export market share. Note that these export numbers, gathered from International Coffee Organization data, are not necessarily the same as *production* numbers, as there are many reasons, like domestic consumption, why countries keep some of their coffee within their own borders. For Hawai'i, I listed the production number calculated from US Department of Agriculture data, as current export and domestic consumption numbers proved difficult to verify. These are meant to give you a rough idea of the particulars, but they are not, of course, inclusive of all variations and subtleties. One of the great things about coffee is there is always more to learn about and explore!

THE BEAN BELT

Arabica coffee typically grows best at higher elevations between the Tropic of Cancer and the Tropic of Capricorn, aka the Bean Belt. Although many more countries grow coffee, these 23 origins are among those you are most likely to see on bags of craft coffee.

KEY

North America
1 Hawai'i
2 Mexico

Central America
3 Costa Rica
4 El Salvador
5 Guatemala
6 Honduras
7 Jamaica
8 Nicaragua
9 Panama

South America
10 Bolivia
11 Brazil
12 Colombia
13 Ecuador
14 Peru

Africa
15 Burundi
16 Democratic
   Republic of
   the Congo
17 Ethiopia
18 Kenya
19 Rwanda
20 Tanzania

Asia and Oceania
21 Indonesia
   a *Sulawesi*
   b *Sumatra*
   c *Java*
22 Papua New
   Guinea
23 Yemen (Mocha)

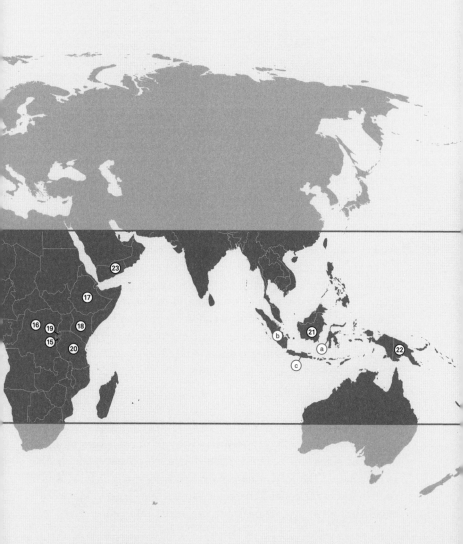

North America

HAWAI'I
100 to 1,000 masl | 45,360 bags | mostly washed

Hawai'i is the only place in the United States that is able to produce high-quality coffee (although I've read that commercial growers are cropping up in California and Georgia). Hawai'i has a handful of growing regions—most of which have mineral-packed, volcanic soil—but the Kona region on the Big Island generally overshadows the rest in the public eye, as it is said to produce some of the world's finest coffee: silky, floral, and with a remarkable balance of sweetness and acidity. However, the Kona growing region is only about 2,000 acres, which means there is never that much available. Kona coffee is incredibly expensive (and some say overrated), and you're unlikely to see it in a pure form outside of a blend. Aside from Kona, many other regions on the Big Island have ideal yet distinct microclimates. Puna, where most coffee grows in or above lava flows, is quite new to the scene but is capable of producing coffee with a lot of acidity and very diverse flavors. Ka'ū, which has been gaining accolades in recent years, is said to be reminiscent of Central American coffees. Hāmākua, home to limited production on very fertile farms, is known for coffee with low acidity and a rich, full body. Coffee is also produced on the islands of Kaua'i, Maui, and Moloka'i.

MEXICO
800 to 1,700 masl | 2,458,000 bags| mostly washed, some natural

Mexico cultivates coffee on about 760,000 hectares across 12 different states. A hectare is equal to about 2.47 acres, so that's roughly 1.88 million acres. The soil in these states tends to be a bit acidic, which contributes to the coffee's character. Most coffee farms in Mexico are small (less than 25 hectares) and organized into cooperatives that specialize in organic coffee. The largest producing region is Chiapas, which shares a mountain range with one of Guatemala's best growing regions and accounts for about a third of Mexico's total production. Other well-established regions include Veracruz, Puebla, and Oaxaca, which, along with Chiapas, account for about 95 percent of all production. You might also see coffee from Guerrero. In the past, Mexican coffee was considered to be low-grown and low-quality, and certain to become filler, but the many small producers growing high-elevation, high-quality coffee in recent years have turned that image around. In the United States, many roasters buy Mexican beans based on the name of respected *beneficios* (coffee processing facilities) or *fincas* (farms). These coffees have the potential to show off interesting mixes of acidity and sweetness, notes of toffee and chocolate, lighter bodies, and creamy textures.

Central America

COSTA RICA
600 to 2,000 masl | 1,133,000 bags | mostly washed

Costa Rican coffee is generally grown and processed with extreme care, which makes it a favorite here in the United States (about half of all Costa Rican coffee makes its way to the US specialty market). Costa Rica's arguably most famous region, Tarrazú, produces nearly a third of the country's total coffee output and uses highly advanced production techniques, which result in extremely clean coffees at scale. Most coffee in Tarrazú, which is surrounded by the peaks of the Cordillera de Talamanca mountain range, is grown at 1,000 to 1,800 meters above sea level. Other regions include West Valley (a quarter of production), Central Valley (where three different volcanoes influence the soil), Brunca, Tres Ríos, and Orosí. The regions of Turrialba and Guanacaste also produce coffee, but suboptimal weather and lower elevations, respectively, make truly stellar coffees a bit harder to come by there. While all of Costa Rica's regions produce coffee with various distinct characteristics, the country's coffees as a whole are widely considered to be the gold standard for Central American coffee: full of nuanced and delicate aromatics, clean, bright, and citrusy, with increased notes of sweetness in higher-grown beans. Small and medium-sized farms that have been producing coffee for hundreds of years have established a reputation for consistent quality among buyers. In recent years, new small estates have been gaining attention, as the farmers there use their own micromills to control all aspects of production and quality. These micromills not only make Costa Rican coffee more traceable, they also make it easier to compare different Costa Rican coffees and taste geographical differences in each cup.

EL SALVADOR
500 to 1,800 masl | 595,000 bags | mostly washed

Although its coffee is not generally considered to be in the same league as Costa Rica's and Guatemala's, El Salvador's volcanic mountain ranges, ideal weather conditions, and deep-rooted coffee tradition make for prime high-quality coffee production. To the northwest, the Alotepec-Metapán growing region, although tiny, produces some of the country's most prized coffees. To the west, Apaneca-Ilamatepec is the largest growing region and is also known for its esteemed beans. From there, traveling eastward, you'll find the regions of El Bálsamo-Quetzaltepec, Cacahuatique, Tecapa-Chinameca, and Chinchontepec. Most (some estimates are as high as 80 percent) of the coffee grown in El Salvador is bourbon (see page 113), which many producers feel is the distinguishing mark of El Salvadoran coffee. In fact, much of it comes from heirloom bourbon trees, which is unique, as most Central American producers have replaced their heirloom varietals with higher-yielding (and some say less yummy) varietals over the years. The coffee, which has a reputation for being very consistent and reliable among professionals, is capable of producing cups that are distinctly sweet and creamy, with flavors of toffee and cocoa. Citrus and fruit notes, like red apple, make their mark in higher-grown beans. While the best Central American coffees often wow people with their powerful, distinct acidity, El Salvadoran coffees tend to be subtler in that arena. If you don't care for acid-forward craft coffees, an El Salvador coffee might be a good option for you. Additionally, the country's producers have been experimenting with varietals and processing lately, so there just may be a surprising bag of El Salvadoran coffee out there waiting to be tasted.

GUATEMALA
1,200 to 1,900 masl | 2,925,000 bags | mostly washed

Coffee from the highlands of Guatemala is considered to be among the finest coffees in the world, the kind that can knock you over the head with its bold acidity and body. One of the country's most famous regions, Antigua, is nestled among three volcanoes, which provide coffee's favorite mineral-rich soil. Antigua often produces cups with dark, earthy notes like spice, flowers, and smoke. Coffees from Fraijanes and Atitlán, both also rich in volcanic soil, are similarly prized. In the southeast corner of the country, Huehuetenango's Caribbean-facing slopes produce distinctly fruit-forward coffees, which may be due in part to how producers dry the coffee during production. Other growing regions include San Marcos with its slopes facing the Pacific, Nuevo Oriente near the Honduran border, and Cobán, which is sandwiched between Antigua and Atitlán. Guatemalan coffees that are sold to roasters under regional names must meet the corresponding flavor guidelines set forth by the Asociación Nacional del Café, the national coffee authority that has been supporting farmers since 1960. Guatemalan coffee has seen an uptick in quality in recent years, owing to Guatemalan producers' high level of participation in the specialty coffee market.

HONDURAS

1,300 to 1,800 masl | 5,020,000 bags | mostly washed

The Honduran coffee program, which was once substantial in the commercial market, was rocked by destruction from Hurricane Mitch and subsequent storms in the late 1990s. It has also traditionally lacked the infrastructure of some of its South American neighbors, so even though the country has prime climate, elevation, and soil quality, it has struggled to keep up with countries like Guatemala and Colombia. However, in the past 10 years, more and more small holders and exporters have entered the specialty coffee market. In 2016, more than 95 small producers collectively cultivated 94 percent of the country's coffee, and today, it is the largest producer and exporter of coffee in Central America. Typical Honduran coffees are mild and medium bodied, and the best tend to be highly complex and juicy. Sometimes Honduran coffee gets knocked for its brief shelf life, which may be related to how rainy the country can be, as that makes drying the coffee difficult. Out of Honduras's 18 departments, 15 grow coffee, although the highest-quality coffee is typically grown in the Marcala region in the southwestern part of the country. Over the past few years, demand for Honduran specialty coffee has increased, and both producers and the Instituto Hondureño del Café have responded in kind—the former by dedicating more land to specialty crops, and the latter by mapping and naming six growing regions based on the high-elevation, shade-grown coffee found in each: Copán, Opalaca, Montecillos (which is marketed under Marcala), Comayagua, Agalta, and El Paraiso. Each region's coffee has defining flavor characteristics, ranging from chocolate to tropical fruit to citrus.

JAMAICA

600 to 2,000 masl | 12,000 bags | mostly washed

Jamaica is the third-largest Caribbean island and home to some of the most expensive specialty coffee on the planet: Blue Mountain. The coffee is named after the (government-designated) region where it's grown, located toward the northeast portion of the island. The elevation of these mountains isn't that high, but it's said that the almost-perpetual blue fog slows down the development of the bean (and increases the flavor). Like Kona coffee in Hawai'i, Blue Mountain is a type of typica that grows under the watchful eye of Jamaican coffee producers and a regulatory board. It's said to have superb cup qualities, including rich flavors, bright acidity, and great body and sweetness. Others say Jamaican coffee lacks the complexity and juiciness that people have come to expect of high-quality specialty beans. Japan snatches up a lot of Jamaica's crop each year, although some of it makes it to the United States. Because it's so rare, fraudulent Blue Mountain labeling is not uncommon.

NICARAGUA
800 to 1,500 masl | 1,810,000 bags | mostly washed

Nicaragua is a relative newcomer to the coffee industry, not getting its start until after a long period of political and economic instability ended in the 1990s. In fact, Nicaraguan coffee imports were banned in the United States until 1990. Nicaragua struggled to compete on the fierce commodity markets and has since rebuilt its coffee program to focus more on high-quality, specialty-grade coffee. Nicaragua, the largest country in Central America, produces a spectrum of coffee across a variety of microclimates in three regions. The North Central region produces the majority (more than 80 percent), and two of the better-known departments, Matagalpa and Jinotega, with their volcanic soil and tropical climates, are contained within it. The next-biggest producing region, the Northeast, accounts for only about 14 percent of total production. Nueva Segovia and Estelí are two of the more well-regarded departments in this region. The last region, the South Pacific, produces the least amount of coffee and has a lower elevation than the other regions. An estimated 95 percent of Nicaraguan coffee is shade-grown across

108,000 hectares. Much of this coffee is certified organic. Nicaraguan coffees tend to hew closely to the typical Central American mode: moderate acidity and body with a range of citrus-fruit notes. Coffees from the Nueva Segovia area have established a reputation for their chocolaty notes as well.

PANAMA
1,200 to 2,000 masl | 43,000 bags | washed and natural

About 80 percent of Panamanian coffee production takes place in the west around the town of Boquete in the mountainous region of Chiriquí, where more than 100 years of coffee tradition inform the cultivation of some of the finest coffees in the world. On the west side of Chiriquí, closer to the Costa Rican border, lies the city of Volcán, around which volcanic soil and warm sea breezes encourage coffee production. Panama has made a concerted effort to prove itself in the specialty coffee market. In 1996, a small group of coffee producers formed the Specialty Coffee Association of Panama (SCAP) to promote high-quality coffee. Today, the organization has more than quadrupled in size and has earned global recognition for its coffees. In the early 2000s, the Panamanian government set aside 8,000 hectares for "quality" and "ecological" coffees. Gesha, one of the finest varietals in the world, thrives in Panama, and many Panamanian producers, like the famed Hacienda La Esmeralda, have dedicated most of their acreage to exclusively cultivating this bean. In 2015, Hacienda La Esmeralda earned the highest bid—a whopping $140.10 per pound—for its gesha at SCAP's annual Best of Panama auction. The best Panamanian geshas bring out the best in the beans: jasmine-like floral aromas, bright citrus acidity, and distinct bergamot notes. Panama's unique landscape provides various microclimates capable of producing flavor notes as diverse as vanilla and maple or citrus and wine.

South America

BOLIVIA

155 to 2,300 masl | 46,000 bags | mostly washed

This landlocked country in central South America is just starting to gain recognition in the specialty coffee market after years of selling lower-quality coffee destined for commercial blends. About 95 percent of Bolivia's coffee production takes place in the Yungas region along the eastern slopes of the Andes Mountains. Other growing regions include Cochabamba, Santa Cruz, and Tarija. While large commercial estates still exist, the government has taken strides to return tracts of land to small producers, who now cultivate 85 to 95 percent of Bolivia's coffee, most of which is grown organically. Although the country has all the necessary qualities (climate, rainfall, elevation) to produce high-quality beans, its lack of infrastructure, technology, and efficient export systems makes growing specialty coffee difficult. Producers are also getting out of the coffee game in favor of more stable ventures, like coca, the plant used to make cocaine, at an alarming clip. Bolivia's coffee exports reached a 10-year record low in 2014–15. That said, Bolivian specialty coffee does show up occasionally in the United States, and infrastructure is improving through programs designed to encourage farmers to grow coffee, rather than coca, as a cash crop. The best Bolivian coffees are said to be sweet, clean, and well balanced.

BRAZIL

400 to 1,600 masl | 36,867,000 bags | natural and pulped natural

Brazil is the biggest coffee producer in the world, accounting for about 30 percent of the world's coffee, and it churns out everything from low-grade commercial coffee to fine specialty beans. Brazil is also the biggest country in South America, which means the terroir across its six major producing regions (Minas Gerais, São Paulo, Espírito Santo, Bahia,

Paraná, and Rondônia, all with various subregions) can vary dramatically. However, Brazil lacks the high elevations you see in Colombia, East Africa, and Central America, which contributes to the beans' mild acidity. Brazilian producers also tend to use natural and pulped natural processes, which add sweetness and complexity to make up for the lack of acid and which contribute to the national flavor. If you don't like acidic coffee, a Brazilian coffee is an approachable alternative. Washed Brazilian coffees do exist, but they are somewhat rare. Although Brazilian coffee gained a strong reputation for quality in the early 2000s, it seems like professionals tend to have mixed feelings about Brazilian coffees now. For what it's worth, some of Andreas's favorite single-origin espresso in recent years has come from Brazil. Brazilian coffees are certainly worth trying, especially if you prefer mild coffee.

COLOMBIA
800 to 1,900 masl | 12,281,000 bags | mostly washed

Colombia, which *invented* the idea of single-origin coffee before specialty coffee existed, competes with Vietnam for the title of second-most productive coffee country in the world, although it ranks first in terms of arabica (97 percent of Vietnam's coffee crop is robusta, and the country is only beginning to develop specialty coffees). Colombian beans generally do not hold as much cachet as, say, Kenyan or Guatemalan beans, but with three mountain ranges and one of the most biodiverse landscapes in the world, Colombia is capable of producing high-quality coffees. As of 2016, nearly 40 percent of all Colombian coffee exports were specialty grade. Unlike those in many other countries, most Colombian producers have processing mills on their property, which helps them control quality; at the same time, they traditionally sort, grade, and bag their beans with other lots without the benefit of cupping, which can diminish overall quality and make it impossible to establish the origin. However, there is a growing trend in Colombia toward cupping and bagging single-farm coffee, which is crucial for the specialty market. If you want to increase your odds of tasting a great Colombian coffee, make sure to choose a bag that identifies the region or farm. Some of the more recognized regions, Nariño, Cauca, and Southern Huila, are in the southwestern part of the country, although the north, including the prominent regions of Antioquia and Santander, produce coffee, too. Colombian coffee has a reputation for being consistent and well balanced. It typically has a medium body with moderate acidity and notes ranging from tropical fruit to chocolate.

ECUADOR
200 to 2,000 masl | 1,089,000 bags | natural, some washed

Although the national government does not offer much support to specialty coffee growers in Ecuador (farms that specialize in low-quality arabica and robusta bound to become instant coffee granules get top priority), some farmers are willing and able to grow coffee that produces interesting, high-quality cups. As of this writing, Ecuador's specialty exports are very small. Café Imports, one of the few buyers that bring Ecuadorian coffee to the United States, posted on its website that in 2014, it had purchased 3 of only 30 total shipping containers of specialty coffee exported from Ecuador. Still, the country has all the right ingredients: It's smack dab on the equator (hence the name), and it has that volcanic soil that coffee loves, not to mention a very wet rainy season and extreme elevations. Growing regions include Loja (where 20 percent of all arabica is grown), Pichincha, Zamora-Chinchipe, Carchi, and El Oro. The best Ecuadorian coffees have a great balance of sweetness and acidity.

PERU
1,200 to 2,000 masl | 2,443,000 bags | mostly washed

Peru does not have the same kind of name recognition in the coffee world as other South American countries, especially those like Brazil and Colombia that benefit from robust national coffee organizations. However, Peruvian coffee has that bright acidity of high-grown coffee—the Andes Mountains run the length of the country, encompassing nearly 28 microclimates. Although Peru struggles with infrastructure issues, in recent years, the Ministerio de Agricultura y Riego del Perú, the body that oversees the country's agriculture, has been offering more modern resources and agricultural education to producers, who tend to be indigenous peoples using traditional processing methods. About 60 percent of Peru's coffee beans are grown in the north in regions such as Cajamarca, Amazonas, San Martín, Piura, and Lambayeque. About 30 percent are grown in the central part of the country, which includes Junín, Pasco, and Huánuco. The southern regions such as Puno, Cusco, and Ayacucho grow the least amount of coffee. Many Peruvian coffees are organic (although Peruvian organic farmers are struggling mightily with coffee leaf rust) and tend to be creamy with sweet notes, such as toffee, caramel, chocolate, and nuts.

Africa

BURUNDI
1,700 to 2,000 masl | 246,000 bags | mostly washed

Burundi is a small country in East Africa, just south of Rwanda. As an extremely mountainous country with a tropical climate, Burundi is well suited to growing specialty coffee. The country grows mostly bourbon or bourbon relatives, which tend to have substantial body and sweetness, while the country's elevation provides complex acidity—an all-around promising combination. The main growing region is Kayanza in the north. When bagged and labeled for sale, Burundian coffee is most likely to be named after the washing station where it was processed. There are more than 20 such stations in the city of Kayanza and about 160 across the entire country. Coffee is an important agricultural crop in Burundi—its number one export, in fact—but due to civil war and other complications, the country has struggled to shine in the specialty market. However, things are starting to turn around, thanks to organizations of producers and specialty coffee exporters. The national industry is also continuing to move toward more privatization after years of governmental control, which has had a positive effect on the quality of the country's coffee crop. Like the coffee in neighboring Rwanda, Burundi's coffee can sometimes fall victim to the *potato defect*, a condition thought to be caused by the antestia bug and a bacterial infection that makes the beans smell and taste like raw potatoes. (Andreas and I think these beans smell just like the freshly cut stems of romaine lettuce.) One defective bean can ruin an entire dose (although that doesn't mean the whole bag is bad—another argument for grinding only what you need), so smell the coffee grounds before using them; you'll be able to tell right away if they've been affected. The frequency of potato defect has greatly declined in recent years, however, due to the significant time and energy invested in figuring out why this defect happens and how to prevent it, so it's unlikely that you will encounter any defective beans.

DEMOCRATIC REPUBLIC OF THE CONGO
700 to 1,500 masl | 135,000 bags | mostly washed

Located in the center of Africa, the Democratic Republic of the Congo (DRC) is currently in the process of rebuilding its specialty coffee program. The country has been ravaged by political conflict and violence for the past few decades, which has dramatically affected its coffee exports: 130,000 tons per year in the mid-1980s dropped to 8,000 tons by 2012. However, you do see DRC coffee in the United States, and efforts are being made to revitalize the industry; in May 2016, the country held its second annual Saveur du Kivu, a national cupping competition. Growing regions are mostly to the east, where the soil is volcanic and the elevations are high. These regions include Beni near the Ugandan border as well as Kivu and Ituri. Lake Kivu influences DRC's (and Rwanda's) coffees (as other large lakes in the area influence the coffee of other East African countries), providing interesting savory notes such as herbs, spices, nuts, or pepper, along with a good balance of acidity and sweetness. These coffees can also suffer from the potato defect.

ETHIOPIA

1,500 to 2,200 masl | 2,872,000 bags | washed and natural

Ethiopia is one of specialty coffee's most respected origins and has some of the finest coffees in all the land. Perhaps it's no coincidence that arabica coffee was first discovered within Ethiopia's borders. One of the most exciting things about this origin is that literally hundreds of heirloom varieties are cultivated by as many small producers (you'll often see the term *heirloom varieties*, as opposed to regions, on bags of Ethiopian coffee). Because of this, Ethiopian coffee can range in flavor, although it is generally known for intensely floral or fruity flavors. That being said, some growing regions are more distinctive than others. For example, Yirgacheffe, a small subset of the Sidama growing region in the south, is known for producing coffee with characteristic Earl Grey flavors. Harar, in the highlands to the east, is known for the unique flavor of its washed and sun-dried coffees. Coffee grown in the west (e.g., Limu, Djimmah, Lekempti, Welega, and Gimbi) is generally fruitier (many Ethiopian coffees taste like blueberries, which is heightened by dry processing) than coffee grown elsewhere. Whatever its flavor, I find Ethiopia's coffee to be big and bold—it's often the first coffee that people say tastes like something more than just coffee. A good Ethiopian coffee gives up its yummy flavors without much fuss, making it a good choice for beginners.

KENYA
1,400 to 2,000+ masl | 720,000 bags | mostly washed

Kenya is another heavy-hitting origin known for some of the highest-quality coffees in the world. Even a middling Kenyan coffee has been known to go toe-to-toe with other countries' highest-quality coffees. High-grown Kenyan coffees have a characteristic sparkling acidity, and certain varietals, including SL28, have very distinct black-currant notes, along with notes of berries, tropical fruits, and citrus fruits (especially grapefruit). Kenyan coffee must often contend with coffee leaf rust and coffee berry disease, and the Kenyan government has taken steps to develop high-quality, disease-resistant plants, such as Ruiru 11 and Batian. Still, quality is king in Kenya; the extreme skill of the producers and the country's unique processing techniques, which are distinguished by a double fermentation process, contribute to the high quality of Kenyan cups. Kenya has several growing regions, although most fall within a swath of land clustered around the slopes of Mount Kenya, which extends south almost to the capital of Nairobi and north to Meru. There is another cluster of growing regions to the west, near the Ugandan border around Mount Elgon, and a few more isolated areas here and there.

RWANDA
1,400 to 1,800 masl | 237,000 bags | mostly washed, some natural

With the help of government programs and investments, Rwanda has been positioning itself as a specialty coffee producer since the early 2000s. Today, it's common to see this origin on the menu at craft coffee shops all over the United States. Like its neighbors, Rwanda mostly grows bourbon and bourbon derivatives, which are generally full bodied and quite sweet. Distinguishing Rwandan flavor notes include raisin and other dried fruits as well as stone fruits, citrus, and sweet spice. Of all the East African coffees affected by the potato defect, Rwandan coffees are often hit the hardest, which tarnishes their image a bit. Most coffee is produced in the north (the region of Rulindo grows some of the country's best coffees) and in the west, particularly around the Albertine Rift mountains and Lake Kivu. The south and east do not yet grow significant amounts of specialty coffee, but they have all the resources (high elevations, good soil, willing producers) to do so in the future.

TANZANIA
1,400 to 2,000 masl | 678,000 bags | mostly washed

Located on the eastern shore of Africa, Tanzania is not as well recognized as Kenya, its superstar neighbor to the north, but its specialty coffee can be top-notch and quite similar to Kenya's. Uniquely, much of Tanzania's coffee is grown under the shade of banana trees on the slopes of Mount Kilimanjaro. The elevation and the shade contribute to a slow-developing bean that offers bright and extremely complex cups. For whatever reason, Tanzanian peaberry coffee is popular in the United States, despite the fact that Tanzania does not produce more peaberries than other countries. Peaberry coffee is not a variety of coffee but rather the name of a naturally occurring mutation in the beans. Most of the time, coffee cherries contain two flat-sided beans. About 5 percent of the time, a coffee cherry produces only one bean (instead of two), which is small and round like a pea (hence the name!). Peaberries are often separated from the regular flat beans before roasting because their shape makes them roast differently, but sometimes they aren't, and you'll find them in a bag of regular coffee. Many people prize peaberries because they believe all the qualities of the two flat beans are concentrated into one bean. Others think they're no different from regular coffee beans. In any case, don't be surprised if you see a Tanzanian peaberry coffee for sale at your local shop.

Asia and Oceania

INDONESIA
8,00 to 1,800 masl | 6,679,000 bags | Giling Basah and washed

Indonesia, located between the Indian and Pacific oceans, is made up of more than 13,000 volcanic islands. Coffee is grown on several of these islands, and a few of them are often treated as their own origin. It's not uncommon to see "Sumatra" on a bag of coffee instead of "Indonesia." Roasters may even go a step further by naming the region or washing station within the island. Because of this, I will break down this origin by some of its most popular islands.

Sulawesi

The Indonesian island of Sulawesi has been a specialty-coffee origin since the beginning of the specialty coffee movement. Most coffee is grown in the Tana Toraja region, located in mountainous South Sulawesi, by small indigenous producers. Many producers in this region tend to use a unique method (called *Giling Basah*, or "wet hulling") for washing the beans, which (at the risk of oversimplifying the process) leaves the beans with a greater moisture content when they leave the farm than other processes do. This method results in coffee with a heavy body and funky earthy notes, including cedar and green pepper, that tend to divide the acidity-loving specialty coffee community. However, more common washing techniques were introduced in the 1970s to help bring out the acidity, sweetness, and fruitiness of Sulawesi beans and provide a more standard way to experience Sulawesi coffee in the specialty world. You may see both kinds available at coffee shops. Other growing regions on the island include Mamasa, Gowa, and Utara.

Sumatra

Sumatra is an island in western Indonesia. Like Sulawesi's crop, much of the coffee produced here is processed with the Giling Basah method, which results in earthy flavors, such as herbs, mushrooms, spices, and mustiness. Again, this goes against the typical acid-forward profile of much of today's specialty coffee. But because this coffee has low acidity and is often quite smooth, it might be a good option for those of you who don't care for acidic qualities all that much. Another unique characteristic of Sumatran coffee beans is their distinctive blue-green color (which can throw off less-experienced roasters and sometimes cause them to overroast the beans). Most Sumatran coffee is produced in the northern highlands. You may see the region of Mandailing listed on a bag of coffee, but this is actually the name of an indigenous tribe that grows coffee in Tapanuli. Other growing regions include Aceh, Lintong, and Lampung.

Java

Java, another Indonesian island, is the birthplace of both typica and one-half of the classic Mocha-Java blend (which you'll still see for sale, despite its being one of the world's oldest blends). In fact, Java is so deeply steeped in coffee's history that the word itself is a slang term for coffee. However, most arabica production in Java (and Indonesia as a whole) has been replaced by robusta, and in Java's case, most high-quality production has been moved to fellow isles Sumatra and Sulawesi. Still, there is some specialty coffee production in the eastern highlands on the Ijen Plateau. Java also produces a significant amount of kopi luwak, the most expensive coffee in the world, which is processed in the intestines of an animal called a civet and then collected as droppings. (For what it's worth, most people seem to think it tastes as you might expect: like something that belongs in the toilet.)

PAPUA NEW GUINEA
1,300 to 1,900 masl | 796,000 bags | mostly washed

Papua New Guinea (PNG) occupies half of the island of New Guinea in the southwestern Pacific Ocean. Although it only produces about 1 percent of the world's arabica (most of it organic), PNG is an interesting origin for specialty coffees; cups tend to be delicate and light bodied, and to vary in flavor from chocolate to citrus depending on the growing region. About 40 percent of PNG's population grows coffee, and 95 percent of them tend tiny plots of a few hundred coffee trees max (but often even fewer than that). These smallholders produce an estimated 90 percent of all of PNG's coffee. As old estates dissolve and small producers become more organized and skilled, coffee in PNG has improved in quality and can sometimes achieve excellent results. Even so, there is very little infrastructure in PNG, and the process of selecting which cherries to harvest tends to be poor, which can lower the overall quality of the coffee. Growing regions include the Western Highlands/Wahgi Valley (you may see bags labeled "Kunjin" or "Ulya," which are regional processing mills), the Eastern Highlands, and Chimbu (often spelled Simbu) Valley.

YEMEN (MOCHA)
1,500 to 2,000+ masl | 20,000 bags | mostly natural

A small country on the Arabian Peninsula just across the way from Ethiopia, Yemen has been growing and exporting coffee since close to the beginning of the coffee trade. Its most famous coffee, Mocha, which has nothing to do with mocha drinks or chocolate, originally got its name from the port city Mokha on the country's western coast. This high-quality coffee is the other half of the famous Mocha-Java blend. Many Yemeni coffees grown today are heirloom varieties, similar to what Ethiopia grows, that are processed via traditional methods. Most of the coffee is produced on the west side of the country, and coffee professionals often describe the flavor profile as "wild," with bright acidity and complexity. However, Yemeni coffee is not all that common in the United States. Exports from Yemen have shrunk over the years as deadly conflict in the country has disrupted its coffee industry, but producers continue to cope and grow with remarkable resilience. In 2015, a group of Yemeni coffee exporters escaped Yemen to attend the annual SCA conference and reintroduce specialty Yemeni coffee to the world. As individuals and organizations help to build the infrastructure necessary for cash-crop specialty coffee cultivation, we may start to see more Yemeni selections on US shelves.

PROCESS

Once a crop of coffee cherries is harvested, the green coffee beans need to be separated from the cherry flesh. The process by which the cherry is removed can greatly affect the taste of the beans. Here are some of the common methods of processing coffee and how they affect flavor:

- **Washed/Wet Process.** At base, this means that water was used to remove the coffee cherry from the beans. Typically, it works like this: the coffee cherries are fed into a machine (called a *pulping machine* or a *depulper*) that removes the outer skin of the cherry. The coffee is then transferred into tanks or troughs of water, where they are left to ferment. The length of the fermentation process and the amount of water used can vary depending on region and producer, but the goal is the same: to remove the rest of the cherry flesh from the bean. After fermentation, the remaining fruit is broken down enough to be washed away with water. Once the beans are clean, they are removed from the water and set out to dry in the sun. The beans are raked periodically so they dry evenly and slowly. Some producers mechanically dry the beans, especially if they grow in an area that doesn't have a long dry season. (Coffee professionals tend to consider this a less desirable method, as it dries the beans more quickly, and research

I've heard (questionable) roasters claim to consumers that washed coffee is cleaner than natural coffee—and that it somehow reduces that number of toxins in coffee beans. This is garbage talk that is based on no empirical evidence. The term *washed* refers only to the fact that water is used during processing. It's true that natural coffee is at greater risk for defects, such as mold and rot, during processing, but proper care eliminates those risks. Besides, defective coffee would likely never make it to the roaster, and if it did, the roaster would know right away that the coffee is off and would not sell it.

suggests that a slow drying process is directly related to how well green beans retain their flavor.) Most coffee in the world is washed. Washing tends to result in a bean that allows the subtle characteristics, including acidity, of the terroir and the varietal to shine through in the cup. It's also a highly controlled process, which makes for consistent lots. Removing the fruit before the beans are dried reduces the chance of something going wrong.

- **Natural/Dry Process.** Before the machinery described earlier was invented, all coffees were naturally processed. In this method, the fruit is not removed from the bean after the coffee cherries are picked. Instead, the cherry is dried fully intact until the fruit dries out enough to be removed by a machine. Because of this, the flavors from the cherry—which are washed away in the wet-process method—actually make their way into the bean during drying. As a result, the flavor of natural coffees is quite distinct: more fruity notes and less acidity than washed coffees. For producers, natural coffees can be challenging to perfect—they require extra time and attention because mold, rot, and other defects love to sleep beneath warm, wet layers of coffee and impart their off flavors.

- **Pulped Natural/Honey.** The pulped natural method was introduced in Brazil and has spread to Central America, where—particularly in Costa Rica—it is called *miel* (Spanish for honey). It is similar to the washed process, except that after going through the pulping machine to remove the outer skin, the coffee is sent directly to the drying phase with part of its fruit still intact. Technically speaking, a true pulped natural/honey coffee is dried with all of the fruit still in place, but there are now many variations of this process that are described with different terms, such as *red honey*, *yellow honey*, *black honey*, and *semiwashed*. The difference among these generally relates to the amount of fruit that is left intact before drying, and the exact processing method can vary greatly from producer to producer. To make things more complicated, it doesn't seem like the industry has settled on firm definitions for these terms, so it's all a bit fluid. As you may guess, honey coffees have some characteristics of washed coffees and some characteristics of natural coffees. They tend to retain the acidity of washed coffees and the body, sweetness, and earthiness of natural coffees but without the strong fruit flavors.

ROAST

Before coffee beans hit store shelves, they need to be roasted. All green coffee beans are kind of boring—they don't smell or taste like much. But it's not their fault—they are largely insoluble, meaning all of their flavor compounds are inaccessible to us. Roasting not only makes coffee soluble (i.e., able to be extracted) but also creates new, wonderful flavors and aromas. More likely than not, you're already familiar with the concept of light, medium, and dark roasted coffee. But how do roasters choose how light or dark to roast the beans? And what do light and dark mean in terms of flavor?

The first thing to realize is that the terms *dark*, *medium*, and *light* do not correlate to some magical roasting time. In general, roasters treat each lot of beans differently by testing a series of roast profiles until the desired result is achieved. Like Q graders, roasters taste each batch and decide what roast profile (a combination of time and temperature) is best for that particular lot of beans. That being said, craft roasters tend to favor roast profiles that highlight certain characteristics of the bean that develop based on where it was grown or how it was processed. This kind of thinking reflects the methods of other artisanal industries, like wine and cheese making.

The science behind coffee roasting is not fully understood, and you can consider the art of roasting to still be in its infancy. What's becoming clear, especially as roasters continue to learn and experiment, is that the idea of "light" and "dark" roast is too simplistic, and it might not be the best way for home brewers to think about coffee as it relates to their preferences. It's really the roast profile—the manipulation of time and temperature—that determines flavor. However, the idea of roast profile is a bit hairy to explain, so I asked Joe Marrocco, who works at Café Imports in Minneapolis and is a member of the Roasters Guild Executive Council, to shed some light on the subject for us:

> A roaster looking for a lively, intensely bright, and complex cup of coffee will likely roast their coffee quickly and to a lower temperature, much like a person who is baking cookies would treat a cookie they want to stay gooey and more like the dough. A roaster who wishes to achieve a mellower, sweeter, and more comforting expression from a coffee would roast the coffee to a higher temperature for a longer amount of time. Finally, a roaster who wants to taste more of their input on the coffee, and less of where the coffee comes from, and who is looking for those dark-chocolate or smoky tones, would want to go even further in the process. Darker roasts are done to much higher temperatures, and so have those charred, heavily cooked flavors.

Generally speaking, the longer and hotter a coffee bean is roasted, the more its flavor changes. Heat exposure tends to cause change on a chemical level, and coffee beans are no different. As green coffee beans are brought to temperature, a few different chemical reactions take place, each of which contributes to the flavor profile of the bean. Very briefly, here are the reactions and stages of roasting:

- **Maillard reaction.** This reaction happens between 150°C and 200°C (302°F to 392°F) and is responsible for a large chunk of the flavor and brown color of roasted coffee. The Maillard reaction is a browning process (actually, it's a lot of different browning processes; *Maillard* is an umbrella term), but it is not a *burning* process—it's a chemical reaction between the amino acids and the reducing sugars in green coffee beans. This is the same reaction that happens during other cooking processes, such as searing meat. All that yummy, crusty goodness of a good sear? That's from the Maillard reaction. The changes to the amino acids and sugars add new flavors (particularly savory flavors rather than sweet flavors) or enhance those already in the beans.

- **Caramelization.** Yum, yum, yum, you know what this stage is! When beans are roasted between 170°C and 200°C (338°F to 392°F), you can think of them as a crème brûlée. Coffee beans contain a fair amount of sugar, and at this stage, those sugars start to brown (i.e., caramelize), releasing acidic and aromatic compounds. These acids and aromatics contribute greatly to the flavor (see chapter 5) and balance of the cup, which is the goal. At the beginning of the process, caramelization deepens the complexity of the flavors. However, counterintuitively, the more the sugars caramelize, the more the perceived sweetness of the beans *decreases*. This means that later in the process, caramelization starts contributing bitter flavors, which can obscure the other flavors in the beans. Caramelization continues into the first crack.

- **First crack.** At about 196°C (385°F), the coffee beans start cracking, and they sound kind of like popcorn. At this point, the beans are under a lot of pressure—both the Maillard reaction and the caramelization process produce volatile gases that add to the water vapor and other gases that have been forming from all of the chemical activity in the beans. When these reach a critical mass, the beans literally crack open to relieve the pressure (they also double in size). Roasters that aim to highlight the unique flavors of the beans (sometimes called the *origin character*) and the "liveliness" Joe described usually roast until somewhere between the first and second crack.

- **Second crack.** The beans continue to cook, and some start to show the first signs of the second crack, which happens around 212°C to 218°C (414°F to 424°F). This time, the cracking sound comes from the walls of the bean cracking open. The heat is breaking down the structure of the bean, and the second crack is essentially the sound of the bean collapsing. Most of the beans will crack a second time by 230°C (446°F). At this point, they are usually medium to medium-dark in color and a bit shiny from the released oils.

If a roaster continues past the second crack (after all of the beans have cracked), the beans plunge deeper and deeper into dark roast territory. They continue to get darker and shinier, and the delicate acids that contribute to brightness continue breaking down into acids that taste more bitter and more robust. In other words, the beans start to take on more flavors associated with roasting (sometimes called the *roast character*), like the chocolaty or smoky notes that Joe described. The sugars start to burn. As the roast continues, the beans become more carbonized, like tiny little bricks of charcoal. At this point, the roasted coffee tastes like any other burnt thing. If the beans continue to roast, they will eventually catch fire, as organic matter is wont to do.

For whatever reason, people tend to fall into one of two camps: those who enjoy the flavors associated with the beans themselves and those who prefer the flavors associated with the roasting process. As craft coffee pioneer George Howell said: "Dark roast covers things like a heavy sauce." Following that analogy, people prefer either a dark or a light roast in the same way that they prefer either the sauce of a meat dish or the meat itself. Another way to think of it is by comparing wine and whiskey. Some people like the terroir of the *plant* associated with wine. Other people like the aging/barreling *process* associated with whiskey.

One certainly isn't better than the other; it depends on preference. Starbucks and other second-wave shops have popularized roasts that tend to favor roast character, and I would argue that the general public associates specialty (that is, high-quality) coffee with those flavors, even today. These roasts tend to be consistent, day after day, year after year, which is an appealing quality. But Starbucks-brand specialty coffee has also been, for many people, a stepping stone into the world of craft coffee, which tends to celebrate the natural nuances found in coffee beans by, as we've seen, experimenting with different roasts. In my mind, these differing roasting techniques are one of the most tangible ways craft roasters distinguish themselves beneath the umbrella of specialty coffee.

It's certainly worth mentioning that coffee isn't automatically good just because it's roasted quickly at lower temperatures. First of all, such roast profiles tend to taste more acidic, and even pleasant acidity can take some getting used to. These beans are also less soluble than their roastier counterparts, which means the coffee particles don't dissolve as easily in water, and it can take a bit more coaxing to get the flavors into the cup. As Mr. Howell noted, roasts like this also don't mask anything, so any small defect that might have been obscured by a longer roast time could be laid bare in the cup. Additionally, there is such a thing as too light a roast, in which the beans aren't given enough time with the heat to develop good flavors. These beans might taste like wood or bread—and not in a good way.

DECAFFEINATION

Most craft coffee roasters offer a high-quality decaf option for those of us who want to cut back on caffeine or limit our caffeine intake after a certain point in the day. To be clear, decaffeinated coffee is not caffeine-*free*. It still contains some caffeine: typically three to six milligrams per six ounces of coffee. For some perspective, a regular cup of drip arabica coffee normally contains 75 to 130 milligrams per six ounces, and green tea packs 12 to 30 milligrams into six ounces. So decaf contains relatively little caffeine, but it's an amount that can add up with multiple cups.

A few plants naturally produce caffeine-free beans, but as far as I can tell, they are not widely cultivated. That means most decaf is green coffee from which the caffeine was extracted. Today, there are four main ways to remove caffeine from coffee beans. All methods first soak the beans in water and then use some kind of additive to extract the caffeine. Water, as you may have guessed, can't do the job alone—yes it will extract caffeine, but it will also extract flavor molecules, which would leave you with tasteless beans. Coffee with no caffeine *and* no taste? There is no point. Some decaffeination methods involve chemical solvents (like methylene chloride, which some suspect is carcinogenic) to remove the caffeine. Craft coffee roasters would likely never choose beans that had been subject to any chemicals because they can diminish flavors and leave a chemical residue—on top of the speculation that some of these solvents could be harmful to human health. The following are two more preferable methods for removing caffeine, the Swiss water process being the most common.

A Note on Caffeination

In scientific terms, caffeine is a naturally occurring, odorless, bitter alkaloid found in coffee beans and other plant products, such as tea, yerba mate, and cocoa. It's technically a psychoactive drug because it stimulates the central nervous system and the autonomic nervous system. And that's why people tend to like it—it can, among other things, temporarily block the receptors that make you feel tired as well as boost your ability to focus.

A six-ounce cup of coffee has about 100 to 200 milligrams of caffeine. Despite what you may have heard, roast doesn't have any bearing on how much caffeine is in a coffee bean, because caffeine is neither created nor destroyed during the roasting process. Bean to bean, the caffeine content is largely stable regardless of the roast level. What can affect the caffeine content of your cup is twofold:

- **Species/Varietal.** Robusta has about twice as much caffeine as arabica: arabica beans have about 100 milligrams per six-ounce cup and robusta beans have closer to 200 milligrams per six-ounce cup. The level of caffeine can also vary slightly among arabica plants depending on the varietal, but the differences aren't all that significant.

- **Roast level.** What? I just said roast doesn't matter! It doesn't on a bean-to-bean level, but in practice, you must take weight into consideration. Lighter beans weigh more than darker beans. (A pound of dark roast coffee can have about 90 more beans in it than a pound of light roast coffee.) Therefore, if you measure your beans by weight, a 20-gram dose of dark-roast beans would have more caffeine than a 20-gram dose of light-roast beans— but only because there would be more beans in the dose. On the flip side, light beans are smaller than dark beans, as they don't expand as much during the roasting process. So, if you measure your coffee in scoops, there will be more light beans per scoop than dark beans, which means there will be slightly more caffeine in your light-roast cup than your dark-roast cup. Science!

Carbon Dioxide Process

Carbon dioxide can be used to rid coffee of most of its caffeine. When compressed, carbon dioxide takes on the properties of both a gas and a liquid. It also has the convenient ability to bind with caffeine molecules, and the carbon dioxide process takes advantage of this ability. First, the beans are soaked in hot water. The heat opens up the beans' pores, which gives the caffeine a way out. The soaked beans are transferred out of the water and into a separate vessel, where they are mixed with compressed carbon dioxide. The carbon dioxide pulls the caffeine from the beans but does not attract the flavor molecules. The carbon dioxide is then removed, leaving the decaffeinated beans. The caffeine can be removed from the carbon dioxide and used for other purposes (like caffeinating soda pop), and the carbon dioxide can be recycled and used again. One advantage that the carbon dioxide process has over the Swiss water process is that the flavor molecules stay in the beans the entire time, which, in theory, lessens the chance that any flavor molecules will be lost or destroyed. However, the equipment for this method is quite expensive, so it's not used very much outside of giant commercial operations. For specialty coffee, the Swiss water process is used most often.

Swiss Water Process

The Swiss water process was developed for the explicit purpose of decaffeinating coffee without using any chemicals—not even carbon dioxide. Instead, this method removes the caffeine through SCIENCE (aka solubility and osmosis). Like in the carbon dioxide process, the green coffee beans are placed in a tank of hot water. They stay there for several hours and essentially start brewing: flavors, oils, and caffeine leach into the water. The coffee water then passes through a carbon filter that is designed to capture only the caffeine molecules. The result is a pile of flavorless caffeine-free beans and a tank of flavored, caffeine-free water.

This water is called *green coffee extract*, or GCE. The GCE is composed of the same oils and other flavor molecules as regular green beans—just without the caffeine.

Here's where osmosis comes in. The flavorless beans are thrown away. *New* beans (full of flavor) are brought in and dumped into the GCE. Through osmosis, the caffeine is drawn out of the new beans and into the water. Because the beans and the water are in balance with regard to their flavor molecules, only the caffeine is lost. This means that the beans lose the caffeine but retain much of their flavor.

Look for bags of decaffeinated coffee that say "Swiss water process," and you'll know that the coffee was processed without potentially harmful chemical solvents. You may also notice that decaffeinated beans may cost a bit more than their caffeinated counterparts, which is due to the extra processing involved.

CHAPTER 4

Buying the Coffee

WHEN YOU ARE BEGINNING your craft coffee journey, simply getting your hands on a bag of the good stuff can be a challenge—deciphering all of the jargon on the label is another story. In this chapter, I explore how to identify a bag of craft coffee, where to purchase it, how to read the label, and how to keep it fresh once you get it home.

WHERE TO FIND CRAFT COFFEE

Craft coffee has never been more accessible than it is right now. If you live in a city, you likely have access to several craft coffee vendors with a multitude of readily available options to choose from. If you live in a more rural area, you may need to rely on the internet instead of a brick-and-mortar store, but you still have plenty of choices. There are hundreds of craft coffee roasters around the country, and you can find their high-quality coffee if you know where to look and what to look for.

If you are unfamiliar with the roasters in your area (or if there aren't any), it can be difficult to differentiate a bag of craft coffee from the other bags on the shelf. A little research can go a long way, but keep in mind that the kinds of roasters I'm talking about likely don't refer to themselves as "craft roasters." You can determine whether or not a roaster qualifies as a craft roaster based on the values they describe on their website and, to some extent, the language they use on their packaging. In general, craft roasters:

- **Are small and (usually) independently owned**. The biggest craft roasters are sometimes referred to as the Big Four: Stumptown (based in Portland, Oregon), Intelligentsia (based in Chicago, Illinois), Blue Bottle (based in Oakland, California), and Counter Culture (based in Durham, North Carolina). These are the brands credited with leading the craft coffee movement. They may be the biggest names in craft coffee, but collectively, they are still dwarfed by the likes of specialty coffee chains like Starbucks. In 2015, the conglomerate that owns Peet's and Caribou purchased a majority stake in both Stumptown and Intelligentsia, although both companies have pledged to uphold quality as they expand. The purchases likely mean these two craft brands will proliferate much more quickly than they would have otherwise. Most other craft roasters are a lot smaller than the Big Four, although you may find that one or two local roasters dominate your market—craft roasters are very much like craft beer in that way.

- **Are explicitly interested in quality.** The website and packaging of a craft roaster is likely to clearly state that quality is important. It might also provide philosophies related to sourcing, buying, roasting, and/or selling coffee. Look for terms like *specialty coffee*, *fostering relationships*, *seed to cup*, *transparency*, *precision roasting*, *partnerships*, *respect*, *ethically grown and purchased*, *responsibly sourced*, *artisanal*, and similar.

- **Are interested in coffee's story.** A craft roaster usually includes a lot of information on their website about where their coffee comes from. They almost certainly will discuss the origin of their coffee, and they might even provide detailed information about the washing station, cooperative, farm, or producer that harvested or processed the coffee. They might also talk about their importers.

- **Provide a lot of information on the bag.** The more information that's on a bag of coffee—particularly about when the coffee was roasted and where it came from—the more likely the bag is from a craft roaster (although not all roasters put a bunch of info on their bags). Learn more about how to decipher a coffee bag and what to look out for on page 163.

In order to find craft coffee, you should start by finding the roaster. Roasters often own their own coffee shops—although the roaster and the shop do not always go by the same name—and they also sell their beans wholesale to other cafés as well as grocery stores. In other words, if there are no roasters near your town, it doesn't mean you are out of luck.

Grocery Stores

If you don't live near any craft roasters, the first place to look for craft coffee is your local grocery store. The selection there will vary greatly depending on where you live. One good thing about grocery stores is that virtually all of them follow the same basic organization no matter where they're located. The lowest-quality commodity coffee, usually sold in large canisters or tins, tends to be grouped together. Similarly, specialty coffee, such as Starbucks, Peet's, and Caribou, as well as the brands that are trying to compete with them, such as Dunkin' Donuts, Panera, and the higher-end "gourmet" or "select" versions of the commodity brands, are commonly bunched together, usually in clusters. If your grocery store sells craft coffee, it is most likely to be near the specialty coffee. I've noticed, however, that a single coffee brand (especially if it's one of the big ones) can span multiple shelves—grocery stores are not necessarily set up like liquor stores where the cheap stuff is on the bottom shelf and the good stuff is up top.

The easiest way to make sure you are purchasing craft coffee is to familiarize yourself with the biggest names in craft coffee, along with the names of your local and regional roasters, as those are the brands your grocery store is most likely to carry. The closer you live to a city, the more selection you likely will have, both in terms of brands and types of coffee. Here in Chicago, my local grocery chain has a surprising selection of craft coffee, although most of the small roasters featured there are from Chicago or nearby midwestern cities. But when I visit my smallish hometown in Indiana, it's difficult to find even whole-bean specialty coffee at the grocery store, let alone craft coffee brands. If your store carries craft coffee but doesn't have a big selection, you are most likely to see one or more of the Big Four. If you're lucky, you'll have a few local roasters thrown into the mix as well. However, roasters are popping up all over the place, even in small cities, so you may be surprised by what you find.

If you aren't familiar with the roasters in your area, you can look out for these sure signs that you're not dealing with craft coffee and avoid them:

- **Canisters.** A craft coffee shop will always package their coffee in bags, not canisters. Usually the bags will have a little plastic contraption that looks like a belly button. That's a one-way valve that releases carbon dioxide while keeping out oxygen, and most craft coffee roasters use them to help keep their coffee fresh.

- **Flavored coffee.** While packages of craft coffee often include flavor notes (see page 176), craft roasters most certainly will not sell coffee with added flavor. Avoid these coffees like the plague.

- **Vague origin.** Craft coffee roasters tend to be very specific about where their coffee comes from, usually indicated by a country and a region within that country. It's a point of pride for the roaster to communicate this information. If a coffee package includes absolutely no information about origin, that is suspect, as is an ambiguous origin like "Island Blend" (unless there is more specific information listed with it). The words "Colombia" and "Brazil" appear frequently, even on lower-grade coffee, so they don't necessarily mean anything.

- **Heavy focus on dark roast.** Any coffee labeled "French Roast" is likely not craft coffee. Actually, if the bag makes any reference to darker roasts (e.g., French or Italian), it's likely not from a craft roaster (some craft roasters do offer darker roasts, but they probably would not use the aforementioned terms). If a coffee's packaging emphasizes words like *bold*, *full-bodied*, or *dark*, it's also unlikely to be craft coffee.

- **Emphasis on organic or fair trade.** A few brands at the grocery store put more effort into promoting the organic and/or fair-trade aspects of their coffee rather than the coffee itself. These qualities aren't necessarily bad, but they aren't the primary focus of most craft coffee packaging.

To some extent, you may have more luck at certain grocery stores than others. Whole Foods and similar stores may be more likely to carry craft coffee than other local or regional grocery chains, especially because they often offer opportunities to buy local. However, it can still be hard for small roasters to get shelf space at chain stores, so be sure to check out independent stores and co-ops in your area, too.

Cafés/Coffee Shops and Roasters

Craft coffee roasters often operate cafés or shops where they sell drinks, bags of their coffee, and equipment. If a small roaster owns a shop, you'll certainly be able to purchase their coffee directly from them at that shop. As a bonus, the people working behind the counter will be able to answer your questions about the coffee and how to brew it before you make a purchase.

Many independent cafés and coffee shops are not directly owned by a roaster. However, these shops may exclusively use coffee from one particular roaster (usually one of the Big Four or a nearby roaster) or from multiple roasters. Normally, these independent specialty shops sell bags of coffee in addition to drinks. If you add up all of the independent specialty shops in the United States, there are more of them than there are Starbucks stores, so there is a good chance you don't live too far away from one and can fulfill all of your craft coffee needs there. To be clear, not all independent specialty shops are craft coffee shops—with highly trained baristas that are deeply invested in their skills and techniques— though they are a step in the right direction and may still carry and use craft coffee. How do you know whether your local coffee shop is a craft coffee shop? Look out for:

- **Knowledgeable baristas.** If you are at a true craft coffee shop, the baristas behind the counter should be able to answer any questions you have about where the coffee comes from, how it tastes, and how it should be brewed. If they have no idea, it's probably not a craft coffee shop.

- **Manual brewing methods.** You might see a Chemex or V60 hanging out on the brew bar. Also, if there is any kind of giant, scientific-looking contraption behind the counter or taking up a wall somewhere, you are probably in a craft coffee shop (it's used to make cold brew).

- **Inscrutable signage.** Craft coffee shops usually have a small menu board by the counter with a list of the day's coffees. They are typically named according to their country of origin, the device, or both—like Guatemala AeroPress, which may have seemed like gibberish before you read this book. If it's a café that's not associated with a roaster, they might list the coffees with more emphasis on the roaster's name.

- **A retail space.** Craft coffee shops usually have a small retail space—sometimes just a few shelves—where they sell devices and other coffee equipment.

- **Latte art.** Baristas at craft coffee shops often pour designs and shapes such as hearts and flowers into lattes and other espresso drinks.

Another recent feature of the craft coffee movement is the emergence of non–coffee shops that sell craft coffee. Back in that small hometown of mine, there are at least two stores that are not dedicated to coffee (one is a frozen yogurt café and one is a doughnut/comic shop) where I can purchase bags from prominent Chicago roasters. This shows just how easy it is to find bags of craft coffee for sale even outside of a craft coffee shop.

Online

Even if you live in a place with no craft coffee vendors, there is still hope. Almost every craft roaster has a website with an online shop and most provide a lot of details about their coffees so you know exactly what you're buying. Most roasters handle their own shipments to ensure that they are sending out only the freshest coffee, so you can be confident that your coffee won't be stale by the time it gets to you. You can try coffee from any roaster in the country this way—there are a lot of options (I provide a very short list of some of my favorites in the Resources section on page 259). Some might say there are too many options. Because of this, several online services offer coffee subscriptions. These services send you curated selections of coffee on a regular basis in exchange for a monthly fee. Subscription programs are often a bit more expensive than individual purchases, and they don't make sense unless you drink enough coffee to keep up with the pace of the shipments. But they are a convenient way to get a lot of different kinds of coffee delivered right to your doorstep.

SEASONALITY

Many craft coffee roasters have become more serious about coffee seasonality in recent years. This is a relatively new concept in the coffee industry (or at least it's a relatively new concept to be widely adopted among craft coffee people). However, coffee has always been a seasonal product. Coffee cherries are fruit and, like most fruit, they grow only during certain times of the year. Most coffee-producing countries have distinct time frames throughout the year for growing, harvesting, processing, and shipping green coffee. On top of that, there is usually a peak season for the coffee harvest—usually in the middle of the harvest period—when most coffee cherries are at their best. Some countries have climates that allow growing and harvesting year round. Others have two distinct periods each for growing and harvesting, and even so, only one of those harvests tends to produce the highest-quality beans.

The belief among many coffee roasters is that they should be roasting and selling their product during peak season: as soon as possible after harvest. Because it can take months to process coffee—and then several more weeks to ship it to the United States—seasonal coffee is generally considered to be any coffee sold within nine months or less of the harvest date.

Other roasters, however, believe coffee seasonality is a bunch of bull hockey that creates an unnecessary sense of scarcity. They say that coffee, if stored properly, stays pretty fresh in its green state. Some even believe green coffee can stay fresh for a year or more. If that's true, then we should be able to enjoy any type of coffee all year long.

Both of these views probably contain a bit of truth. Some green coffees with certain characteristics may be able to stay very fresh for a long time. Other types might go stale more quickly. Andreas has seen cases when coffee at the roaster has actually diminished in quality and flavor before the shipment could be fully roasted. At other times, he has trained new employees with seemingly old (older than a year) leftover green coffee, and it still tasted great after roasting. Others argue that perhaps we should enjoy coffee seasonally because with all of the origins that regularly produce high-quality coffee beans, another great cup of coffee is always just around the bend—there's simply no reason to store coffee at all.

What does all of this mean for you, the home coffee brewer? The biggest takeaway is that it's unlikely you'll be able to find your favorite single-origin coffee the entire 12 months out of the year. You'll also notice that most roasters will release certain origin coffees around the same time each year. For example, Ethiopias generally start hitting shelves in June and July, while a lot of Brazils tend to be seen in the winter months. The chart on the next page outlines the average peak harvest times and the corresponding market availability (when you might see roasted coffee for sale) of the most popular coffee-producing origins. Note that these are just estimates—harvests and shipments can be delayed for any number of reasons, the weather being chief among them.

HARVEST SCHEDULE

Origin	Jan.	Feb.	March	April	May	June	July	Aug.	Sept.	Oct.	Nov.	Dec.
Bolivia	○	○						●	●	●		○
Brazil	○					●	●	●	●	○	○	○
Burundi						●	●	●		○	○	○
Colombia		○	○	◉	●			○	○	●	●	●
Costa Rica	●	●	●	○	○	○	○					●
DRC	◉	○	◉	◉	◉	●	○	○	◉	◉	●	●
Ecuador						●	●	●		○	○	○
El Salvador	●	●	●	○	○	○	○					●
Ethiopia	●	●	○	○	○	○					●	●
Guatemala	●	●	●	○	○	○	○					●
Hawai'i	●	○	○	○	○					●	●	●
Honduras	●	●		○	○	○						●
Jamaica	●	●			○	○						
Java	○					●	●	●			○	○
Kenya	●	●	○	○	○	◉	●			○	◉	●
Mexico	●	●	◉	○	○	○	○				●	●
Nicaragua	●	●	●	○	○	○	○					●
Panama	●	●	●		○	○	○					
Papua New Guinea						●	●	●		○	○	○
Peru	○	○						●	●	●		○
Rwanda				●	●	●	●	○	○	○	○	
Sulawesi	○	○	○				●	●	●	●	◉	○
Sumatra	●	◉	◉	○	○	○	○			●	●	●
Tanzania		○	○	○						●	●	●
Yemen		○	○	○						●	●	●

KEY: ● Harvest ○ Market ◉ Both

DECIPHERING THE COFFEE BAG LABEL

At times, coffee bags from craft roasters can seem to display a bunch of esoteric information, and I have yet to see any that come with a decoder ring. How much of this information is necessary for the home coffee brewer? It depends on what you care about and what you want to know. In general, a lot of this information is just the roaster's way of showing you they have done their homework and know where their coffee came from and how it was processed. The more information roasters include on their bags, the more likely they will be able to answer questions you may have about how the coffee was produced, which is important because, as you'll see, official designations on bags only mean so much in the coffee world. The fact that this information is listed in the first place is one way you can distinguish craft coffee from specialty coffee and specialty coffee from commodity coffee when you are staring at rows and rows of bags at the grocery store. Let's break down the basic pieces of information you're most likely to see on a typical craft coffee bag.

Whole or Ground Beans

This one is self-explanatory, but I'll take this opportunity to emphasize that if you want to make better coffee at home, you shouldn't be buying preground beans (see page 84).

Blend versus Single Origin

One of the first things you should notice about a bag of coffee is whether the beans inside are from different origins or one location. The former is known as a *blend*, while the latter is known as a *single-origin coffee*. Some craft roasters are resistant to selling blends—I guess because they are not considered as pure as single-origin coffees or because of rumors that roasters try to get rid of stale scrap beans by adding them to blends. But when done well, blends can be a good go-to option for home brewers.

Ideally, blends mix and match different types of beans to create a balanced, consistent cup. Many of us tend to like consistency (or at

DECIPHERING THE COFFEE BAG LABEL

KEY

1. Whole or Ground Beans
2. Blend versus Single Origin
3. Farm/Finca, Producer, and Processing Station
4. Varietals
5. Elevation
6. Process
7. Roast/Roast Date
8. Flavor Notes
9. Certifications

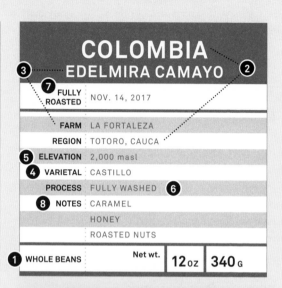

COLOMBIA
EDELMIRA CAMAYO

FULLY ROASTED	NOV. 14, 2017
FARM	LA FORTALEZA
REGION	TOTORO, CAUCA
ELEVATION	2,000 masl
VARIETAL	CASTILLO
PROCESS	FULLY WASHED
NOTES	CARAMEL
	HONEY
	ROASTED NUTS
WHOLE BEANS	Net wt. **12**oz **340**g

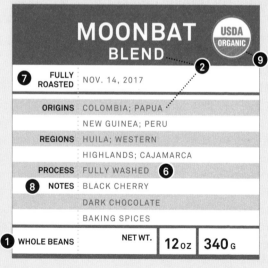

MOONBAT
BLEND

USDA ORGANIC

FULLY ROASTED	NOV. 14, 2017
ORIGINS	COLOMBIA; PAPUA
	NEW GUINEA; PERU
REGIONS	HUILA; WESTERN
	HIGHLANDS; CAJAMARCA
PROCESS	FULLY WASHED
NOTES	BLACK CHERRY
	DARK CHOCOLATE
	BAKING SPICES
WHOLE BEANS	NET WT. **12**oz **340**g

least the illusion of it), and a blend is one way to get consistent coffee. As you've seen, single-origin coffees can vary widely in flavor. If that's not your style, a blend—although still seasonal and subject to some variation—will never veer too far from what you liked about it in the first place. It takes *a lot* of planning and skill on the part of the roaster to offer a consistent flavor profile in a blended product month after month, so for roasters who know what they're doing, it is certainly not a cop-out.

Blends also give roasters a way to use up perfectly good leftover beans and less expensive beans while still offering a high-quality product. Blends can make good use of inexpensive beans—beans that might be considered boring on their own but that may offer pleasant qualities when used as one of several beans in a blend. Because of this, blends tend to be less expensive than single-origin coffees, which can be appealing.

At the very least, bags of blends usually list the countries of origin of the beans and may even delve into regions. While blends are often named something cute, sometimes the origin is right there in the name— Mocha-Java is a classic example (although some blends labeled as Mocha-Java might come from neither Yemen nor Indonesia; *Mocha-Java* is often used as a generic marketing term, and some claim such blends are intended to replicate classic Mocha-Java flavors). I tend to feel that roasters that list the origins have more accountability—and generally a higher-quality product. I would be slightly suspicious of a craft roaster that did not disclose at least the countries of origin behind a blend and highly suspicious of a craft roaster that protected all of the details surrounding a "secret" blend.

Single-origin coffee is usually named after at least the country of origin and usually a growing region or washing station within that country, although many roasters include the most specific information available about where the coffee was grown (more on that later). Craft roasters often strive to highlight the unique qualities of their beans, and one way to do that is by grouping them by origin. Origin certainly affects how a coffee tastes because everything related to the plant's terroir (soil, climate, sunlight, weather, elevation) contributes to the coffee's flavor development. Because these factors can vary significantly from year to year—or even from one corner of a farm to another—single origins from the same country can taste surprisingly different from each other. It's hard to say that *all* Ethiopias are this way or *all* Panamas are that way.

Buying Tip

Commodity coffee is almost always a blend, and it would be unusual to find many details about its origin on the bag. However, you may see a bag of commodity coffee labeled "Colombia," because that country has been marketing its coffee that way since the early days of the coffee trade. Despite the outlier of Colombia, single-origin coffee is a very craft concept. Big specialty coffee brands sell mostly blends as well, although they are more likely to include information about origin on their bags. Recently, big specialty coffee companies have also been more visibly pushing a couple of their own single-origin coffees—usually marketed as "premium" or "limited edition"—but you are more likely to find those bags at a coffee shop than a grocery store.

Farm/Finca, Producer, and Processing Station

More and more, craft roasters are including the small farm or estate (or *finca*, in Spanish) on their packaging. In some cases, such as the prized Panamanian gesha from Hacienda La Esmeralda, the estate may have more cachet than the region itself. Some bags even include the name of the individual producer and/or the cooperative (a group of producers that pool resources) that grew and processed the coffee. As opposed to simply listing the information, the coffee is often named for the washing station, producer, or estate itself. For example, Halfwit Coffee Roasters' Rwanda Kanzu is named after the country of origin and the Kanzu cooperative that produced it, and Blue Bottle's Burundi Kayanza Heza is named after the country, region, and washing station, respectively. In the example on page 164, the single-origin coffee is named for the country (Colombia) and the producer (Edelmira Camayo).

Companies use different naming methods, but these general conventions are partly for traceability, which is the cornerstone of the craft coffee ethos, and partly out of respect for the coffee producers and their product. In general, the more traceable a coffee is, the higher quality it is—and the more likely that the coffee producer was paid a higher price. That's because if you can trace coffee back to a specific place, you can learn exactly how it was grown, harvested, processed, and sorted, as well as how it was traded and sold. Typically, the more care that is taken in each of these areas, the higher the quality and price of the coffee.

However, different countries and regions have varying levels of traceability because not all parts of the world are equipped with the infrastructure necessary to keep coffee traceable. Areas with limited access to washing stations, for example, will process all of the coffee from the surrounding farms together. Some coffee may even need to be shipped to a processing facility. This doesn't mean that coffee that cannot be traced back to a farm or producer is automatically of lower quality—some great coffees are not easily sourced.

Varietals

Craft coffee roasters often list varietals on their bags of coffee, especially on bags of single-origin coffee. If varietals are listed, you're likely to see more than one, because producers often grow more than one plant in the same field. Additionally, in some countries, it's common for producers to process their beans together, which can mean that multiple varietals end up in one bag. However, it's not uncommon to see a bag of only one varietal, especially if the beans were carefully sorted. Coffee that comes from rare or specially sorted lots may even be named after the varietal. For example, Intelligentsia's Santuario Colombia Red Bourbon includes the varietal in the name, along with the farm and country of origin.

Certain varietals, such as bourbon, gesha, and SL34, are associated with high quality, but I don't think consumers can assume a certain level of quality based solely on the varietal (although if a coffee is named after the varietal, the roaster likely considers that coffee to be special in some way). As discussed in chapter 3, varietals can be associated with certain characteristics, but because the terroir and the roast can affect coffee's taste so drastically, you can't glean many details about flavor from the name of the varietal alone.

At the very least, the presence of varietals on a coffee bag is a marker of care and traceability. However, a lack of varietals on the bag does not necessarily mean the coffee is of poor quality.

Elevation

Many coffee packages will tell you how many meters above sea level (masl) or feet above sea level (fasl) the coffee was grown. Generally speaking, higher-quality beans are grown at higher elevations. According to the Coffee Research Institute, in subtropical climates, the best elevation for growing coffee is about 550 to 1,100 masl, and in places close to the equator, the sweet spot is generally between 1,000 and 2,000 masl—although it's important that the plants don't suffer frost, no matter where they are.

It's much cooler at these high elevations; according to a 2005 article in

Roast magazine, experts have found that for every 100-meter increase in elevation, expect a 33.8°F (0.6°C) drop in temperature. Cooler temperatures and lower levels of oxygen cause coffee beans to mature more slowly because they are essentially under stress. In this state, most of the coffee plant's energy goes toward making seeds (as opposed to developing leaves and branches), which makes the coffee beans hard and dense. The beans also have more time to develop and store nutrients, mostly in the form of sugars. In fact, experts say that every 300-meter jump in elevation is associated with a 10 percent increase in sucrose (sugar) production in coffee beans. These sugars play a big role in the development of flavor—specifically acidity, which is why higher-elevation coffee also tends to have a high perceived acidity, a trait many coffee connoisseurs value. Other experts point out that the soil is of better quality up in the mountains, and certain coffee-plant pests cannot live at such high climes. All of these factors combine to make higher-elevation coffee more desirable. The chart below shows a very generalized way to think about how elevation affects flavor:

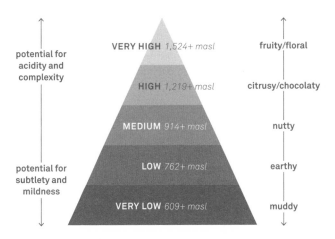

potential for acidity and complexity

VERY HIGH *1,524+ masl*   fruity/floral

HIGH *1,219+ masl*   citrusy/chocolaty

MEDIUM *914+ masl*   nutty

LOW *762+ masl*   earthy

potential for subtlety and mildness

VERY LOW *609+ masl*   muddy

If the roaster lists elevation on the bag, the upshot is twofold: (1) it shows that the roaster knows where the coffee came from, and (2) a higher elevation might indicate a higher-quality coffee. Of course, there are exceptions. Hawaiian Kona coffee, often considered one of the best coffees in the world, is grown at relatively low elevations. And a certain elevation does not guarantee a high-quality bean. Plenty of gross coffee is grown at 1,500 meters. Elevation cannot make up for poor soil, wonky weather, or poor farming practices.

Process

The way a bag of coffee beans was processed can tell you a lot about how that coffee will taste—in fact, this is one factor (unlike origin) that has a fairly predictable outcome when it comes to coffee characteristics. Many roasters will include information about how the coffee was processed on

> ### A Note on Elevation and Brewing
>
> Because high-elevation beans are denser and harder, you may notice that water takes noticeably longer to drain through them. For an extremely high-elevation bean, this doesn't necessarily mean you have to change anything. Dense, hard beans take longer to extract, so the slower drawdown might be just what they need. As always, let the taste of the cup guide you. On the flip side, lower-elevation beans tend to extract more quickly. If you have tried everything and your cup is still overextracted, try reducing your water temperature.

the bag. Since we already discussed what these processes are on page 142, here we will focus on flavor and the terms you might see on the bag.

WASHED/WET PROCESS

On a bag of coffee, "washed" and "wet process" refer to the same thing. Because this method is the one most commonly used on arabica coffee throughout the Bean Belt, it is the processing term you'll see most frequently on coffee packaging. Washed processing tends to produce "clean" coffee in which multiple flavors and attributes can be detected. This is one reason why craft roasters tend to like this process—it allows the origin character, as well as a good deal of acidity, to shine through. The list of potential flavor notes is essentially endless when it comes to washed coffee, as flavor notes are so influenced by terroir. Remember that washed coffee needs to be dried, too, before it can be sold, so it's not uncommon for roasters to explain what drying method they used. On your bag, you may see phrases that describe this stage, such as "dried on patios" or "dried on raised beds."

NATURAL/DRY PROCESS

The terms *natural* and *dry process* are used interchangeably in the coffee world, so you may see either one on a coffee bag. Unlike washed coffees, natural coffees tend to produce very, very distinct fruit notes, often those of blueberry and stone fruit. These are actual fruit notes that almost anyone would be able to discern; they will likely surprise you the first time you taste a natural coffee. In fact, if you aren't sure whether you can tell two different coffees apart, I encourage you to seek out a naturally processed coffee and compare it with a washed one. In addition to their distinctive fruitiness, natural coffees tend to have fuller bodies and less perceived acidity than washed coffees.

Natural arabica coffees are most common in Brazil, Ethiopia, and Yemen. Consistently good naturals are often highly prized, although they still tend to spark controversy in the coffee world because some say they are all essentially the same and lack the nuance and variation you see in washed coffees. (I don't agree.) In any case, natural coffees seem to have a polarizing effect on people: you either love them or you hate them.

PULPED NATURAL/HONEY

As you might guess with a process that borrows a little from the washed method and a little from the natural method, the pulped natural process tends to result in a coffee that has a mix of washed and natural characteristics. Beans processed this way tend to keep the acidity of washed coffees and the earthiness of natural coffees. Because the exact processing method can vary from producer to producer, there can be a lot of variation among pulped naturals when it comes to taste.

This is not the most common processing method, although more producers are starting to experiment with different pulped natural techniques. You are most likely to see a pulped natural coffee from Brazil, where the technique was invented, or in Central America, where they call it *honey*. More recently, new terms, such as *red honey*, *yellow honey*, and *black honey*, have cropped up—all of them are related to how much fruit is left on the beans before they are set out to dry. Another word you may see on a coffee bag is *semiwashed*, which also means that, unlike a true pulped natural coffee, not all of the fruit was left on before the beans were dried.

Some professionals have found that naturally processed coffees tend to extract more quickly than washed coffees. This means it may be easier to overextract these beans. If you find this is the case, try lowering your water temperature by a few degrees.

Roast

I've already talked a good deal about roast, but when choosing a bag of coffee, it's important to keep in mind that there is very little standardization when it comes to naming roasts. Many craft roasters appear to have abandoned the traditional language you might still see on some commodity and specialty coffee bags (City, American, Vienna, French, etc.), likely because those names and their loose definitions are very subjective and not immediately understood. When it comes to craft coffee, it is far more common to see language that references color (light, medium, medium dark, dark), but there still aren't any scientific parameters you can use to figure out what these terms actually mean. A lot of craft roasters don't even mention roast on the bag (like the example on page 164)—in fact, many consider the terms *light, medium,* and *dark* to be overly simple when it comes to describing roast, as roasters use time and temperature to achieve certain roast profiles, which may not always correlate with the color of the beans. In other words, two beans that look exactly the same shade of brown can produce two wildly different flavors.

However, that (lack of) information is not all that helpful to you. It's usually safe to assume that most craft roasters' beans would be considered light to medium roast by the majority of people who use that scale. As a general rule of thumb, the lighter the roast, the more of the beans' flavors you'll get, and the darker the roast, the more of the roast's flavors you'll get. Although the color of the beans does not necessarily correlate with their flavor, you can generally expect certain qualities from these descriptors.

When in doubt, talk to the roaster or a barista in a café of high regard. They will be able to describe the characteristics of the coffee in detail. If you live in an area with a dearth of craft coffee shops, you can find roasters online, and they tend to provide a lot of detail on their websites. Alternatively, you can pay more attention to the flavor notes listed on the coffee bag (see page 164) than to the color of the roast to get an idea of what the coffee might taste like.

As a final note, it's important to keep in mind that certain large specialty coffee chains use a different language from the rest of the coffee industry to communicate with the general public. Their blonde roasts may not even be in the same zip code as what others in the industry would call a light roast. This is just one more (extreme) example of how roast color and process are highly subjective.

ROAST DATE

I'm going to put my foot down here and say that a bag of high-quality coffee should have a roast date on it. It's the only way to tell whether the coffee is fresh or already stale from sitting on the shelf too long. I've said it before, and I'll say it again: coffee is incredibly delicate; its flavors just don't last that long, even in its whole state. Industry wisdom says that coffee shouldn't necessarily be consumed immediately after roasting because it needs time to off-gas a certain amount of carbon dioxide, which can otherwise make it taste bitter. How much time? Some say at least 24 hours, some say 48 hours, and others say at least one week (and still others say the need to off-gas is a myth). Like most things having to do with coffee, the time needed to off-gas likely depends on the beans. Different beans (and different roasts) vary in their peak freshness. Some say that lighter roasts in particular may need more time to off-gas than other roasts.

ROAST DEFINITIONS

Roast	Characteristics
Light	• Light body • Notes of seeds, malt, grain, grass, corn
Medium-Light	• Bright acidity • More complexity • Clear origin character • Notes of fruit, nuts, spice, brown sugar
Medium	• Balanced acidity and sweetness • Full body • Clear origin character • Notes of caramel, honey, brown butter, cooked fruit, cooked vegetables, darker spices like black pepper, cloves, plum, cooked apple
Medium-Dark	• Emerging bittersweetness • Slightly muted acidity • Potential for heavy body • Notes of tobacco, vanilla, bourbon, porter beer, stewed meat, smoked fruit
Dark	• Prominent bittersweetness • Muted acidity • Light body • Notes of burnt tobacco, very dark cocoa, bitter black tea, charred vegetable, very dark toast
Very Dark	• Dominant bitter/bittersweet tones • Light body • Fully muted origin character • Notes of cigar smoke, smoked meat, liquid smoke, soy sauce, fish sauce, burnt toast
Extreme-Dark	• Dominant burned/bitter tones • Flavorless except for notes of smoke, ash, aspirin

Andreas and I tend to think that peak freshness of whole roasted beans is somewhere between 7 and 10 days after roasting, although you can likely get great results in your kitchen up to 21 days after roasting. After that, the flavor quality diminishes. This doesn't mean the coffee goes bad or will poison you after 21 days; it will just seem duller, like a carbonated beverage gone flat. One way to determine how fresh your coffee is to pay attention to the bloom while you brew it (see page 42)—this is the coffee off-gassing carbon dioxide, so if it doesn't bubble much or at all when you pour water over it, then you know it's probably stale.

A good rule of thumb is to buy only as much coffee as you are going to consume in a week. If you're giving coffee as a gift and it won't be consumed right away, consider buying a bag with a very recent roast date (or buy a gift card). If you are buying directly from a roaster, you should, of course, follow their advice, as they know their beans best. Some roasters put a best-by date on their coffee, especially if it's going to be sold in a grocery store. I don't really like this practice, because the best-by date doesn't indicate when the coffee was roasted, and there's no way to know what metrics the roaster used to come up with that date. Your safest bet is to stick with coffee that lists the roast date on the bag and to choose bags with recent roast dates.

Flavor Notes

Flavor notes are little descriptors of things you might taste in the coffee, such as caramel or pear. They can seem like a bunch of baloney, especially when you brew a cup and taste none of those flavors. An experience like this can make home coffee brewers feel like outsiders, leading them to think that they made a mistake while brewing or that they apparently don't speak the same language as the coffee professionals.

But here's the thing: you might taste a flavor note—especially if it's very exaggerated—but you might not, and that's not necessarily because you did anything wrong. The flavor notes are what the *roasters* experienced when *they* tasted the coffee. It's based on a roaster's palate, not on a universal ideal. As we've seen, coffee can be influenced by many outside factors, including water composition. While these outside factors may not make your coffee taste bad, they may prevent you from tasting the flavor notes when you make the coffee at home.

Additionally, taste is necessarily subjective and so is the way taste is described. One person's "almond" might be another person's "cashew." If both parties have not agreed on what an almond note tastes like, then there's a bit of a language barrier: the flavor cannot be understood beyond the broad stroke of "nutty," perhaps. This is compounded by the fact that people can only recognize flavors that they're familiar with: if you've never tasted an almond, you're certainly not going to taste one in your coffee. Roasters and baristas have highly trained palates that they exercise every day. Unless you, too, taste things for a living, you likely won't be able to taste on the same level as a coffee professional—unless you practice, of course (see chapter 5).

It's also worth mentioning that even if you can taste all of the flavor notes listed on a bag, the coffee still won't taste exactly like those things because coffee flavors are subtle—except for that one time my Ethiopia tasted like a blueberry muffin in liquid form. But usually, coffee flavors are subtler than that, especially because coffee is always going to involve bitterness.

In other words, you should not strive to create the flavor notes listed on the bag in your brew at home. Instead, you should use flavor notes as guideposts that direct you toward the broader flavor category the coffee falls into, like earthy, fruity, floral, or sweet. If you know you don't really like fruity coffees, then you'll want to stay away from a bag that lists stone fruit as one of its flavor notes. If you want something sweet, you might look out for notes like "milk chocolate" or "nougat."

I want to emphasize that flavor notes are not completely useless; they can often give you a better idea of what a coffee might taste like than the roast can, so I don't recommend dismissing them entirely. However, from a consumer's perspective, it's important to acknowledge that most roasters don't always do the best job communicating with us, especially when it comes to flavor. In general, coffee bags tend to be more industry facing, which makes sense, because many roasters sell their beans to other coffee professionals through wholesale accounts like coffee shops. But as more of us become interested in buying beans ourselves and making coffee at home, I think the language used on bags needs to change to be more accessible, and when it comes to flavor notes, that means the language needs to become more general.

Some roasters have already reexamined how they communicate to consumers through their packaging. Blueprint Coffee in St. Louis uses an easy-to-read graphic that shows what consumers can expect from the coffee's body, sweetness, and brightness (acidity).

Certifications

Coffee, like many products, often comes with certifications on its packaging. These may or may not mean anything. I'll say up front that I don't think you should be discouraged from buying a bag of coffee just because it doesn't have any certifications on it nor should you be encouraged to buy one just because it does. The best way to find out more about your coffee is by talking to the roaster or a barista familiar with the beans. I encourage you to look into these certifications on your own, but here are the basics:

- **USDA Organic.** This means that the coffee was produced in compliance with the guidelines established by the US Department of Agriculture's National Organic Program. It also means the producer is able to afford the fees associated with the certification. It does not necessarily mean that *no* synthetic substances were used, as the USDA's National Organic Program has a list of allowable synthetic substances. It also doesn't mean that any coffee without the USDA Organic label is not organic. Many coffee producers already farm organically out of tradition or necessity (synthetic chemicals are expensive), but they might not have the extra funds required to put the certification on the bag. The roaster should be able to provide you with the best information about where the coffee came from and how it was grown.

- **Fair Trade.** This is probably one of the most common certifications for coffee, and it's one that helps many consumers make purchasing decisions. In the beginning, fair-trade certification was intended to help smaller coffee producers survive in a competitive marketplace. A fair-trade label on a bag of coffee is supposed to mean that the coffee was purchased from the producer at a fair market value. In exchange for the fair price, the coffee producer is expected to adhere to certain environmental, ethical, and social standards (although their coffee does not need to be organic). In the United States, fair-trade certification is governed by Fair Trade USA, which broke off from Fairtrade Labelling Organizations International in 2012. In recent years, Fair Trade USA has come under fire for a variety of reasons. For one thing, Fair Trade USA started allowing big corporations to become fair-trade certified, which made it seem like the fair-trade mission had moved away from trying to help smaller producers. For another, Fair Trade USA's minimum price of fair-trade coffee isn't that much higher than the price of regular commodity coffee, and it hasn't increased very much in the past 20-something years, leading some to wonder how fair these fair-trade prices actually are. Additionally, critics wonder whether the extra money is really making it to the producers and not being siphoned off by some corrupt body along the way, as there is not much oversight of each transaction. As previously mentioned, transparency is a big part of the craft coffee movement, so many craft roasters skip the drama of fair trade altogether by directly trading with producers. This allows them to pay fair prices while establishing a relationship with their producers; however, their coffee won't have any fair-trade labels on it. Don't let the lack of a fair-trade label stop you from buying a bag of coffee—talk to the roaster!

- **Bird Friendly.** This certification, developed by the Smithsonian Migratory Bird Center, relates to shade-grown coffee. To receive this certification, coffee producers must meet requirements related to the percentage of shade coverage on their farms, the height of their trees, and the diversity of the tree species they grow—plus their coffee must be certified organic. What do birds have to do with coffee? It's not uncommon for forests to be cleared to make way for coffee plantations. This reduces the habitat for migratory birds, which are essential to the ecosystems they inhabit. Maintaining native shade trees on coffee plots helps restore a safe haven for these birds. It also helps reduce water waste, maintain healthy soil, and produce more delicious coffee. That's right: birds aside, shade-grown coffee is often prized for its quality. It develops more slowly, similar to coffee at high elevations, which increases the nutrients (like sugar) in the bean. While this is certainly an admirable certification (especially because the fees go toward migratory bird research), some coffee farms produce organic, shade-grown coffee without the label.

- **Rainforest Alliance.** This certification comes from the Rainforest Alliance and requires adherence to a number of standards related to the environment, ecology, and labor. No organic or shade-grown requirement is needed to receive this certification. Unlike other certifications, the Rainforest Alliance requires that only 30 percent of a producer's coffee beans meet its conditions in order for its seal to be used on the packaging. The seal discloses this percentage.

It's worth noting that coffee producers can often negotiate better prices for certified coffee, and the value of this negotiating power should not be underestimated. It ensures that coffee producers, who often live in impoverished countries, receive better prices that help them to maintain their livelihood. The ethics of coffee growing—which has largely been ignored throughout coffee's entire history—is certainly something to be concerned about. The main idea here is that it is difficult to determine from a bag alone whether the coffee inside was produced and purchased ethically.

If you care about the way your coffee is grown and sold, a better course of action than purchasing based on certifications alone is to look for direct-trade coffee or to ask a roaster how they source their coffee. *Direct trade* is a term used by roasters that have built relationships with producers, purchased coffee directly from them, and likely paid a premium for it. In the case of direct trade, the roaster can tell you exactly where the coffee came from and how it was grown. However, direct trade isn't practical for all roasters because it takes time and skills related to shipping logistics. Many roasters instead rely on like-minded importers to help them source their coffee. In fact, many small roasters would not survive without the help of these importers, which invest a lot of time and resources building long-term relationships with producers and, in some cases, help them improve their quality and, of course, reach customers. The takeaway? Direct-trade coffee is usually a good thing, but that's not to say that importers are money-grabbing middlemen. They are a vital part of the industry, and ethics-conscious home brewers would be wise to get to know their roaster's importers, too!

STORAGE

To get the most out of your new bag of coffee beans, proper storage is essential. It's best to think of coffee as a spice: buy it both fresh and whole. It's not uncommon for folks to dry-toast spices before using them, but it's not recommended to store them that way long term, as toasting speeds up the staling process. Coffee is essentially a toasted spice, and it loses flavor even more quickly than most spices (that's why I recommend you only purchase what you think you will consume in a week).

Most coffee people recommend that you store your coffee, again like spices, in an airtight container in a cool, dark, dry place. Air, heat, light, and moisture will expedite the staling process. At our house, Andreas and I find that keeping coffee in its original bag is fine as long as we are careful to squeeze out as much air as possible between uses. Many people transfer their beans to a jar, but I still prefer the bag—you can't squeeze extra air out of a jar. Bags are also opaque; therefore, the beans have very limited exposure to light. Most bags also have a one-way valve, the nifty little invention that greatly improves the longevity of roasted coffee.

You might not think your coffee is at risk of coming into contact with moisture in your kitchen, but that's not entirely true. Be sure to keep your bags away from water and steam (think stoves, electric kettles, radiators, brewing devices, humidifiers, dishwashers, and open windows). In certain climates, humidity could also be an issue.

Many people have been told to store their coffee in the refrigerator in order to keep it fresh. This is horrible advice. The refrigerator isn't cold enough to keep your beans fresher than, say, the cabinet, but there is a bigger danger: rogue odors. Coffee beans absorb odors like a sponge, and refrigerators tend to be smelly places. Just don't risk it.

Storing beans in the freezer is a hotly debated topic. Some feel it does nothing to extend the shelf life of coffee, others believe it works in a vacuum at extremely low temperatures (not exactly practical for most home brewers), and still others swear by it. A couple of studies suggest that immediately freezing very fresh coffee does extend its life span—some say for up to eight weeks—so it might be worth trying. Andreas and I have casually kept beans in the freezer just to see what would happen. I'm not entirely convinced that freezing beans keeps them at peak freshness any longer (we have been pleasantly surprised by old freezer beans, but I think it had more to do with the heartiness of the beans themselves), but it certainly hasn't *negatively* impacted our beans' flavor. We are more convinced by the research suggesting that cold coffee beans break apart in the grinder more consistently, which improves extraction. The pleasant flavor that some attribute to the freshness of freezer beans may actually be due to improved fracturing and extraction.

CHAPTER 5
The Flavor

C OFFEE FERVOR IS A SPECTRUM. It's nice to keep that in mind. Somewhere on that spectrum is a line that declares that analyzing the flavor of coffee is a valid and worthy pursuit. Directly above, a cloud of shame casts its shadow in a wide perimeter. On either side of the line, people fret.

What we know is a typical roasted bean contains somewhere between 900 and 1,000 scientifically identified flavor-producing molecules, and their various combinations can produce seemingly infinite results. To the average coffee drinker, these flavors may not be immediately clear. Coffee just tastes like coffee, and when you taste one you like, you know it—it hits you like a sock full of coins. You don't need to know why you like it to enjoy it.

But if you drink enough cups of different kinds of coffee, chances are good that you'll start to differentiate among them whether you want to or not. You don't have to study anything, and you certainly don't need the skill of a sommelier or a scientist. Humans' senses of taste and smell are remarkably refined; millions of years of evolution have left them capable of distinguishing among a multitude of tastes and textures. The more you taste, the more refined your palate naturally becomes—and the more you can discern what you like from what you don't. In the end, that's what matters most.

If you are interested in optimizing your cup to suit your individual preferences (or in selecting a bag that you're most likely to love), it helps to have a rudimentary understanding of why coffee tastes the way it does. There are five basic tastes: acidity (sourness), sweetness, bitterness, saltiness, and umami (savoriness). The last two aren't usually present in coffee. In this chapter, I will focus on the first three, bring the senses of touch and smell into the mix, explain how flavor works in general, and provide some tips for those of you who want to refine your coffee-tasting palate.

ACIDS AND (PERCEIVED) ACIDITY

When acidity is mentioned in relation to coffee, it's often misunderstood. You might think of something sour, sharp, tangy, and relatively unpleasant, like pure lemon juice. But in the context of coffee, acidity is often a desirable characteristic. In a well-balanced cup, it's the sensation that can make coffee taste like biting into an apple: fruity, juicy, bright, lively, crisp, refreshing. Coffee professionals use these words to describe the nuanced flavors and sensations that come from the more than 30 individual acids present in a cup of coffee. Acidity in coffee is kind of abstract—in fact, you're actually tasting *perceived* acidity, because pH is generally not involved. This is why you'll hear so many poetics used to describe acidity in coffee.

Science doesn't have all the answers for how, exactly, different acids affect coffee flavor. But it knows enough to conclude that not all acids taste great (and not all of them contribute to perceived acidity), so it's really the combination and balance of different acids and other flavor compounds that provide that pleasant zing in coffee. As a whole, acidity is a counterpoint to perceived sweetness (see page 188), and its presence prevents a cup from tasting dull or flat. One way to think about this

---

Tasting Tip

Having trouble discerning acidity in your coffee? You're not alone! Try tasting something you know is acidic, like a lemon. Pay close attention to the parts of your mouth that react to it and how they react to it. Then drink some coffee and see whether your mouth reacts in the same way. It also helps to take a sip of coffee, hold it in your mouth, and move your tongue around before swallowing it. Everyone is different, but for me, acidity in coffee feels like a tart tingle on the tip of my tongue and a mouthwatering sensation on the walls of my cheeks, which is the same feeling I get when drinking orange juice.

combination is by comparing it to homemade salad dressing: the right proportion of, say, lemon juice to olive oil produces something that is more pleasing to the senses than the individual parts alone. Here are a few of the most important acids found in coffee and how professionals think they affect flavor:

- **Chlorogenic acids.** Most of the organic acid in roasted coffee is made up of chlorogenic acids (this is actually a group of acids, not the name of an individual acid). These acids are largely responsible for perceived acidity—the zingy or sparkling quality—in a cup of coffee. They are destroyed more and more the longer the coffee roasts, which is why beans with shorter roast times are referred to as "bright" more often than beans with longer roast times.

- **Citric acid.** This is usually the second-most prevalent organic acid in roasted coffee. It's actually produced by the coffee plant itself, not by the roasting process (although roasting degrades it). The citric acid in coffee is the same as that in citrus fruit. As you might guess, it's associated with citrus flavor notes, such as orange and lemon—even grapefruit when phosphoric acid is also present. Citric acid also contributes to the perceived acidity of a cup, and in high concentrations, it can make coffee taste unpleasantly sour.

- **Malic acid.** This sweet, crisp acid is said to contribute flavors of stone fruit (such as peaches and plums), as well as notes of pear and apple. In fact, this type of acid is found in high concentrations in apples, making it familiar enough for some coffee drinkers to more easily distinguish it from other acids.

- **Quinic acid.** Quinic acid forms as chlorogenic acids decompose during the roasting process. Therefore, it is present in higher concentrations in darker roast coffees than in lighter roast coffees. This acid contributes to coffee's body and perceived bitterness, and it can produce an astringent (drying) quality. Quinic acid continues to form in a cup of coffee if it's left to sit, which is why coffee that's been left on a hot plate for hours (don't do this) tastes bitter. It's also present in greater quantities in stale coffee than in fresh.

- **Caffeic acid.** This acid (unrelated to caffeine) is also formed as chlorogenic acids decompose. It's found only at low levels in coffee, but it's thought to contribute to astringency.

- **Phosphoric acid.** This inorganic acid is believed to taste sweeter than most other acids. When combined with strong citrus flavors, phosphoric acid can mellow those flavors to taste more like grapefruit or mango. It can also add a cola flavor to coffee and may contribute to the overall perceived acidity in a cup.

- **Acetic acid.** The main acid in vinegar, acetic acid can give coffee an unpleasant, fermented taste if present in high concentrations. However, in proper balance, it is said to provide notes of lime and sweetness. The concentration of acetic acid in green coffee can increase as much as 25 percent during shorter roasting periods, but it drops off if roasting continues.

Coffees grown at high elevations or in mineral-rich or volcanic soil often contain more perceived acidity. Further, washed coffees are generally more acidic than naturally processed coffees, which might be because naturally processed coffees usually contribute more body to a cup, and body often diminishes perceived acidity.

Some people find that coffee is too harsh on their stomachs and causes acid reflux. It should be noted that coffee isn't all that acidic. Regardless of the acid combination in any given cup, coffee is usually around a 5 on the pH scale. For some perspective, pure water is a 7 (neutral), saliva is a 6, and orange juice is a 3. However, there is evidence that the chlorogenic acids in coffee increase the level of acid in a coffee drinker's stomach, which can trigger acid reflux. According to a 2005 article in *Roast* magazine, as little as 200 milligrams of chlorogenic acids can increase stomach acid (in a typical cup, you'll find between 15 and 325 milligrams). A few friends have shared anecdotal evidence that lighter roast coffee tends to affect their stomachs more than darker roasts, which lends some support to that conclusion.

A Love Affair with Acidity

Acidity is a prized characteristic among many craft coffee professionals. It's probably safe to say that professionals like acid-heavy coffee more than the general public does. Coffee that your barista might describe as "balanced" might have a zing to it that you just can't take. I personally like some acidity, but I think it's an acquired taste, and you shouldn't let anyone shame you about it. Plenty of coffees, particularly naturals and those from lower elevations, have less perceived acidity. If you don't like acidity, look for flavor notes related to chocolate, caramel, and flowers as opposed to those related to fruit, particularly citrus fruit.

(PERCEIVED) SWEETNESS

When it comes to coffee, sweetness is a counterintuitive concept. Coffee is objectively bitter; otherwise, there wouldn't be so many of us taking sugar in our daily brew. Yet, it isn't uncommon to find a coffee bag labeled with flavor notes such as chocolate, strawberry, caramel, and other sweet-sounding items. When coffee people talk about sweetness, they aren't talking about added sugar—or even about the sucrose naturally found in some coffee beans. A chocolate flavor note on a bag does not mean that chocolate has been added to the coffee. It just means that the combination of the flavor molecules in the roasted coffee can leave the impression of a chocolate flavor on your tongue.

As discussed, there is a decent amount of sugar (not the white stuff but rather compounds like sucrose and glucose) in green arabica beans, but it makes up a smaller percentage than other components, and much of it is destroyed during roasting. Therefore, coffee will always be a bitter drink and will never be overtly sweet like, for example, hot chocolate. Instead, coffee has a subtle, perceived sweetness that is based on the balance of its flavor compounds. Sweetness can also be perceived in coffee through its ability to add definition to flavors. For example, sweetness can take coffee from tasting vaguely acidic to having very clear flavors of red apple.

Like a lot of things related to coffee, the jury is still out on what definitively creates sweet notes. Some people believe sweet aromatics, fewer caramelized sugars from roasting, and trace amounts of natural sugars contribute to coffee's sweetness. Others feel that the amount of truly perceptible sweetness in coffee is mostly caused by flavor compounds that happen to remind us of sweet things (e.g., strawberries). Some people think a heavier mouthfeel can enhance or contribute to sweetness.

Sweetness can be elusive to a tasting novice. It's certainly subtle, but it likely will become easier to distinguish the more coffee you taste.

BITTERNESS

Coffee is inherently bitter, and many people point to bitterness as the reason why coffee in general is gross or why a particular cup is off. In my experience, people often say a coffee is too bitter when they really mean it's too sour or it dries out their mouth in an unappetizing way, neither of which is the fault of bitterness.

Still, human tongues are inherently very sensitive to bitterness (probably for self-preservation; many toxic substances are bitter), so its demonization is somewhat understandable. In fact, bitterness is often characterized as unpleasant by definition, and on its own or in large amounts, it is. But in concert with other flavor elements, such as sweetness and acidity, bitterness can add dimension and complexity to coffee. Bitterness also balances perceived acidity, which makes it an essential component to a well-balanced cup. Several elements are thought to contribute to bitterness in coffee, some of which include:

- Quinic acid (see page 186)
- Trigonelline, a bitter plant alkaloid
- Furfuryl alcohol
- Caffeine
- Carbon dioxide (see page 16)

Coffee that has been roasted for a long time often supplies more bitterness to a cup than coffee that has been roasted for a short time. This is partially because quinic acid continues to build as coffee is roasted. On top of that, coffee that has been roasted for a relatively short period of time has fewer soluble solids (as well as more acidity and more aroma), which means it generally tastes less bitter than coffee that has been roasted longer.

While many bitter compounds take longer to extract than sweet and acidic compounds, because bitterness is so potent to our senses, its compounds can quickly dominate a cup if given the chance. Therefore, bitterness is a sign of overextraction. It's also important to remember that robusta coffee is bitterer than arabica coffee, regardless of all other factors.

MOUTHFEEL

A lot of people find the word *mouthfeel* to be elitist, but I think it's very practical. It describes how coffee feels in your mouth—what else would it be called? Does coffee feel like anything? Of course it does. If you pay close attention, you'll realize it has heft, texture, and viscosity. Mouthfeel is not one of the five basic tastes, but it does contribute to how you *experience* a cup of coffee, and it may even work its magic to influence certain flavors. One way to think about mouthfeel is to break it out into its components: body, oiliness, and astringency.

Body

Technically, body is a characterization of strength (see page 19), which, if you'll remember, is defined by the concentration of TDCS in a cup. Strong coffee can feel thick or muddy and leave a film on your tongue. Weak coffee feels almost like water; it's thin, and there is little to no feeling that lingers on your tongue. If they aren't filtered out during brewing, insoluble particles (like fines) can also contribute to body, making it thicker. Some people use various kinds of milk to describe body because milk is familiar: the feel of whole milk is analogous to a heavier, thicker-bodied coffee, while the feel of skim milk is analogous to a lighter, thinner-bodied coffee.

When it comes to describing body, the terms *thick* and *thin* can have negative connotations—they both imply that something went wrong during the brewing process. Instead, professionals use two other words to describe body: *heavy* and *light*. Stay with me now—*heavy* and *light* may seem just as bad as *thick* and *thin*, but in the context of describing body, neither is necessarily better or worse than the other.

Origins and processing methods can strongly influence the body of a cup of coffee, which means different kinds of coffees inherently have different bodies. For example, Sumatran coffees tend to have heavy bodies while Mexican coffees tend to have lighter bodies. Natural coffees (see page 143) tend to have more body than washed coffees. Heavy bodies, light bodies, and everything in between can be considered desirable, depending on the coffee, which is why coffee professionals need a neutral way to talk about them. When analyzing coffee, professionals tend to judge the body based on what is expected of the beans, not on a universal ideal. So if a natural coffee has a light body, that might be considered a flaw if the coffee was expected to have a heavy body.

Another potential benefit of body, according to some professionals, is that it can influence the way we perceive flavors. For example, body might contribute to a perceived sense of sweetness in a cup. Similarly, body can help balance acidity. I recommend trying different coffees and different brewing methods to figure out what kind of body you like. One easy way to test your preference is to compare French press coffee with filter coffee. French press coffee tends to have more body because the French press does not have a filter to remove sediments from the brew.

How Filters Affect Body

Strength only measures the soluble (dissolved) coffee solids in a cup, not the insoluble (undissolved) solids that were mentioned earlier, but both contribute to body. That means a cup made with a paper filter, which traps insoluble solids, and a cup made with a metal filter, which doesn't trap as many insoluble solids, could have the same strength, but the metal-filter coffee might have more body because it contains more insoluble solids.

Oiliness

Lipids (fats, oils, and waxes) can also affect the way coffee feels on the tongue. The quantity of lipids in a finished cup of coffee directly relates to the quantity found in the coffee beans. Arabica beans have about 60 percent more lipids than robusta beans. Unlike many other compounds in coffee, lipids are virtually unchanged after roasting. However, a lot of the oil in coffee beans is trapped behind sturdy cell walls, and as these cell walls break down during roasting, the oil is free to escape, making the outside of the beans appear shiny.

In my experience, the mere presence of oil on the outside of the beans doesn't contribute significantly to the oiliness of the cup. What *does* contribute is the kind of filter you use (see page 52). Paper filters trap most coffee oil, so not much makes it into the cup. Cloth filters also trap a lot of oil, but not as much as paper filters do. Metal filters let through the most oil of any filter. The more oil in your cup, the thicker and more "buttery" your coffee may feel on your tongue.

Astringency

Astringency is a term that describes a drying or puckering sensation in your mouth. Many people mistake this sensation for bitterness, but the two are distinct. In fact, when you experience astringency, certain molecules are binding to your tongue and causing a drying feeling. You may be more familiar with the astringency in red wine and tea, which is caused by compounds called *polyphenols* (tannins are well-recognized polyphenol compounds in tea and wine). Coffee also contains polyphenols, which likely contribute to its astringency. Two polyphenols that are often linked to astringency in coffee are chlorogenic acids (see page 186) and dicaffeoylquinic acid. Caffeine may also play a role. Too much astringency in coffee is unpleasant and may be a sign of overextraction.

AROMA

Ah, the smell of freshly brewed coffee. So distinct! So beloved! Even people who don't like to drink coffee often enjoy the warm, comforting embrace of its aroma. Aroma is the counterpart to taste and is thus essential to coffee's flavor; you can't have flavor without aroma. As anyone who has had a stuffed-up nose can attest, our senses of smell and taste are inextricably linked, which means aroma plays an important role in the character of our coffee.

Aroma isn't just what you smell when you bend down and take a big whiff of your steaming cuppa joe. Retronasal olfaction, smelling that happens from inside your mouth, is incredibly important when it comes to tasting flavors in coffee (or flavors in anything). Nasal congestion diminishes this kind of smelling, which is why food often tastes bland when you have a cold. When you take a sip of coffee, hundreds of volatile aromatics are bouncing around in your mouth and making their way to the back of your throat and up into your nose. Once detected by your olfactory system, the aroma, along with the taste and mouthfeel, helps your brain discern and log flavors.

You may notice that coffee professionals often slurp their coffee when they taste it. This is meant to aerate the coffee so that it hits the entire palate at once and gets the nose involved quickly. (Without slurping, the coffee will hit the front part of the tongue first and then hit the back on its way down.) Is slurping necessary for you? Probably not, but it's kind of fun to try!

Professional baristas are often trained to detect nuances in aroma at different stages of the coffee life cycle, from when the beans are freshly ground to after the coffee is swallowed. When training employees and wholesale customers, Andreas uses a product called Le Nez du Café, which contains 36 unmarked vials of different aromas that are commonly found in coffee. To use it, you smell each vial and try to identify its aroma. The goal is both to introduce you to the aromas most often found in coffee and to train your nose to identify those aromas. Why? Well, it's incredibly difficult to identify a scent or flavor in coffee if you've never smelled or tasted it before! I've tried Le Nez du Café and was able to correctly identify only a few scents—those related to items I'd been exposed to the most.

> ### Retronasal Olfaction Action
>
> One fun way to better understand how retronasal olfaction works is to purposefully exhale through your nose after swallowing some coffee and compare what you taste to what you taste after inhaling. The difference should be quite distinct.

Aroma is determined by volatile aromatics, of which more than 800 have been identified in coffee. Although it's unlikely that *all* of them contribute to that distinct coffee smell, there are a few broad categories to help you understand where coffee aromas come from:

- **Enzymatic.** These aromas originate in the coffee plant itself and are often described as floral, fruity, or herbal. This makes a lot of sense because coffee beans are technically the seeds of fruit.

- **Browning.** Browning aromas are the result of the Maillard reaction (see page 146) and the caramelization of sugars, both of which happen during roasting. These reactions are the same as those responsible for the delicious smell of baking bread. These mostly sweet aromas are often described as nutty, caramely, chocolaty, or malty, and they likely contribute to perceived sweetness in the cup.

- **Dry distillation.** If coffee beans get far enough along in the roasting process, parts of them will actually start to burn. The aromas associated with this burning are often described as wood, clove, pepper, or tobacco. It goes without saying that the longer the beans roast, the more present these aromas will be.

The ways that coffee beans are grown, processed, and roasted can all affect how aromatics present themselves in the cup, and there is no right or wrong combination. It's worth emphasizing the *volatile* nature of coffee's aromatic compounds: they disappear quickly at room temperature, which is a major reason why coffee can go stale so quickly.

HOW TO ASSESS FLAVOR

Flavor is where smell and taste come together. These two senses are so closely connected, it can be hard for us to differentiate smell from taste or taste from smell. One of the remarkable things about coffee is that such a simple seed can contain such depth and breadth of flavor across its species. Most coffee lovers have a detailed memory of the first time they sipped a coffee that surprised them. It's a singular, startling moment in the life of a coffee drinker. For Andreas, it was when he was working at a midwestern coffee chain in 2010 and tasted one of their special offerings: it tasted exactly like Cap'n Crunch Crunch Berries cereal. For many of us, this experience fuels a lifelong obsession with replicating that moment of recognition. Yet, many flavors in coffee tend to be subtle and elusive to the point that some of us begin to doubt their existence. Notes of black plum and cardamom in my coffee, you say? I don't think so.

Flavor can be a divisive subject, and esoteric flavor notes often build a wall between baristas and customers. But flavor is not objective. It's dependent on a number of factors, including genetics and personal experience. Our genes influence the way we taste. They can cause some of us to be more sensitive to bitterness or make others of us think cilantro tastes like soap—some people even have more taste buds than the rest of us, which makes them more sensitive to flavors in general. Perhaps most important, when it comes to coffee at least, are our taste memories. If you've never tasted a black plum, for example, you'd be hard-pressed to identify that note in your coffee. When Andreas tasted a fruity, sugary cereal in his coffee, he was probably tasting notes of blueberry; however, he was more familiar with Crunch Berries, so that's where his mind went.

Obviously, being able to identify flavors is not a requirement of enjoying coffee. If you drink coffee regularly, you'll likely develop preferences for certain flavors and be able to identify them using your own terminology without much conscious thought—and it's fine to draw the line there. But if you do want to learn how to consciously taste your coffee, it takes practice. Your palate is malleable and must be trained to be more sensitive. The more you taste and smell something, the more likely it is that you will be able to detect it in your coffee. Remember how I could identify only the few aromas in Le Nez du Café that were most familiar to me? The more familiar you are with tastes and smells in general, the better your chance of finding their subtle variations in your cup. Baristas and other coffee professionals have a leg up on the rest of us because they spend hours a day tasting coffee. Not only that but they also spend a lot of time *comparing* different coffees. It's much easier to suss things out of coffee if you have multiple samples to compare with each other.

Of course, recognizing a flavor in a cup of coffee does not necessarily mean you'll be able to articulate that idea to someone else. We're back to the language barrier. If I say a coffee reminds me of my grandmother's basement, that doesn't help anyone who hasn't been in my grandmother's basement understand what that coffee tastes like. This type of communication gap happens between roasters and consumers all the time. I've seen roasters use flavor notes that are whimsically meaningless ("autumn breeze") or deceivingly specific ("peanut brittle"). These ultimately leave customers confused because they don't know what an autumn breeze is supposed to taste like, or disappointed because the coffee tastes nothing like a dessert. Too often, flavor notes don't mean what they say and don't say what they mean—and consumers' expectations often aren't set correctly in the first place.

That's what I appreciate about the new and improved SCA Coffee Taster's Flavor Wheel, which was developed to help coffee professionals, scientists, and coffee lovers describe the taste and smell of coffee in a common language. At the beginning of 2016, the SCA updated the wheel for the first time since 1995 to account for a growing body of research in sensory science. The new terms, which align with the Sensory Lexicon developed by World Coffee Research and Kansas State University's Sensory Analysis Center, replace decades-old jargon from the previous wheel and are recognizable even to people who aren't involved in the coffee industry. The Lexicon provides a catalog of physical references for the flavor notes (scientists call them *flavor attributes*) and aromas on the wheel, so anyone can replicate them at home and improve their taste and smell memories.

First and foremost, the Flavor Wheel offers an opportunity for roasters and consumers to get on the same page when describing flavor. Ideally, roasters would use the new Flavor Wheel's descriptors to replace any obscure or misleading flavor notes on their packages. Flavor notes could become so standardized that two different coffees with "raisin" listed among their flavor notes would both taste like raisins—and the flavor could be measured by a common reference. This sounds obvious enough, but flavor notes have not yet reached this level of consistency, neither among coffee professionals nor between consumers and roasters. Unfortunately, not all roasters have adopted the Flavor Wheel yet, so the language barrier remains. But it serves as a reminder of the ideal: a world where any given flavor note would mean the same thing to everyone.

I should note that coffee professionals who use standardized language to describe flavor can taste the same cup of coffee blindly and each come up with the same flavor notes for it. I am in no way trying to imply that flavor notes are imaginary or something—there's just no universal language we can use to talk about them. The wine industry is far more advanced in this area than the coffee industry. Sommeliers are trained to pick out characteristics in wine and communicate them in a very specific way that other professionals can understand immediately.

The new version of the Flavor Wheel can help consumers communicate about flavor as well. It is a great way for home coffee brewers to casually identify and explain the flavors in their coffee, as it provides the words needed to describe actual flavors based on mere impressions. In my example of the coffee that tastes like my grandmother's basement, I could use the Flavor Wheel to find a description that more people would be able to understand, such as "musty" or "stale." Changing my description from personal (my grandmother's basement) to universal (musty) allows me to talk about that flavor, and part of the joy of coffee is being able to talk about it with other coffee enthusiasts.

Before using the Flavor Wheel for the first time, familiarize yourself with it, starting with the broadest categories in the center and working your way outward to the more detailed descriptors around the edge. Then, smell or taste your coffee with purpose. You can try to do this at every stage of your brew: after grinding the beans, while the coffee is brewing, and, of course, once the brew is in the cup. When tasting, move your tongue around and see whether you can detect any specific flavors.

If you smell or taste something familiar but can't quite put your finger

If you are really getting into this tasting thing, you can access the Sensory Lexicon on which the Coffee Taster's Flavor Wheel is based. It lists all of the flavor attributes with definitions and references, which identify real-world items that you can taste or smell to fine-tune your palate. A free download is available at worldcoffeeresearch.org.

on it, go ahead and prompt yourself with the wheel. Again, start from the center with the general categories. Ask yourself questions like, "Does this taste like spices?" or "Does this smell sweet?" Pay attention to your first impressions, even if they don't quite seem to make sense. If, like Andreas, you taste a sugary cereal, you might be able to match that to Sweet or Fruity or both. Once you think you have a flavor or aroma nailed down, double-check it by mindfully tasting your coffee again.

Although, due to the constraints of publishing, this book reproduces it in shades and tints of brown, the original Flavor Wheel (see page 200) was designed so that people could use color to discern flavors. Using research, the wheel's designers matched each flavor to the color most commonly associated with it. So, if you can't find the right words but the coffee somehow reminds you of something green, there's a good chance the flavors fit into the Vegetative category. The wheel is also designed so that you can be as specific as you want to be. Because of the way it is tiered, you can try to move outward into increasingly specific flavors and aromas—or not.

As you make your way through the wheel a second time, you might notice the different-sized gaps between the flavor attributes. Like the colors, these gaps have a purpose too. Flavors identified as being closely related to each other (e.g., raisin and prune) have the smallest gaps between them. A bigger gap, like that between peanuts and clove, means the two flavors are less related.

COFFEE TASTER'S FLAVOR WHEEL

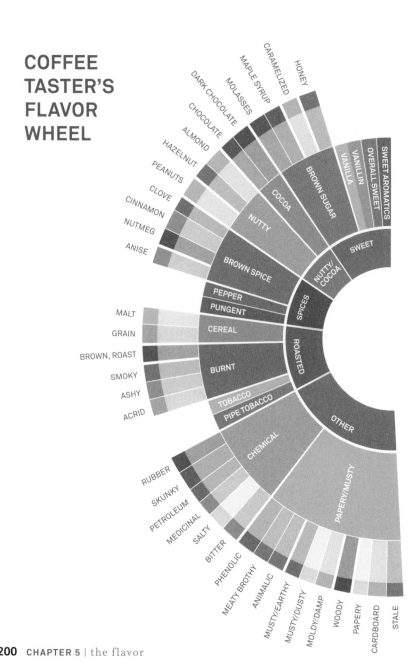

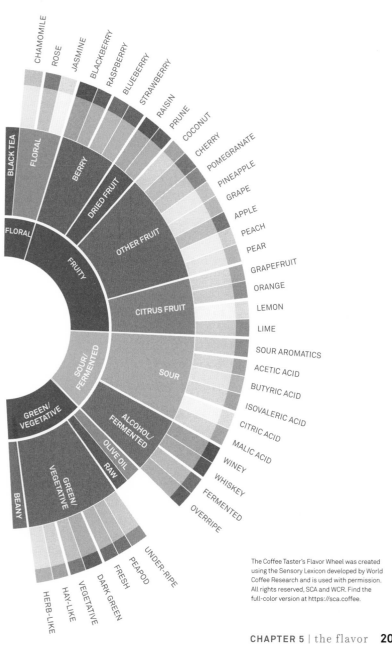

The Coffee Taster's Flavor Wheel was created using the Sensory Lexicon developed by World Coffee Research and is used with permission. All rights reserved, SCA and WCR. Find the full-color version at https://sca.coffee.

The Flavor Wheel, in my opinion, is a beautiful thing, and if roasters insist on putting flavor notes on bags, they should use the terms from the wheel so that coffee enthusiasts can understand them. However, you shouldn't feel like you have to use it. If you still can't taste any specific flavors in your coffee, even with the Flavor Wheel, then give up. Seriously. Who cares? Coffee is supposed to be enjoyable, and forcing your brain to find a flavor where you perceive none seems like an unfun exercise in futility to me.

Coffee-Tasting Party!

Honing your coffee-tasting skills is more fun with other people. If you're having fun in a casual, relaxed environment with your coffee comrades, you'll probably enjoy your brew that much more.

To kick off your coffee-tasting party, select two different kinds of coffee to taste and compare. You can select more than two kinds, but note that you'll be trying to brew all of them around the same time, so things can spiral out of control fairly quickly (she did not say from experience). What two kinds should you choose? A washed coffee versus a naturally processed coffee is a classic choice, but you can also try two coffees from two different origins or two coffees from the same origin that were roasted at different levels or by different roasters or that were processed in different ways. The possibilities are endless!

Make sure you have a device (or two) big enough to serve your guests. You'll likely need some kind of thermal carafe or thermos so you can brew both coffees and make sure they both stay warm. The key is to be able to taste the two coffees side by side. It's easier to distinguish differences when comparing them in the moment, rather than relying on your memory. (Also, be sure to pick up some baked goods for, um, scientific purposes—I mean, there is probably a reason why coffee and doughnuts go so well together. If you're trying to be pure about this, you'll need to hold off on eating the baked goods until you've tasted both coffees with an unadulterated tongue—the baked goods will absolutely influence the taste. You probably already know this about coffee and delicious breakfast food, but it's kind of mind-blowing to consciously taste coffee both before and after eating a doughnut.)

If you want to write down your thoughts, use the following chart as a template. You'll want to taste each coffee four times, concentrating on only one of the four categories each time. Together, body, sweetness, and acidity determine whether or not a coffee is balanced (coffee is always bitter, so you don't need to taste for that. However, if it's overly bitter—i.e., you taste only bitterness and nothing else—then your coffee is probably overextracted.) Each can influence the flavors present in the cup. You may find it helpful to sip the first coffee and then the second before moving on to the next category. You might not think you notice any sweetness in one of the coffees, but after comparing it to the other cup, you might be able to tell that one is at least sweeter than the other. Gut reactions are usually the best reactions, and remember, if you can't detect anything in a certain category, don't search too hard. Just move on to the next one.

Here's how each round breaks down:

1. **Body.** For the first taste, try to focus only on how the coffee feels in your mouth. Hold the coffee in your mouth and move your tongue around. Does its consistency feel more like water or more like

COFFEE TASTING CHART

Coffee		
Body		
Sweetness		
Acidity		
Flavor Notes		
Overall Impressions		

whole milk? Does it feel heavy on your tongue? Gritty? Buttery? Creamy? Does it seem to leave a coating on your tongue or cheeks, or does your mouth feel clean? Does any part of your mouth feel dry or puckered?

2. **Sweetness.** Before tasting for sweetness, breathe in your coffee's seductive vapors. Let them envelop you. Think about sweetness and all of its variations: fruit, syrup, caramel, cooked carrots, wine, chocolate, nuts. Now taste the coffee. Move your tongue around. Does anything in there remind you of something sweet? Sweetness is most often associated with a flavor—not an actual sweet taste. Sweetness in coffee tends to be incredibly subtle, and it's not caused by sugar. Coffee's natural bitterness, understandably, makes sweetness even harder to discern. Sweetness might sneak in as a tangential feeling. If your immediate reaction is to describe a coffee as "smooth," for example, it likely contains a fair amount of sweetness. If you taste two coffees side by side and the first one seems sharp or biting and the second one doesn't, the second one probably contains more sweetness.

3. **Acidity.** Unlike sweetness, acidity might knock you over the head and be quite easy to detect. People often mistake acidity for bitterness—if you want to avoid this, try my tip on page 252. Acidity usually presents itself as an overall feeling or quality. If the coffee feels bright, juicy, zingy, sparkling, or sharp in your mouth, that's likely acidity. Another way to think about acidity is by comparing the coffee to how your mouth feels when consuming other acidic foods, like salad dressings, vinegars, wines, apples, or citrus fruits. However, the coffee shouldn't taste sour or unpleasant. If it does, it is likely underextracted.

4. **Flavor Notes.** On the fourth taste, you'll be thinking only about what flavors this coffee reminds you of. During this stage,

alternating between the first coffee and the second coffee might be most helpful. Write down whatever comes to mind, even if it sounds silly. You might be surprised that your friends write down different but related tastes and associations.

CHAPTER 6

Brewing Methods

B Y NOW YOU'VE PROBABLY COME TO REALIZE that coffee is a fickle beast. Just when you think you have it figured out, its taste changes, it behaves differently, or it becomes stale. It's easily swayed by external factors, from the weather to the water to your eager hand. When making coffee, the goal is to repeat delicious results. There is no point otherwise. But how do you repeat results when the primary ingredient seems comfortable wallowing in a dark, inscrutable pit of inconsistency? You need to know where to start.

That's why this chapter provides you with base specs and suggested methods for each of the 10 devices covered in chapter 2. Some devices include more than one method. For each method, Andreas and I dialed in the base specs across multiple brews using different kinds of coffee and consistently saw good results. These specs are a good place to start. You may find they work perfectly for your setup, or you may find you need to adjust them here and there to account for your environment or your preferences. But to get started, here's the information we included:

- **Base specs.** Each method offers a snapshot of the base specs that Andreas and I tested with, including the grind size, brew ratio, temperature, and timing. These are the items you can play around with to perfect your cup. You can use the brew ratio to scale the yield up or down, but note that some other variables, like time and grind size, might also need to be adjusted.

- **Water.** Most of the recipes call for water *off boil*, by which we mean 30 seconds to 1 minute after it's been brought to a boil. A couple of methods require more specific temperatures. I also indicate that you should boil more water "as necessary" along with the amount needed for the recipe. I find it's easiest to fill the kettle with a couple hundred grams more water than necessary.

Keep in mind that you can literally just dump water into a lot of the devices in this chapter and end up with something better than what a typical automatic machine can make. All of the details included here are aimed at optimizing the cup and replicating the results.

You can use the extra water to wet your filter beforehand (which we always recommend) or to immediately rinse your device afterward, which keeps cleanup quick and easy.

- **Grind size.** Our descriptions of grind size correspond with the chart on page 29. I've also included the Baratza Virtuoso grind setting that we used for our tests. If you don't have a Virtuoso, you may be able to find conversion numbers online—Baratza doesn't have consistent settings even among its own models. This lack of grind size standardization is certainly one of the most annoying things about home brewing today, but there's nothing we can do about it. Physics! At the very least, you'll be able to get close to the right grind size by using the grind references in the aforementioned chart.

- **Equipment icons.** Each method includes icons that indicate the minimum amount of equipment we recommend using for an optimized cup: either one device (burr grinder), two devices (burr grinder and scale), or three devices (burr grinder, scale, and gooseneck kettle). These mostly correspond with the information on page 83, but there are a couple of fun surprises, too. I am assuming that

Burr grinder

Scale

Gooseneck kettle

Thermometer

everyone has a kitchen thermometer already, but in general, I don't think thermometers are strictly necessary for home brewers. The few methods I strongly recommend a thermometer for are marked with a corresponding icon. A stopwatch, on the other hand, is always necessary. I use the one on my phone. Obviously, you can make any method with a full brew bar or you can choose to use no coffee equipment. You do you.

- **Grams.** It should come as no surprise by now that I strongly suggest the use of a gram scale for most methods—except, of course, for the ones I don't think benefit from it (which are marked). In other words, most of these recipes were developed using grams to measure both coffee and water. Because I know some of you still don't believe me about the life-changing magic of a kitchen scale, I have also included conversions for US customary units. You're welcome! Keep in mind that these measurements are nowhere near as accurate as the gram measurements. For one thing, I had to round them in some cases in order for them to be actually useful. But also, measuring by volume is fundamentally inconsistent for all the reasons described in chapter 1 (see page 24). It also won't be easy to use the brew ratios to scale up the recipes if you measure by volume.

In case you're curious or want to use your knowledge to create your own recipes, I've included some conversion charts on the opposite page to help you swap between grams and US customary units. Again, the US customary units have been rounded. If you are familiar with measuring water in milliliters, you are in luck, as 1 gram of water equals 1 milliliter of water.

One last word of advice: in the beginning, I recommend that you choose one brewing device—based on the considerations you learned about in this book—and keep at it until you perfect it. Once you know a device inside and out and understand all of its idiosyncrasies, manual coffee brewing will become that much easier and that much more intuitive. Practically speaking, even if you have a bunch of devices, like we do, you'll probably gravitate toward one or two of them most of the time anyway. Happy brewing!

WATER MEASUREMENT CONVERSION CHARTS

Water (fl. oz)	Water (g)
1	29.57
6	177.42
8	236.56
12	354.84
16	473.12
24	709.68

Water (g)	Water (fl. oz)
1	0.03
50	1.7
100	3.4
200	6.8
400	13.5
600	20.3

WHOLE COFFEE MEASUREMENT CONVERSION CHARTS

Coffee (Tbsp.)	Coffee (g)
1	6
2	12
3	18
4	24
5	30
6	36

Coffee (g)	Coffee (US customary)
2	1 teaspoon
6	1 tablespoon
24	¼ cup
48	½ cup
72	¾ cup
96	1 cup

THE FRENCH PRESS
(Press Pot, Coffee Press, or Cafetière)

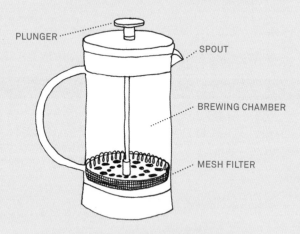

PLUNGER

SPOUT

BREWING CHAMBER

MESH FILTER

The Eight-Minute French Press Method

Most coffee guides will tell you that to make French press coffee, you should pour water over the grounds and let them sit for four to five minutes. I used to make it that way, too. However, thanks to barista Nick Cho of Wrecking Ball in San Francisco, I've found that extremely coarse grounds and longer steep times (up to eight minutes) produce a more even, delicate cup. Because of this, Andreas and I have included specs for both the eight-minute method and the five-minute method here—shorter brewing times do have an early-morning appeal, after all.

The eight-minute method works best with a very coarse grind. Start with the coarsest setting on your grinder that still produces an even grind (the coarsest setting on our Virtuoso chews up the beans).

BASE SPECS	Grind: extra coarse (39 on Baratza Virtuoso)
	Brew ratio: 1:14
	Water temp: off boil
	Total brewing time: 8 minutes

INGREDIENTS	28.5 grams (¼ cup + 2 teaspoons) fresh whole coffee
Makes 400 grams	400 grams (13.5 fluid ounces) water, plus more as needed
(13.5 fluid ounces)	

METHOD

1. Pour the water into a kettle and set it over medium-high heat. Bring to a boil.

2. While the water heats, set a timer for 8 minutes but don't start it yet. Grind the coffee to an extra coarse size, transfer it to the brewing chamber of a French press, and gently shake the chamber to level the grounds. Set it on a kitchen scale and zero the scale.

3. When the water just starts to boil, remove the kettle from the heat. Start the timer and quickly but carefully add the water to the French press until the scale reads **400 grams**.

4. After 30 to 45 seconds has elapsed on the timer, gently stir the water with a spoon until most of the grounds start to sink to the bottom (there will still be a froth with some grounds at the top). Place the plunger over the vessel, but do *not* depress it.

(continued)

The Eight-Minute French Press Method

(continued)

5. When the timer sounds, slowly and gently depress the plunger. It's important to do this carefully. Forcefully depressing the plunger will result in an unwanted amount of agitation, and you'll risk ruining your balanced cup by unleashing the bitter, astringent flavors that are still in the bean.

6. Serve immediately or transfer to a separate carafe. Use any extra hot water to rinse the device. Enjoy!

BREWING TIPS

Most of the methods in this section call for a stopwatch. For this method (and the Five-Minute French Press Method), it's easier to set a timer and wait for it to sound.

One of the best things about using a French press is that it's quick and easy to make coffee for multiple people. But remember, there is still sediment in your brew, and the bulk of it has sunk to the bottom. If you serve multiple people by filling each cup one at a time, the first cup will contain very little sediment, and the last cup will contain a lot—and it won't necessarily taste that good. To avoid this, pour each cup in waves to distribute the sediment evenly.

The Five-Minute French Press Method

In our home experiments, Andreas and I found that limiting the brewing time for this method to four minutes or less made it too difficult to achieve a balanced cup. It's often not enough time for the water to fully penetrate coarse grounds and extract delicious flavors. If you tighten the grind, it's *too* easy for the water to penetrate, which leads to a bitter, filmy brew (no matter what anyone else says, you do not need to resign yourself to bitter, filmy coffee when using a French press!). We settled on five minutes.

Aside from the time involved, the main difference between the eight-minute method and this shorter method is that it requires a different kind of agitation to extract properly. Also, due to the shorter brewing time, you do not need as coarse of a grind as in the eight-minute method.

BASE SPECS

Grind: coarse (34 on Baratza Virtuoso)
Brew ratio: 1:16
Water temp: off boil
Total brewing time: 5 minutes

INGREDIENTS
Makes 400 grams
(13.5 fluid ounces)

25 grams (¼ cup + ½ teaspoon) fresh whole coffee
400 grams (13.5 fluid ounces) water, plus more as needed

METHOD

1. Pour the water into a kettle and set it over medium-high heat. Bring to a boil.

2. While the water heats, set a timer for 5 minutes but don't start it yet. Grind the coffee to a coarse size, transfer it to the brewing chamber of a French press, and gently shake the chamber to level the grounds. Set it on a kitchen scale and zero the scale.

(continued)

The Five-Minute French Press Method

(continued)

3. When the water just starts to boil, remove the kettle from the heat. Start the timer and quickly but carefully pour the water into the French press until the scale reads **400 grams**.

4. After 1 minute has elapsed on the timer, gently stir the water in a circle with a spoon, about 10 times. Place the plunger over the vessel, but do *not* depress it.

5. When the timer sounds, slowly and gently depress the plunger. It's important to do this carefully. Forcefully depressing the plunger will result in an unwanted amount of agitation, and you'll risk ruining your balanced cup by unleashing the bitter, astringent flavors that are still in the bean.

6. Serve immediately or transfer to a separate carafe. Use any extra hot water to rinse the device. Enjoy!

BREWING TIPS

If you'd like to see how different brewing methods can change the taste of the same coffee beans, compare your French press coffee with a cup of the same coffee brewed with any pour-over method.

Even once you depress the plunger of a French press, the grounds at the bottom of the container will continue to extract, so make sure to remove the coffee from the device as soon as it's done brewing.

The French Press Cold Brew Method

Cold brewing is one of the easiest ways to make a great cup of coffee. This method is a combination of a traditional method and a special French press technique Andreas and I picked up from James Hoffmann, author of *The World Atlas of Coffee* and the 2007 World Barista Champion (although he used it for a hot brew, not a cold brew). If you don't have a French press, this method can also be done in any old jar with a lid. Instead of pouring the concentrate through the French press screen, gently and carefully pour it through a paper or cloth filter. A batch of cold-brew concentrate can make upward of five cups after dilution. Depending on the size of your vessel, you can make even more with the ratios listed below.

BASE SPECS	**Grind:** medium coarse (25 on Baratza Virtuoso) **Brew ratio:** ~1:6 **Water temp:** cold (from fridge or from tap) **Total brewing time:** 12 hours
INGREDIENTS Makes 600 grams (20.3 fluid ounces) of concentrate	**96 grams** (1 cup) fresh whole coffee **600 grams** (20.3 fluid ounces) cold water
METHOD	1. Grind the coffee to a medium-coarse size, add it to the brewing chamber of a French press, and gently it shake to level the grounds. Add the water. Insert the plunger, but do *not* depress it all the way. The mesh filter should just rest on the grounds, keeping them submerged. Transfer the French press to the refrigerator and let the coffee brew for **12 hours**.

(continued)

The French Press Cold Brew Method

(continued)

2. Remove the French press from the refrigerator and remove the lid. Stir 3 times, just until the crust starts to sink. Set it aside for 5 to 10 minutes to allow most of the tiny coffee particles to sink to the bottom of the vessel. Then insert the plunger, but do *not* depress it all the way. Plunge it just enough so the mesh filter rests gently on top of the coffee. It's untraditional, but depressing the plunger will agitate your perfect cold brew and stir up all the tiny particles that you waited so patiently to sink to the bottom. The goal is to keep them out of the filtered cold brew so they do not continue to extract!

3. Gently pour the cold brew concentrate into a separate container. To enjoy, dilute with fresh, cold water using a 1:1 ratio, or to taste. Refrigerate in an airtight container for 1 to 2 weeks.

THE AEROPRESS

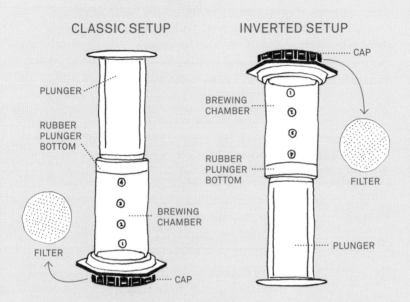

CLASSIC SETUP

PLUNGER

RUBBER PLUNGER BOTTOM

④
③
②
①

BREWING CHAMBER

FILTER

CAP

INVERTED SETUP

CAP

BREWING CHAMBER

①
②
③
④

RUBBER PLUNGER BOTTOM

FILTER

PLUNGER

Classic AeroPress Method

This method is adapted from the manufacturer's original instructions. Many professionals tend to dislike this method, as water will start to leak from the device into your cup before you depress the plunger. The method calls for a fairly low water temperature—without an electric kettle with temperature settings, I've found it can take a good while off boil for the water to reach that temperature. If you're using medium- to dark-roast beans, you may need to go as low as 175°F to achieve a pleasing extraction. Of course, you can always measure the temperature of the water as it heats, but that can be tricky without a clip-on thermometer!

For a bounty of other recipes, check out the World AeroPress Championship website, which features winning recipes from the past several years.

BASE SPECS

Grind: fine (6 on the Baratza Virtuoso)
Brew ratio: 1:12
Water temp: 185°F
Total brewing time: 50 to 90 seconds

INGREDIENTS
Makes 138 grams
(4.7 fluid ounces)

11.5 grams (2 tablespoons) fresh whole coffee, or 1 AeroPress scoop ground coffee (see Tip)
138 grams (4.7 fluid ounces) water, plus more as needed

METHOD

1. Pour the water into a kettle and set it over medium-high heat. Bring to a boil, then remove the kettle from the heat and set aside to cool.

2. While the water cools, place a filter in the cap and twist the cap onto the brewing chamber to attach it. Place the brewing chamber on top of a mug. Thoroughly wet the filter (50 to 60 grams of water) with the hot water and discard the rinse water. Set the whole rig on a kitchen scale, if using. Grind the coffee to a fine size. Using the AeroPress funnel, carefully add the grounds to the device and gently shake to level the bed. Remove the funnel and zero the scale.

3. When the water reaches the right temperature, start a stopwatch and quickly add water to the AeroPress until the scale reads **138 grams**, or until the water level reaches **the middle of the number 2** on the brewing chamber. This should take about

20 seconds—it's important to move fast because water will start dripping through the grounds and into your mug, which will mess up your measuring. Using the AeroPress paddle, stir in a circular motion for 10 seconds, making sure all the grounds are saturated. By this point, the stopwatch should read **0:30**.

4. Remove the rig from the scale, insert the plunger, and with one hand placed where the mug and device meet and the other hand on the plunger, gently depress it for 20 to 60 seconds. Be sure to keep one hand on the mug to prevent sliding. When the plunger is fully engaged (you'll hear hissing), the stopwatch should read between **0:50** and **1:30**.

5. Discard the coffee grounds, clean up, and enjoy!

BREWING TIPS

The manufacturer's website states that one level AeroPress scoop is equal to "11.5 grams of coffee," so that is the measurement Andreas and I used for testing. However, during our tests (with more than five different kinds of coffee), we found that one level scoop of whole coffee usually weighed between 15 and 16 grams, while one level scoop of ground coffee usually weighed between 12 and 13 grams. If you're not using a scale, you may want to measure ground coffee instead of whole to get closer to the 11.5-gram mark.

Some professionals say that an AeroPress should be bone-dry in order to work properly. It can be very difficult to depress the plunger of a dry AeroPress, which will mess up your timing. I like to wet the pieces of my AeroPress before I brew, to make plunging easier.

Inverted AeroPress Method

This method is based on the method Andreas uses at work. The classic and inverted AeroPress methods essentially work the same way, but in the inverted method, you are measuring everything with the device upside down. This prevents water from dripping through the cap before you're finished pouring, which allows for more accuracy. Obviously, you'll want to be careful as you flip the device upside down. If you are not using a scale, I've found that filling the AeroPress cap with whole beans so that they are level, but not heaping, gets you close to the 16 grams this method calls for.

BASE SPECS	**Grind:** fine (6 on the Baratza Virtuoso) **Brew ratio:** ~1:14 **Water temp:** off boil **Total brewing time:** 1 minute and 50 seconds
INGREDIENTS **Makes 220 grams** **(7.4 fluid ounces)**	**16 grams** (2 tablespoons + 2 teaspoons), or 1 AeroPress scoop fresh whole coffee **220 grams** (7.4 fluid ounces) water, plus more as needed
METHOD	1. Pour the water into a kettle and set it over medium-high heat. Bring to a boil. 2. While the water heats, place the cap of the AeroPress on a mug (if the mug is the correct size for the device, it should hang there) and add an AeroPress filter. Prepare the device by inserting the plunger into the brewing chamber so that the width of the rubber bottom just fits inside (it should be right by the top of the first circle, the number 4), and set it aside. Grind the coffee to a fine size and set it aside.

3. When the water just starts to boil, remove the kettle from the heat. Thoroughly wet the filter (50 to 60 grams of water), discard the rinse water, and set the mug aside. Set the prepared AeroPress upside down (flared side up) on a kitchen scale, if using. Using the AeroPress funnel, carefully add the grounds to the device and gently shake to level the bed. Remove the funnel and zero the scale. By now, the water temperature should be about right.

4. To bloom the coffee, start a stopwatch and add water until the scale reads **50 grams**, or until the water level reaches the **midpoint of the number 3** on the brewing chamber. With the AeroPress paddle, swish one time in the pattern of a plus sign (down and up, then left to right and back again) and once around the walls of the device (I find two half-circle motions works best). Make sure you are inserting the paddle as far as it will go.

5. Immediately after agitating, add the water until the scale reads **220 grams**, or until the water level reaches the **bottom edge of where the brewing chamber starts to flare**. Twist the cap on, remove the device from the scale, and remove the air pocket by gently pushing down the sides of the brewing chamber until liquid (usually a foam) just starts to bubble up through the cap. With one hand on the brewing chamber and one on the plunger, flip it, quickly (and carefully) enough not to spill, onto the mug. At this point, the stopwatch should read **0:50**.

6. Let the coffee brew until the stopwatch reads **1:20**. Then, with one hand placed where the mug and device meet and the other on the plunger, slowly and gently depress the plunger until the stopwatch reads **1:50**, about 30 seconds. Be sure to keep one hand on the mug to prevent sliding.

7. Discard the coffee grounds, clean up, and enjoy!

BREWING TIP

It might take a couple of tries to get the timing of this method down. Steps 4 through 6 must happen quickly, so you may feel a bit rushed at first, but it doesn't take too much practice to get it right!

THE ABID CLEVER

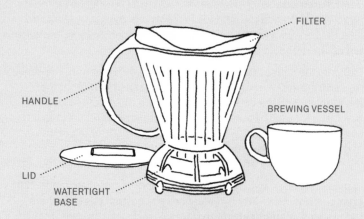

FILTER

HANDLE

BREWING VESSEL

LID

WATERTIGHT
BASE

The Clever Dripper Method

During our home tests of this method, in a couple of instances the brew stopped draining completely because of the Clever's tendency to clog when used with finer grind sizes. On the other hand, Andreas and I don't feel like long, French-press style brewing times (and the requisite very coarse grounds) work all that well with the Clever either. This is partially because it seems like the longer the hot water is in contact with the paper filter, the more likely that a papery taste will leach into the brew. We settled on a three-minute brewing time here, which we feel delivers a well-balanced cup.

BASE SPECS	**Grind:** medium fine (14 on Baratza Virtuoso)
	Brew ratio: ~1:15
	Water temp: off boil
	Total brewing time: 4 minutes

INGREDIENTS	**26.5 grams** (¼ cup + 1 teaspoon) fresh whole coffee
Makes 400 grams	**400 grams** (13.5 fluid ounces) water, plus more as needed
(13.5 fluid ounces)	

METHOD

1. Pour the water into a kettle and set it over medium-high heat. Bring to a boil.

2. While the water heats, grind the coffee to a medium-fine size and it set aside. Then, set up your rig: filter and device.

3. When the water just starts to boil, remove the kettle from the heat. Thoroughly wet the filter (50 to 60 grams of water), discard the rinse water, and set the rig on a kitchen scale. Add the grounds, gently shake the rig to level the bed, and zero the scale.

4. To bloom the coffee, start a stopwatch and slowly pour **50 grams** of water evenly in concentric circles, making sure to thoroughly saturate the grounds. When the stopwatch reads **0:30**, continue to step 5.

5. Continue adding water, in half-dollar-sized circles in the center of the bed, until the scale reads **400 grams**. Cover the Clever and let the coffee brew until the stopwatch reads **3:00**.

(continued)

The Clever Dripper Method

(continued)

6. Decant the Clever by placing it on top of a brewing vessel. The coffee should take about 1 minute to draw down; the stopwatch should read **4:00**. Remove and discard the filter and rinse the device with any extra hot water. Enjoy!

BREWING TIP

You may notice a pocket between the bottom of the filter and the bottom of the Clever. It's along the sides, where the shape changes from the wedge to the neck. During the beginning of the brew, coffee gets trapped in the neck, and the filter blocks it from the rest of the slurry. If your bloom is too heavy, you end up with pockets of underextracted coffee. That's why this bloom weight is lower than in other methods.

The Clever Dripper Cold Brew Method

The Clever seems perfectly designed for cold brew: it's a self-contained vessel with a filter and a lid! The only downside is that it doesn't hold as much coffee as other devices do. The 400 grams tested here pretty much maxes it out.

BASE SPECS

Grind: medium coarse (25 on Baratza Virtuoso)
Brew ratio: ~1:7
Water temp: cold (from fridge or from tap)
Total brewing time: 15 hours

INGREDIENTS
Makes 400 grams
(13.5 fluid ounces)
of concentrate

58 grams (½ cup + 2 tablespoons) fresh whole coffee
400 grams (13.5 fluid ounces) cold water

METHOD

1. Insert a filter into the Clever, thoroughly wet the filter, and discard the rinse water. Grind the coffee to a medium-coarse size, add it to the Clever, and gently shake to level the bed. Add the water.

2. Cover the Clever with the lid and transfer it to the refrigerator. Make sure you place it on the bottom shelf or set it on a flat surface, or else it will drain into the refrigerator. Let the coffee brew for **15 hours**.

3. Remove from the refrigerator and decant the cold brew concentrate into a separate lidded container. To enjoy, use fresh, cold water to dilute the concentrate using a 1:5 ratio, or to taste. Refrigerate in an airtight container for 1 to 2 weeks.

THE SIPHON
(Vacuum Pot)

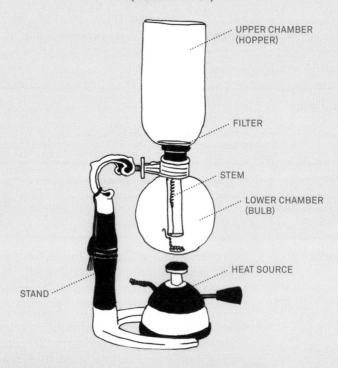

UPPER CHAMBER
(HOPPER)

FILTER

STEM

LOWER CHAMBER
(BULB)

HEAT SOURCE

STAND

Three-Cup Siphon Method

This method was adapted from the siphon method used by Blue Bottle, a coffee company based in San Francisco. Being able to measure temperature is important in this method, so you will need a thermometer. To help you visualize the key parts of the process, I have included a panel on page 231.

BASE SPECS	**Grind:** medium fine (15 on Baratza Virtuoso)
	Brew ratio: ~1:14
	Water temp: 202°F
	Total brewing time: 1 minute and 55 seconds

INGREDIENTS	**22 grams** (3 tablespoons + 2 teaspoons) fresh whole coffee
Makes 300 grams	**300 grams** (10.1 fluid ounces) water, plus more as needed
(10 fluid ounces)	

METHOD

1. If using a new filter, boil it for 5 minutes. If using a filter you've been storing in water in the refrigerator, soak it in warm water for about 5 minutes. While the filter preps, grind the coffee to a medium-fine size and set it aside. Set the siphon stand (with bulb) on a kitchen scale, zero it out, and add the water to the bulb until the scale reads **300 grams**. At this point, you will no longer need the scale.

2. Add the prepared filter to the hopper by gently lowering it so that the ball chain hangs through the stem. Pull down on the ball chain and attach the hook to the side of the stem. Loosely attach the hopper to the bulb. It should be leaning slightly to the side; do not seal it yet (PANEL A).

3. Turn on the heat source. When the water starts to boil, adjust the hopper so that it's upright and firmly sealed. Wait until the water works its way up through the filter and into the hopper; the stem doesn't reach to the bottom of the bulb, so some water will remain (PANEL B).

(continued)

Three-Cup Siphon Method

(continued)

4. Turn down the heat source (if using a butane burner, it should be on the lowest possible setting). When an instant-read thermometer placed in the water registers **202°F**, add the coffee grounds and start a stopwatch (**PANEL C**). Quickly push the dry grounds down into the slurry with a butter knife. When the stopwatch reads **0:30**, stir the slurry three times with the butter knife.

5. When the stopwatch reads **1:20**, turn off the heat source and stir the slurry 10 times as the water drains from the hopper into the bulb below (**PANEL D**); the water level in the bulb will stop and there will be bubbles. All the coffee should drain by the time the stopwatch reads **1:55**.

6. Carefully remove the hopper from the device. To do this, you may need to hold the bulb steady, as it can spin. It will be hot, so use a kitchen towel to hold it steady as you gently twist off the hopper. Set it aside to cool (if your device comes with a lid, it usually doubles as a hopper stand). Serve the coffee directly from the bulb. Enjoy!

BREWING TIPS

This method is quicker if you boil the water before pouring it into the bulb. Your heat source will boil it eventually, but it takes much longer, and you'll need to actively watch it. When you use hot water, the active time you spend with the device is much shorter.

When you serve the coffee, it will be hotter than normal because the bulb was over direct heat. Let the coffee cool longer than you normally would before enjoying it.

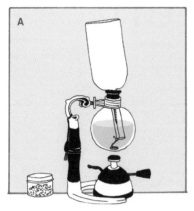

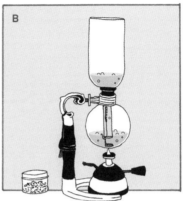

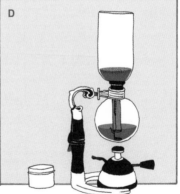

THE MELITTA

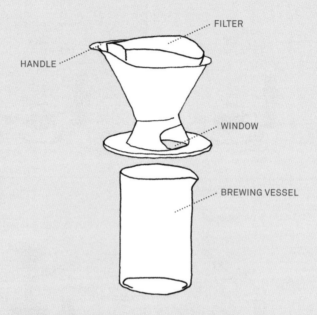

HANDLE

FILTER

WINDOW

BREWING VESSEL

Single-Cup Melitta Pulse Method

We tested this method on the Ready Set Joe model, but you can scale up these specs for larger models and yields.

BASE SPECS	**Grind:** medium (20 on Baratza Virtuoso)
	Brew ratio: 1:17
	Water temp: off boil
	Total brewing time: 3 minutes and 30 seconds

INGREDIENTS	23.5 grams (¼ cup) fresh whole coffee
Makes 400 grams	400 grams (13.5 fluid ounces) water, plus more as needed
(13.5 fluid ounces)	

METHOD

1. Pour the water into a kettle and set it over medium-high heat. Bring to a boil.

2. While the water heats, grind the coffee to a medium size and set it aside. Then, set up your rig: filter, device, and brewing vessel.

3. When the water just starts to boil, remove the kettle from the heat. Thoroughly wet the filter (50 to 60 grams of water), discard the rinse water, and set the rig on a kitchen scale. Add the grounds, gently shake the brewing vessel to level the bed, and zero the scale.

4. To bloom the coffee, start a stopwatch and slowly pour **50 grams** of water evenly in concentric circles, making sure to thoroughly saturate the grounds. When the stopwatch reads **0:45**, continue to step 5.

(continued)

Single-Cup Melitta Pulse Method

(continued)

5. Start your first pulse by adding **50 grams** of water, beginning in the middle and pouring in slow, concentric circles over the next 10 seconds. By this point, the scale should read **100 grams** and the stopwatch should read **0:55**. Wait 15 seconds, then pulse about three more times, in 100-gram increments, until the scale reads **400 grams** and the stopwatch reads **2:40** (see Brewing Tip).

6. Let the coffee draw down; it should take about 50 seconds and the stopwatch should read **3:30**. Remove and discard the filter, rinse the device with any extra hot water, and enjoy!

BREWING TIP

Want a better handle on your pulse timing? Here are some guidelines:

0:45 to 0:55: end at 100 grams

1:10 to 1:30: end at 200 grams

1:45 to 2:05: end at 300 grams

2:20 to 2:40: end at 400 grams

THE BEEHOUSE

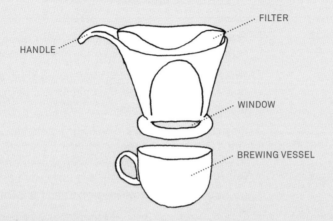

HANDLE

FILTER

WINDOW

BREWING VESSEL

The Large BeeHouse Pulse Method

The design of the BeeHouse restricts water flow quite a bit, so I think the pulse method is the easiest way to go. Your pouring pattern doesn't really matter that much, as long as you are evenly applying the water. Andreas prefers concentric circles, while I am better at keeping a figure-eight pattern. If you notice grounds clinging to the sides of the filter as the bed height reduces, take a quick, gentle lap around the perimeter to push those puppies back into the brew water.

BASE SPECS

Grind: medium fine (14 on Baratza Virtuoso)
Brew ratio: 1:16
Water temp: off boil
Total brewing time: 3 minutes and 30 seconds

(continued)

INGREDIENTS
**Makes 400 grams
(13.5 fluid ounces)**

25 grams (¼ cup + ½ teaspoon) fresh whole coffee
400 grams (13.5 fluid ounces) water, plus more as needed

METHOD

1. Pour the water into a kettle and set it over medium-high heat. Bring to a boil.

2. While the water heats, grind the coffee to a medium-fine size and set it aside. Then, set up your rig: filter, device, and brewing vessel.

3. When the water just starts to boil, remove the kettle from the heat. Thoroughly wet the filter (50 to 60 grams of water), discard the rinse water, and set the rig on a kitchen scale. Add the grounds, gently shake the rig to level the bed, and zero the scale.

4. To bloom the coffee, start a stopwatch and slowly pour **50 grams** of water evenly in concentric circles, making sure to thoroughly saturate the grounds. When the stopwatch reads **0:45**, continue to step 5.

BREWING TIP

*Want a better
handle on your
pulse timing?
Here are some
guidelines:*

0:45 to 0:55:
end at 100 grams

1:10 to 1:30:
end at 200 grams

1:45 to 2:05:
end at 300 grams

2:20 to 2:40:
end at 400 grams

5. Start your first pulse by adding 50 grams of water, beginning in the middle and pouring in slow, concentric circles over the next 10 seconds. By this point, the scale should read **100 grams** and the stopwatch should read **0:55**. Wait 15 seconds, then pulse about three more times, in 100-gram increments, until the scale reads **400 grams** and the stopwatch reads **2:40** (see Brewing Tip).

6. Let the coffee draw down; it should take about 50 seconds and the stopwatch should read **3:30**. Remove and discard the filter, rinse the device with any extra hot water, and enjoy!

THE WALKÜRE

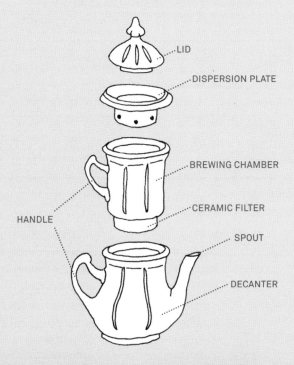

LID

DISPERSION PLATE

BREWING CHAMBER

CERAMIC FILTER

HANDLE

SPOUT

DECANTER

Medium Walküre Method

While the pour for this method doesn't require much technique beyond aiming for the center of the dispersion plate, the Walküre does,
like many methods, benefit from a slow, controlled pour. Its brewing
chamber is quite small, and it's easily overwhelmed with water. I've
also discovered that it's important to pour the bloom weight quickly,

as it seems to affect how the grounds settle in the brewing chamber. When I've poured slowly, my drawdown time has been out of control. Because the Walküre is made of porcelain, it retains heat very well. This thing can get hot as hell, so be careful when decanting!

BASE SPECS

Grind: medium (20 on the Baratza Virtuoso)
Brew ratio: 1:17
Water temp: off boil
Total brewing time: 3 minutes and 45 seconds

INGREDIENTS
Makes 350 grams
(11.8 fluid ounces)

20.5 grams (3 tablespoons + 1 teaspoon) fresh whole coffee
350 grams (11.8 fluid ounces) water, plus more as needed

METHOD

1. Pour the water into a kettle and set it over medium-high heat. Bring to a boil.

2. While the water heats, grind the coffee to a medium size and set it aside. Then, set up the rig: decanter, brewing chamber, and dispersion plate. Set the lid aside.

3. When the water just starts to boil, remove the kettle from the heat. Preheat the device by pouring water directly into the center of the dispersion plate. Discard the rinse water, and set the rig on a kitchen scale. Add the grounds to the brewing chamber, gently shake it to level the bed, replace the dispersion plate, and zero the scale.

4. To bloom the coffee, start a stopwatch and very quickly pour **45 grams** of water directly into the center of the dispersion plate. The pour should take no more than 10 seconds. Allow the coffee to bloom until the stopwatch reads **0:40**.

5. Begin continuously adding the water as slowly as possible, so that the scale reads **350 grams** when the stopwatch reads **3:00**. If using a gooseneck kettle, you should be able to pour slowly enough that the dispersion plate "sings." That's a good sign. When the brewing chamber fills up (a ring of bubbles and light brown liquid will emerge from the holes of the dispersion plate), pause for a few moments to allow the brewing chamber to drain. If the pour is slow enough and the grind is right, you should need to stop two or three times.

6. Let the coffee draw down; it should take 30 to 45 seconds and the stopwatch should read no more than **3:45**. Rinse the device with any extra hot water and enjoy right away!

BREWING TIPS

Sometimes if you pour the grounds into the Walküre's brewing chamber when it's already assembled, some of them will fall into the decanter. Either remove these grounds before brewing or level them before placing the brewing chamber on top of the decanter.

The device is designed so that all of its component parts fit together. Be sure to remove the brewing chamber and dispersion plate from the decanter and add the lid before serving! It will be much harder to pour if you do not remove these items.

Because this device does allow sediment through, decant it like a French press (see page 214).

THE KALITA WAVE

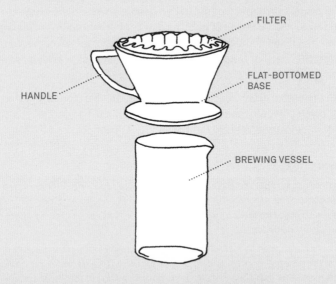

FILTER

FLAT-BOTTOMED
BASE

HANDLE

BREWING VESSEL

The Kalita Wave #185 Pour-Over Method

Andreas and I adapted this method from one used by craft coffee
pioneer George Howell. Although folks often use continuous pour for
this method, I went with a pulse. Because the bloom serves as the
first pulse, note that you may need to adjust your pulse timing if your
bloom needs more time, which it might if you are using super-fresh
coffee. Also, be aware that the sides of the Kalita filter can be
somewhat delicate. It's best to avoid pouring water directly onto the
filter (when you wet it or while you're brewing), as it could collapse
and ruin everything.

BASE SPECS	**Grind:** medium (18 on Baratza Virtuoso)
	Brew ratio: 1:17
	Water temp: off boil
	Total brewing time: 3 minutes and 45 seconds

INGREDIENTS	23.5 grams (¼ cup) fresh whole coffee
Makes 400 grams	400 grams (13.5 fluid ounces) water, plus more as needed
(13.5 fluid ounces)	

METHOD

1. Pour the water into a kettle and set it over medium-high heat. Bring to a boil.

2. While the water heats, grind the coffee to a medium size and set it aside. Then, set up your rig: filter, device, and brewing vessel.

3. When the water just starts to boil, remove the kettle from the heat. Thoroughly wet the filter (50 to 60 grams of water), discard the rinse water, and set the rig on a kitchen scale. Add the grounds, gently shake the rig to level the bed, and zero the scale.

4. To bloom the coffee, start a stopwatch and slowly pour **50 grams** of water evenly in concentric circles, making sure to thoroughly saturate the grounds. When the stopwatch reads **0:35**, continue to step 5.

(continued)

The Kalita Wave #185 Pour-Over Method

(continued)

5. Start your first pulse by adding 100 grams of water, beginning in the middle and pouring in slow, concentric circles over the next 15 seconds. By this point, the scale should read **150 grams** and the stopwatch should read **0:50**. Wait 10 seconds, then repeat the process five more times, in 50-gram increments, until the scale reads **400 grams** and the stopwatch reads **3:00** (see Brewing Tip).

6. Let the coffee draw down; it should take about 45 seconds. Remove and discard the filter, rinse the device with any extra hot water, and enjoy!

BREWING TIP

Want to make sure your pulses are staying on track? Here are some guidelines:

0:35 to 0:50: 150 grams

1:00 to 1:15: 200 grams

1:25 to 1:40: 250 grams

1:50 to 2:05: 300 grams

2:15 to 2:30: 350 grams

2:45 to 3:00: 400 grams

THE CHEMEX

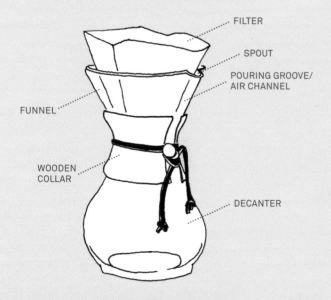

FILTER

SPOUT

POURING GROOVE/
AIR CHANNEL

FUNNEL

WOODEN
COLLAR

DECANTER

The Six-Cup Chemex Pour-Over Method

It's more important to wet your filter with the Chemex than with other devices. Chemex filters are thicker, so they tend to have more of a papery taste than other filters, which water can help alleviate. Additionally, the way a wet filter sticks to the sides of the device is part of the Chemex design: it helps regulate airflow. If you've thoroughly wetted the filter, you should be able to simply pour the water through the spout without it spilling out.

BASE SPECS	**Grind:** medium fine (17 on Baratza Virtuoso)
	Brew ratio: ~1:16
	Water temp: off boil
	Total brewing time: 3 minutes and 45 seconds

INGREDIENTS	**31 grams** (¼ cup + 1 tablespoon) fresh whole coffee
Makes 500 grams	**500 grams** (16.9 fluid ounces) water, plus more as needed
(16.9 fluid ounces)	

METHOD	

1. Pour the water into a kettle and set it over medium-high heat. Bring to a boil.

2. While the water heats, grind the coffee to a medium-fine size and set it aside. Then, set up your rig: filter and device.

3. When the water just starts to boil, remove the kettle from the heat. Thoroughly wet the filter (50 to 60 grams of water), discard the rinse water, and set the rig on a kitchen scale. Add the grounds, gently shake the rig to level the bed, and zero the scale.

4. To bloom the coffee, start a stopwatch and very slowly pour **70 grams** of water evenly in concentric circles, making sure to thoroughly saturate the grounds. This should take you at least 20 seconds. When the stopwatch reads **0:45**, continue to step 5.

5. Slowly and continuously add water to the center of the coffee bed in a nickel-sized circular pattern until the scale reads **200 grams**. (You won't be pouring as slowly as you did for the bloom.) Take two quick laps around the perimeter of the coffee bed, taking care not to hit the sides of the device.

Continue pouring toward the center of the bed in the nickel-sized circular pattern until the scale reads **400 grams**. By this point, the stopwatch should read **2:00**. Take one more quick lap around the perimeter of the coffee bed, taking care not to hit the sides of the device. Continue pouring toward the center of the bed in the nickel-sized circular pattern until the scale reads **500 grams** and the stopwatch reads **2:30**.

6. Let the coffee draw down; it should take about 75 seconds and your stopwatch should read **3:45**. Remove and discard the filter and enjoy!

BREWING TIP

No matter the shape of your filter, the multilayered side should always be placed on the pouring-groove side of the Chemex. The layers make the filter sturdy even when wet, which prevents the paper from collapsing and blocking the flow of air through the spout.

THE HARIO V60

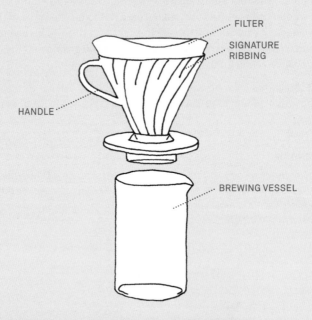

FILTER

SIGNATURE
RIBBING

HANDLE

BREWING VESSEL

The #2 V60 Continuous Pour Method

This is the tried-and-true spec and method combination that Andreas uses as a starting point for dialing in V60s at work. It has never once led him astray. However, please note that this particular method is nearly impossible without a gooseneck kettle to help you pour in circles and avoid hitting the steep sides of the device, which allow water to bypass most of the coffee bed.

BASE SPECS	**Grind:** medium fine (12 on Baratza Virtuoso)
	Brew ratio: 1:17
	Water temp: off boil
	Total brewing time: 3 minutes and 30 seconds

INGREDIENTS	**23.5 grams** (¼ cup) fresh whole coffee
Makes 400 grams	**400 grams** (13.5 fluid ounces) water, plus more as needed
(13.5 fluid ounces)	

METHOD

1. Pour the water into a kettle and set it over medium-high heat. Bring to a boil.

2. While the water heats, grind the coffee to a medium-fine size and set it aside. Then, set up your rig: filter, device, and brewing vessel.

3. When the water just starts to boil, remove the kettle from the heat. Thoroughly wet the filter (50 to 60 grams of water), discard the rinse water, and set the rig on a kitchen scale. Add the grounds, gently shake the rig to level the bed, and zero the scale.

4. To bloom the coffee, start a stopwatch and very slowly pour **60 grams** of water evenly in concentric circles, making sure to thoroughly saturate the grounds. This should take you at least 20 seconds. When the stopwatch reads **0:45**, continue to step 5.

5. Slowly and continuously add water to the center of the coffee bed in a nickel-sized circular pattern until the scale reads **200 grams**. Take two quick laps around the perimeter of the coffee bed, taking care not to hit the sides of the device. Continue pouring toward the center of the bed in the nickel-sized circular pattern until the scale reads **300 grams**.

(continued)

**The #2 V60
Continuous
Pour
Method**

(continued)

By this point, the stopwatch should read **2:00**. Take one more quick lap around the perimeter of the coffee bed, taking care not to hit the sides of the device. Continue pouring toward the center of the bed in the nickel-sized circular pattern until the scale reads **400 grams** and the stopwatch reads **2:30**.

6. Let the coffee draw down; it should take about 1 minute and your stopwatch should read **3:30**. Remove and discard the filter, rinse the device with any extra hot water, and enjoy!

The #2 V60 No-Gooseneck Method

During our research and testing, Andreas and I found a fantastic V60 method from Tonx, a coffee subscription service that was acquired by Blue Bottle, that is suitable for those of you who don't have a gooseneck kettle. We've adapted it here. A V60 method without a gooseneck kettle may be difficult for many coffee people to believe, but believe it—and the fact that devices are endlessly versatile.

BASE SPECS

Grind: medium fine (16 on Baratza Virtuoso)
Brew ratio: ~1:15
Water temp: off boil
Total brewing time: 3 minutes or less

INGREDIENTS
Makes 400 grams
(13.5 fluid ounces)

26.5 grams (¼ cup + 1 teaspoon) fresh whole coffee
400 grams (13.5 fluid ounces) water, plus more as needed

1. Pour the water into a kettle and set it over medium-high heat. Bring to a boil.

2. While the water heats, grind the coffee to a medium-fine size and set aside. Then, set up your rig: filter, device, and brewing vessel.

3. When the water just starts to boil, remove the kettle from the heat. Thoroughly wet the filter (50 to 60 grams of water), discard the rinse water, and set the rig on a kitchen scale. Add the grounds, gently shake the rig to level the bed, and zero the scale.

4. To bloom the coffee, start a stopwatch and slowly pour **60 grams** of water evenly in concentric circles, making sure to thoroughly saturate the grounds. When the stopwatch reads **0:30**, continue to step 5.

5. Add water in a small circular pattern, starting from the center of the coffee bed and working outward. Continue pouring in a circular pattern toward the center, which should push the grounds outward, until the scale reads **400 grams**. By this point the stopwatch should read near **1:30**. If the device is filled before the target weight is reached, allow the water to drain, but continue to add water as you can.

6. Let the coffee draw down. By the end of the draw, the stopwatch should read **3:00** or less. A thick layer of grounds should cover the filter all the way up. If there is balding, take more care not to hit the sides of the device next time. Remove and discard the filter, rinse the device with any extra hot water, and enjoy!

APPENDIX

Troubleshooting, Tips, and Tricks

USE THIS SECTION AS A GUIDE for how to resolve the issues you are most likely to encounter when brewing coffee at home. Remember, all base specs tend to need tweaking from time to time in order to get your coffee to taste just the way you like it. What works on one day might not work on the next. What works on one kind of bean may not work on another. When you do adjust your specs, be sure to make only one change at a time. Otherwise, you won't be able to tell which change resulted in what outcome!

TOO WEAK (THIN/WATERY)

This likely means your brew ratio is off—there is too much water and not enough coffee, which makes the coffee's body feel too thin or watery in your mouth. Try this:

1. **Increase the dose.** Technically, you can also decrease the amount of water in your brew ratio to correct this problem, but I'm assuming you don't want to end up with less coffee. Therefore, it's easier to just add more coffee to your dose. If you are using my brew ratios, increase your dose by only half a gram at a time, since you should already be close to the right dose.

2. **Tighten the grind.** Do this only if the coffee's thinness is accompanied by a sour taste, which likely means your grind is way too coarse.

TOO STRONG (THICK/HEAVY)

This likely means your brew ratio is off—there is too much coffee and not enough water, which makes the coffee's body feel too thick or heavy in your mouth. Try this:

1. **Decrease the dose.** Technically, you can also increase the amount of water in your brew ratio to correct this problem, but I'm assuming you don't want to end up with more coffee. Therefore, it's easier to just use less coffee in your dose. If you are using my brew ratios, decrease your dose by only half a gram at a time, since you should already be close to the right dose.

TOO ACIDIC (SOUR)

This likely means your brew is underextracted—the water didn't spend enough time with the coffee to extract all of its flavor molecules. (It might also mean that your coffee is brewed well but has a bright acidity that you don't prefer. If that's the case, there isn't much you can do but log it for future reference. Live and learn!) Keep in mind that some people confuse sourness with bitterness, which is a separate issue that the solutions here can't resolve. If you think this might be the case, try the tasting tip on page 185 to teach yourself how to identify acidity. Otherwise, let's get that brew less sour. Try one or a few of these:

1. **Decrease the dose.** Using less coffee gives the water more opportunity to extract. However, this will weaken the body of the coffee. If you already like the way the coffee feels in your mouth (not too watery and not too heavy), skip this adjustment. If you do need to decrease your dose, decrease it by only half a gram at a time.

2. **Tighten the grind.** Do this only if the body is in a good spot and you don't want to change it. If so, tighten the grind, but only in small increments, because this adjustment tends to both increase your contact time and make finer particles that are easier to extract. You don't want to accidentally muddy the texture!

3. **Decrease the bloom weight.** Try this adjustment for pour-over methods only. Decreasing the bloom weight allows less water to drip through into your brewing vessel. Remember, the most acidic-tasting parts of the coffee extract first (see page 16). Decreasing the bloom weight means less acidity makes it into the cup. Decrease it by only half a gram at a time.

4. **Increase the contact time.** More contact time means more extraction. This is a better adjustment to make with immersion methods (for pour-over methods, pouring more slowly doesn't just increase the contact time; it can have a number of different effects and make results harder to predict).

5. **Increase the agitation.** Agitation helps coffee extract. For immersion methods, more agitation might mean more stirring. For pour-over methods, it might mean adding another interval of

rest to your pulse method. It's harder to increase agitation with continuous pouring. Also note that agitation can muddle flavors, making the cup feel dirtier (i.e., stronger).

6. **Increase the temperature.** If you are using very dense (high-grown) light-roast beans and/or a lower-temperature method, you may try increasing the water temperature. Both of these conditions make it harder for coffee solids to dissolve, and more heat can help address that.

TOO BITTER

This likely means your brew is overextracted—the water spent too much time extracting the coffee's flavor molecules. All coffee is bitter, but this is an overly unpleasant bitterness. Let's get that brew less bitter. Try this:

1. **Increase the dose.** Using more coffee gives the water less opportunity to extract. However, this will strengthen the body of the coffee. If you already like the way the coffee feels in your mouth (not too watery and not too heavy), skip this adjustment. If you do need to increase your dose, increase it by only half a gram at a time.

2. **Loosen the grind.** Do this only if the body is in a good spot and you don't want to change it. If so, loosen the grind, but only in small increments, because this adjustment tends to both decrease your contact time and make coarser particles that are harder to extract. You don't want to overcompensate and end up with underextracted coffee!

3. **Increase the bloom weight.** Try this adjustment for pour-over methods only. Increasing the bloom weight allows more water to drip through into your brewing vessel. Remember, the most acidic-tasting parts of the coffee extract first (see page 16). Increasing the bloom weight means more acidity makes it into

the cup, which balances the bitterness. Increase it by only half a gram at a time.

4. **Decrease the contact time.** Less contact time means less extraction. This is a better adjustment to make with immersion methods (for pour-over methods, pouring more quickly doesn't just decrease the contact time; it can have a number of different effects and make results harder to predict).

5. **Increase the bloom time.** If your coffee is very fresh, it has a lot of carbon dioxide in it, and carbon dioxide is bitter. This means you may want to increase the bloom time because a longer bloom time will ensure that this gas escapes into the air and not into your cup. You shouldn't increase the bloom time by more than five seconds at a time. When in doubt, pay attention to the bubbling in the bloom.

6. **Decrease the agitation.** Agitation helps coffee extract. For immersion methods, less agitation might mean less stirring. For pour-over pulse methods, it might mean removing a pulse. If you are continuous pouring, try to pour more gently.

7. **Decrease the temperature.** If you are using less dense (low-grown) medium- to dark-roast beans and/or a higher-temperature method, you may try decreasing the water temperature. Both of these conditions make it easier for coffee solids to dissolve, and less heat causes extraction to slow down.

ASTRINGENT QUALITY

Astringency, or the drying effect on your tongue that's often associated with eating underripe fruit, is a sign of overextraction. See the Too Bitter section (previous page).

FILMY QUALITY

The coffee has a mouth-coating quality that feels oily. It indicates that the body is too heavy. In other words, the coffee is too strong. See the Too Strong section (page 252).

POWDERY QUALITY

You may feel a powdery texture on your cheeks (not on your tongue). This is an indication of bitterness, and it usually means that your grind is too fine. This is a case when you might try loosening the grind before you try increasing the dose. See the Too Bitter section (page 254) for more.

BURNT QUALITY

This is an indication of overextracted coffee. See the Too Bitter section (page 254) for more. It also could be just a quality of a darker-roast coffee that you might not like. Nothing you can do there but log your preference for future reference. If your method involves boiling the coffee together with the water, then your coffee could be literally burnt.

MUTED FLAVORS

This is an indication that your coffee is Too Strong (page 252). Sometimes coffee with a heavy body has a muting effect on flavors, even if the coffee doesn't feel heavy in your mouth. The body can cover up flavors that you would otherwise perceive. Your coffee might also be too strong if the flavors seem fleeting or if you find you can kind of taste something but not really. If your coffee tastes flat and lacks complexity, it could also be old and stale. If it doesn't bubble very much (or at all) when you bloom, then it's likely stale.

MUDDY COFFEE BED

This is a sign your grind is too fine. Your coffee likely is overextracted. See the Too Bitter section (page 254) for more. If you continue to encounter this problem despite using your same tried-and-true process, the burrs in your burr grinder might be dull.

DRAWDOWN TOO SLOW

This mostly applies to pour-over methods. If your coffee takes forever to draw through the bed, your grind is likely too fine. Try loosening your grind. Alternatively, your filter might be getting clogged with fines. If the sides of your filter are bare in places (known as "balding"), you are likely hitting the sides of the device and washing fines to the bottom, causing a clog. To avoid this, try aiming your pour away from the sides of the device as much as possible.

DRAWDOWN TOO FAST

This mostly applies to pour-over methods. If you are pouring as slowly as you can and your coffee is still drawing through the bed too quickly, your grind is likely too coarse. Try tightening your grind.

Resources

All About Coffee
by William H. Ukers

Atlas Coffee Importers
www.atlascoffee.com

*The Blue Bottle Craft of Coffee:
Growing, Roasting, and Drinking,
with Recipes*
by James Freeman and Caitlin Freeman

Blueprint Coffee
https://blueprintcoffee.com

Boxcar Coffee Roasters
www.boxcarcoffeeroasters.com

Brandywine Coffee Roasters
www.brandywinecoffeeroasters.com

Café Imports
www.cafeimports.com

Cat and Cloud podcast
www.catandcloud.com/pages/podcast

Christopher H. Hendon
http://chhendon.github.io

Coffee Chemistry
www.coffeechemistry.com

Coffee Research
www.coffeeresearch.org

Coffee Review
www.coffeereview.com

Colectivo Coffee Roasters
www.colectivocoffee.com

Counter Culture Coffee
www.counterculturecoffee.com

Fresh Cup Magazine
www.freshcup.com

Gaslight Coffee Roasters
www.gaslightcoffeeroasters.com

George Howell Coffee
www.georgehowellcoffee.com

Halfwit Coffee Roasters
www.halfwitcoffee.com

Heart Coffee Roasters
www.heartroasters.com

Houndstooth Coffee
www.houndstoothcoffee.com

*How to Make Coffee: The Science
Behind the Bean*
by Lani Kingston

Huckleberry Roasters
www.huckleberryroasters.com

Intelligentsia Coffee
www.intelligentsiacoffee.com

International Coffee Organization
www.ico.org

Ipsento Coffee
www.ipsento.com

Madcap Coffee
www.madcapcoffee.com

Metric Coffee
www.metriccoffee.com

National Coffee Association USA
www.ncausa.org

Onyx Coffee Lab
www.onyxcoffeelab.com

Opposites Extract
www.oppositesextract.com

Panther Coffee
www.panthercoffee.com

Passion House Coffee Roasters
www.passionhousecoffee.com

Perfect Daily Grind
www.perfectdailygrind.com

Portola Coffee Roasters
www.portolacoffeelab.com

Prima Coffee Equipment
www.prima-coffee.com

Ritual Coffee Roasters
www.ritualroasters.com

Roast Magazine
www.roastmagazine.com

The Roasters Guild
www.roastersguild.org

Ruby Coffee Roasters
www.rubycoffeeroasters.com

Sightglass Coffee
https://sightglasscoffee.com

Specialty Coffee Association
https://sca.coffee/

Specialty Coffee Association of Panama
www.scap-panama.com

Sprudge
www.sprudge.com

Spyhouse Coffee Roasters
https://spyhousecoffee.com

Stumptown Coffee Roasters
www.stumptowncoffee.com

Sump Coffee
www.sumpcoffee.com

Supremo Coffee
www.supremo.be

Uncommon Grounds: The History of Coffee and How It Transformed Our World
by Mark Pendergrast

USDA Foreign Agricultural Service
https://gain.fas.usda.gov

USDA National Agricultural Statistics Service
www.nass.usda.gov

Variety Coffee Roasters
www.varietycoffeeroasters.com

Water for Coffee
by Maxwell Colonna-Dashwood and Christopher H. Hendon

The World Atlas of Coffee: From Beans to Brewing—Coffees Explored, Explained and Enjoyed
by James Hoffman

World Coffee Research
www.worldcoffeeresearch.org

Wrecking Ball Coffee Roasters
www.wreckingballcoffee.com

Index

Bold page numbers refer to brewing method recipes.

prewetting of filters with, 54–56, 93, 103

prewetting of grounds with, 42–44

temperature of, for brewing, 34–37, 208–209

weighing in grams before brewing, 23–26, 91, 95

Water for Coffee (Colonna-Dashwood and Hendon), 33

Wedge-shaped filters, 69–70, 78

Weight, measuring beans and water by, 23–26, 91, 95, 150, 211

Well water, brewing and, 31–32

White filters, 53, 54, 55, 63, 78

Y

Yama, 67

Yemen, coffee cultivation in, 141–142

Yield, extraction and, 19–20

Z

Zeroing, of scale, 43, 93

Acknowledgments

FIRST AND FOREMOST, I would like to thank my husband, personal barista, and coffee mentor, Andreas Willhoff, not only for all the insight and input he provided to this project but also for his patience, which I threatened to destroy on numerous occasions to no avail. A special thank you goes to all my coffee tasters and testers, especially to Jacqueline, Deirdre, Helena, and Morgan, who also helped bring this little coffee baby into the world with their various professional talents and inclinations. Morgan gets a second thank you—THANK YOU—for drawing all the illustrations found throughout these pages. They are perfect. A huge thank you goes to my editor, Amanda Brenner, who tirelessly helped me rein in this beast, and to my publisher and fellow coffee enthusiast, Doug Seibold, who believed in this project and my ability to write it before I did. My sincerest gratitude to all the coffee professionals I've met along the way, particularly Joe Marrocco, who is so generous with his time and knowledge, and Travis, Kamila, and the Halfwit and Wormhole crews for their support and well wishes! Thank you, of course, to my friends: specifically, those from MFA school, whose successes and ambitions inspire me to peel supine body from the couch, apply butt to chair, and type with, if nothing else, back support; Bailey, who has been listening to, participating in, and instigating my crazy tales for actual decades; and Victoria, whose wisdom and candor can halt an insecurity spiral like no one's business. Last but not least, I would like to thank my family, who have been so enthusiastic and supportive, and my parents, who are probably going to read this really long book about coffee even though they don't drink it or like it in general—true love!

About the Authors

JESSICA EASTO received a degree in journalism from the University of Tennessee and an MFA in creative writing from Southern Illinois University. She works as a book editor. Her writing has appeared in the *Chicago Tribune*, *Gapers Block*, and more. She has been brewing craft coffee at home for more than eight years.

ANDREAS WILLHOFF is the director of education at Halfwit Coffee Roasters and the director of operations at The Wormhole Coffee, a Chicago coffee shop that has been recognized by *Food and Wine* magazine, *Fresh Cup* magazine, Sprudge.com, and CNN.com, among others. He has competed at the SCA Brewers Cup and often represents Halfwit at trade events, such as the annual Specialty Coffee Association Expo, Coffee Fest, and CoffeeCon Chicago.